D0344522

MADE LOVE
GOT WAR

Also by Norman Solomon

War Made Easy: How Presidents and Pundits Keep Spinning Us to Death

Target Iraq: What the News Media Didn't Tell You (with Reese Erlich)

The Habits of Highly Deceptive Media

Wizards of Media Oz (with Jeff Cohen)

The Trouble With Dilbert: How Corporate Culture Gets the Last Laugh

Through the Media Looking Glass (with Jeff Cohen)

False Hope: The Politics of Illusion in the Clinton Era

Adventures in Medialand (with Jeff Cohen)

The Power of Babble

Unreliable Sources: A Guide to Detecting Bias in News Media (with Martin A. Lee)

Killing Our Own: The Disaster of America's Experience with Atomic Radiation (with Harvey Wasserman)

MADE LOVE GOT WAR

CLOSE ENCOUNTERS WITH AMERICA'S WARFARE STATE

NORMAN SOLOMON

PoliPointPress

Made Love, Got War: Close Encounters with America's
Warfare State

Copyright © 2007 by Norman Solomon

All rights reserved including the right to reproduction in
whole, in part, or in any form.

"All Aboard" written by McKinley Morganfield, © 1956,
1984 (renewed) Watertoons Music (BMI) Administered by
BUG. All Rights Reserved. Used By Permission.

Song lyrics from "Cakewalk to Baghdad" words and music by
Bruce Barthol, © 2003 Bruce Barthol. Used by permission.

This edition published in the United States of America by
PoliPointPress, P.O. Box 3008, Sausalito, CA 94966-3008
www.p3books.com

Production management: BookMatters
Book design: BookMatters
Cover design: Lisa Fyfe

Library of Congress Cataloging-in-Publication Data

Solomon, Norman, 1951–
    Made love, got war : close encounters with America's
warfare state / Norman Solomon ; foreword by Daniel
Ellsberg.
        p.   cm.
    Includes bibliographical references and index.
    ISBN-13: 978-0-9778253-4-9 (alk. paper)
    ISBN-10: 0-9778253-4-5
    1. Nuclear weapons—United States.   2. Cold War.
3. United States—History—1945–   4. Solomon, Norman,
1951– 5. Journalists—United States—Biography.   I. Title.
    UA23.S52693   2007
    303.6'60973—dc22   2007026903

Printed in the United States of America
July 2007

Published by:
PoliPointPress, LLC
P.O. Box 3008
Sausalito, CA 94966-3008
(415) 339-4100
www.p3books.com

Distributed by Ingram Publisher Services

uA
23
552693
2007

Contents

Foreword
by Daniel Ellsberg

During the Second World War, my father was the structural engineer in charge of designing the Ford Willow Run plant, a factory that made B-24 bombers for the Air Corps. He was proud of the fact that it was the largest industrial building under one roof in the world. It put together bombers the way Ford produced cars, on an assembly line. The assembly line was a mile and a quarter long.

Once my father took me out to Willow Run to see the line in operation. For as far as I could see, the huge metal bodies of planes were hanging from hooks moving along a belt, with workers installing parts as they moved. It was like pictures I had seen of the steer carcasses in a Chicago slaughterhouse. Finally, the planes were lowered to the floor, one after another, rolled out the hangar doors at the end of the factory, filled with gas, and flown out to war. It was an exciting sight for a thirteen-year-old. I was proud of my father. His next wartime job was to design a still larger airplane factory, again the world's largest plant under one roof, the Dodge Chicago plant.

When the war ended, Dad accepted an offer to oversee the buildup of the plutonium production facilities at Hanford, Washington. That project was being run by DuPont under contract with the Atomic Energy Commission. To take the job of chief structural engineer on the project, Dad moved to the Giffels and Vallet company, which became Giffels and Rossetti. Later he told me the firm had the largest volume of construction contracts in the world, and his project was the world's largest at that time. I grew up hearing these superlatives.

The Hanford project gave my father his first really good salary. But while I was away as a sophomore at Harvard, he left his job with Giffels and Rossetti, for reasons I never learned at the time. He was out of work for almost a year. Then he went back to Giffels and Rossetti as chief engineer for the whole firm.

Thirty years later, when my father was eighty-nine, I happened to ask him why he had left Giffels and Rossetti. He said, "Because they wanted me to help build the H-bomb."

This was a rather startling statement for me to hear that year. It was 1978, I was in full-time opposition to the nuclear arms race, and specifically to the deployment of the neutron bomb—a small H-bomb—which President Carter was proposing to send to Europe. (I was arrested four times that year on the railroad tracks at Rocky Flats Nuclear Weapons Production Facility, which produced all the plutonium triggers for H-bombs and was going to produce the cores for neutron bombs.) I had never heard anything like this before from my father, who wasn't particularly wired in to my antinuclear work or to any of my activism since the Vietnam War had ended. I asked him what he meant.

"They wanted me to be in charge of designing a big plant that would be producing material for an H-bomb."

I guessed that might have been the Savannah River plant in Georgia. He said he thought so. I asked him when this was.

"Late '49."

I said, "You must have the date wrong. You couldn't have heard about the hydrogen bomb then, it's too early." I'd just been reading about that. The General Advisory Committee of the Atomic Energy Commission (chaired by Robert Oppenheimer and including James Conant, Enrico Fermi, and I. I. Rabi) was considering that fall whether or not to launch a crash program for an H-bomb. They had advised against it, but President Truman overruled them.

"Truman didn't make the decision to go ahead till January 1950.

Meanwhile the whole thing was super-secret. You couldn't have heard about it in '49."

My father said, "Well, somebody had to design the plant if they were going to go ahead. I was the logical person. I was in charge of the structural engineering of the whole project at Hanford. I had a Q clearance."

That was the first I'd ever heard that he'd had a Q clearance—an AEC clearance for nuclear weapons design and stockpile data. I'd had that clearance myself in the Pentagon, after I left RAND in 1964. It made sense that he would have needed one, for Hanford. I said, "So you're telling me that you would have been one of the only people in the country who knew we were planning, or considering building, the H-bomb in 1949?"

He said, "I suppose so. Anyway, I know it was late '49, because that's when I quit."

"Why did you quit?"

"I didn't want to make an H-bomb. Why, that thing was going to be a thousand times more powerful than the A-bomb." I thought, score one for his memory, at eighty-nine. He remembered the proportion right. That was the same factor Oppenheimer and the others predicted in their report in 1949. (An H-bomb, a thermonuclear fusion weapon, requires a Nagasaki-type A-bomb, a plutonium fission weapon, as its trigger, to set it off. The first explosion of an H-bomb had more than a thousand times the explosive power of the Hiroshima blast.)

He went on: "I hadn't wanted to work on the A-bomb, either. But then Einstein seemed to think that we needed it, and it made sense to me that we had to have it against the Russians. So I took the job, but I never felt good about it.

"Then when they told me they were going to build a bomb a thousand times bigger, that was it for me. I went back to my office and I said to my deputy, 'These guys are crazy. They have an A-bomb, now they want an H-bomb. They're going to go right through the alphabet till they have a Z-bomb.'"

I said, "Well, they've only gotten up to N so far."

He said, "There was another thing about it that I couldn't stand. Building these things generated a lot of radioactive waste. I wasn't responsible for designing the containers for the waste, but I knew they were bound to leak eventually. That stuff was deadly forever. It was radioactive for twenty-four thousand years."

Again he had turned up a good figure. I said, "Your memory is working pretty well. It would be deadly a lot longer than that, but that's about the half-life of plutonium."

There were tears in his eyes. He said huskily, "I couldn't stand the thought that I was working on a project that was poisoning parts of my own country forever, that might make parts of it uninhabitable for thousands of years."

I thought over what he'd said, then I asked him if anyone else working with him had had misgivings. He didn't know.

"Were you the only one who quit?" He said yes. He was leaving the best job he'd ever had, and he didn't have any other to turn to. He lived on savings for a while. I thought about Oppenheimer and Conant and Fermi and Rabi, who had, that same month, expressed internally their opposition to the superbomb in the most extreme terms possible: potentially "a weapon of genocide . . . whose power of destruction is essentially unlimited . . . a threat to the future of the human race which is intolerable." Likewise Fermi and Rabi: "a danger to humanity as a whole . . . necessarily an evil thing considered in any light."

Yet these men didn't risk their clearances by sharing their anxieties and the basis for them with the American public, though they had urged the government to do so. Oppenheimer and Conant considered resigning their advisory positions when the president went ahead with the H-bomb. But they were prevailed on not to quit, lest that draw attention to their expert judgment that the president's course fatally endangered humanity.

I asked my father what had made him feel so strongly, to act in a way that nobody else had done. He said, "You did."

That didn't make any sense. I said, "What do you mean? We didn't discuss this at all. I didn't know anything about it."

Dad said, "It was earlier. I remember you came home with a book one day, and you were crying. It was about Hiroshima. You said, 'Dad, you've got to read this. It's the worst thing I've ever read.'"

I said that must have been John Hersey's book, *Hiroshima*. I didn't remember giving it to him.

"Yes. Well, I read it, and you were right. That's when I started to feel bad about working on an atomic bomb project. And then when they said they wanted me to work on a hydrogen bomb, it was too much for me. I thought it was time for me to get out."

I asked if he told his bosses why he was quitting. He said he told some people, others not. The ones he told seemed to understand his feelings. In fact, in less than a year, the head of the firm called to say that they wanted him to come back as chief structural engineer for the whole firm. They were dropping the DuPont contract (they didn't say why), so he wouldn't have to have anything to do with the AEC or bomb-making. He stayed with them until he retired.

I said, finally, "Dad, how could I not ever have heard any of this before? How come you never said anything about it?"

My father said, "Oh, I couldn't tell any of this to my family. You weren't cleared."

Thirty years after my father finished working on the Hanford buildup, Norman Solomon went to that nuclear site. Like so much else in this book, the story of what he found there is a personal account with great relevance for the present. *Made Love, Got War* helps us understand where we are now and how we got here.

The United States is a warfare state, but not just any old warfare state. It is what historian E. P. Thompson called, along with the former Soviet Union, "an exterminist state." Today, the Defense Department's least acknowledged mission is mass extermination. Our nuclear planning continues to provide for destroying thousands of cities and towns—the "urban-industrial base" of Russia,

China, and lesser potential adversaries. After President Nixon finally signed the Genocide Convention, he and his successors have denied targeting simply "cities" or "population per se" as the plans did explicitly in my day, but the planned destruction of people is essentially the same: up to hundreds of millions, perhaps billions, of deaths.

Political leaders are not any more candid about such information than President Truman was when he told the public in August 1945, "The world will note that the first atomic bomb was dropped on Hiroshima, a military base. That was because we wished in this first attack to avoid, in so far as possible, the killing of civilians." It was days before the American public picked up that Hiroshima was the name of a city, not a camp: the targeted ground zero was the center of the city.

In the early twenty-first century, it is still the U.S. government's policy to initiate nuclear warfare if the American military is met by overwhelming conventional force—which could easily happen at the periphery of our empire, in the neighborhood of our adversaries. The use of nuclear weapons is the apex of the contingency plans; it's certainly not the first step. But if things get out of hand, the endgame of the U.S. warfare state is mass extermination. And the point of the endgame is to throw its shadow before it—to make clear to the other side that the endgame is their total extermination. This policy is based on the ability to destroy cities and surrounding towns, by blast, fire, and widespread fallout. We checkmate with that ability.

To this day, as a matter of policy, planning, deployment, and readiness, the U.S. government keeps open the option of first use of nuclear weapons, in a wide variety of circumstances: including escalation preemptively to all-out, multi-genocidal attack.

We have lived with a god, our savior the bomb, that (the fable goes) won a war while saving us from an otherwise-inevitable invasion of Japan that would have cost the lives of a million GIs: fathers, brothers, and sons. Though historians know that story of "necessity" to be deliberate mystification, since 1945 the American public has lived not only with this positive attitude toward the bomb, but also in a state of near-total denial as to what our military machine has actually become.

I doubt that one American in a hundred has a clear understanding that the devastation at Nagasaki was the result of being hit by what is now just a detonator to a modern nuclear weapon, of which we possess some ten thousand (as does Russia). Our image of nuclear war from 1945 only shows what happens when a detonating cap for a thermonuclear weapon is set off.

Hanford and other facilities have produced the plutonium for scores of thousands of thermonuclear bombs. By the late 1950s, an era described in this book's first chapter, our leaders contemplated killing more than half a billion people under various circumstances. The leaders built, and since then have maintained, the machinery to destroy billions of humans—possibly all life on Earth, though that "nuclear winter" effect wasn't recognized till the early '80s—at a moment's notice. As citizens, we didn't shrink from what little we knew of that prospect—which was far short of the reality, but already horrendous—and we still don't. Our imperial attitudes and those of our leaders are not significantly different from earlier empires—but the physical capability for destruction our leaders wield is thousands of times greater.

I was born in 1931, and my generation had to reorient itself to the unprecedented threat of planetary nuclear suicide-murder. Norman Solomon was born twenty years later, and his generation has never lived under any other circumstance. The strands of this book form a unique weave of personal narrative and historical inquiry. *Made Love, Got War* lays out a half century of socialized insanity that has brought a succession of aggressive wars under cover of—but at recurrent risk of detonating—a genocidal nuclear arsenal. We need to help each other to awaken from this madness.

*You think when you wake up in the mornin yesterday
don't count. But yesterday is all that does count. What
else is there? Your life is made out of the days it's made
out of. Nothin else. You might think you could run
away and change your name and I don't know what
all. Start over. And then one mornin you wake up and
look at the ceilin and guess who's layin there?*

No Country for Old Men, Cormac McCarthy

*You may leave here for four days in space
But when you return, it's the same old place*

"Eve of Destruction," sung by Barry McGuire

*When we review the past and observe it deeply, if we
are standing firmly in the present, we are not overwhelmed by it. The materials of the past which make
up the present become clear when they express themselves in the present. We can learn from them. . . . The
ghosts of the past, which follow us into the present,
also belong to the present moment.*

Thich Nhat Hanh

1

COLD WAR CHILDHOOD

A story could start almost anywhere. This one begins at a moment startled by a rocket.

In the autumn of 1957, America was not at war . . . or at peace. The threat of nuclear annihilation shadowed every day, flickering with visions of the apocalyptic. In classrooms, "duck and cover" drills were part of the curricula. Underneath any Norman Rockwell painting, the grim reaper had attained the power of an ultimate monster.

Dwight Eisenhower was most of the way through his fifth year in the White House. He liked to speak reassuring words of patriotic faith, with presidential statements like: "America is the greatest force that God has ever allowed to exist on His footstool." Or: "Without God there could be no American form of government, nor an American way of life. Recognition of the Supreme Being is the first—the most basic—expression of Americanism." Such pronouncements drew a sharp distinction between the United States and the Godless Communist foe.

But on October 4, 1957, the Kremlin announced the launch of *Sputnik*, the world's first satellite. God was supposed to be on America's side, yet the Soviet atheists had gotten to the heavens before us. Suddenly the eagle of liberty could not fly nearly so high.

Sputnik was instantly fascinating and alarming. The American press swooned at the scientific vistas and shuddered at the military implications. Under the headline "Red Moon Over the U.S.," *Time* quickly explained that "a new era in history had begun, opening a

bright new chapter in mankind's conquest of the natural environment and a grim new chapter in the cold war." The newsmagazine
was glum about the space rivalry: "The U.S. had lost its lead because, in spreading its resources too thin, the nation had skimped
too much on military research and development. Russia's victory in
the satellite race proved that the U.S. had not tried hard enough."

At a diplomatic party, Washington's famed "hostess with the
mostest" Perle Mesta bristled when an administration official told
her that *Sputnik* would be forgotten in six months. Mesta shot back:
"And in six months we may all be dead." The White House tried to
project calm; Eisenhower said the satellite "does not raise my apprehension, not one iota." But many on the political spectrum heard
Sputnik's radio pulse as an ominous taunt.

A heroine of the Republican right, Clare Boothe Luce, said the
satellite's beeping was an "outer-space raspberry to a decade of
American pretensions that the American way of life was a gilt-
edged guarantee of our material superiority." Newspaper readers
learned that Stuart Symington, a Democratic senator who'd been
the first secretary of the air force, "said the Russians will be able to
launch mass attacks against the United States with intercontinental
ballistic missiles within two or three years." Most worrisome was
the fact that *Sputnik*'s first-stage rocket had more than 200,000
pounds of thrust—eight times what the USA was prepared to put
behind its first satellite launch, set for a few months later.

The heft of *Sputnik* made America seem like a space-age light-
weight. "The few who are allowed to know about such things and
are able to understand them are saying that the launching of so big
a satellite signifies that the Soviets are much ahead of this country
in the development of rocket missiles," columnist Walter Lippmann
wrote a week after the 184-pound *Sputnik* went aloft. He added: "In
short, the fact that we have lost the race to launch the satellite
means that we are losing the race to produce ballistic missiles. This
in turn means that the United States and the western world may be
falling behind in the progress of science and technology. This is a
grim business."

A *New York Times* article matter-of-factly referred to "the mild panic that has seized most of the nation since Russia's sputnik was launched two weeks ago." In another story, looking forward, *Times* science reporter William L. Laurence called for bigger pots of gold at the end of scientific rainbows: "In a free society such as ours it is not possible 'to channel human efforts' without the individual's consent and wholehearted willingness. To attract able and promising young men and women into the fields of science and engineering it is necessary first to offer them better inducements than are presently offered."

As if to underscore that *Sputnik* hadn't been a fluke, on November 3 the Soviet Union followed up by launching a second satellite—at 1,100 pounds, six times the weight of the first. While it orbited the Earth, the new capsule housed a dog whose live countenance, circling the planet every hour and three quarters, became a canine symbol of Russia's triumph in space.

The autumn satellites of 1957 lit a fire under the federal government and the scientific establishment in the United States. For the U.S. space effort, progress came in fits and starts. On December 6, a test satellite dubbed *Vanguard* blew up seconds after firing. At last, in early February 1958, an American satellite—the thirty-pound *Explorer*—went into orbit. But four days later, a *Vanguard* launch again quickly fizzled with an explosion in the air. That month, the government set up its first space agency.

What had succeeded in powering the *Explorer* satellite into space was a military rocket, developed by a U.S. Army research team. The head of that team, the rocket scientist Wernher von Braun, was boosting the red-white-and-blue after the fall of his ex-employer, the Third Reich. In March 1958 he publicly warned that the U.S. space program was a few years behind the Russians.

Soon after dusk, while turning a skate key or playing with a hula hoop, children might look up to see if they could spot the bright light of a satellite arching across the sky. But they could not see the fallout from nuclear bomb tests, underway for a dozen years by 1958. The conventional wisdom, reinforced by the press, down-played fears while trusting the authorities; basic judgments about the latest weapons programs were to be left to the political leaders and their designated experts.

Even with all the assurances during the decade, worries grew about health effects of radioactivity from above. But apologists often blamed the nefarious enemy. "On Your Guard: Reds Launch 'Scare Drive' Against U.S. Atomic Tests," said a 1955 *Los Angeles Examiner* headline over one nationally distributed column, which told of "a big Communist 'fear' campaign to force Washington to stop all American atomic hydrogen bomb tests." The *Washington Post*, the *Chicago Daily News*, and other major newspapers pub-lished similar messages from another syndicated columnist, David Lawrence, who wrote in a typical piece: "Evidence of a world-wide propaganda is accumulating. Many persons are innocently being duped by it and some well-meaning scientists and other persons are playing the Communist game unwittingly by exaggerating the im-portance of radioactive substances known as 'fallout.'" Lawrence portrayed the star-spangled bomb explosions as beneficial: "The Nevada tests are being conducted for a humanitarian purpose—to determine the best ways to help civilian defense—and not to de-velop stronger weapons of war." Such claims were ludicrous. And dangerous.

In the community of Railroad Valley not far north of the Nevada Test Site, a boy named Martin Bardoli died of leukemia months after entering grade school in 1956. When his parents cir-culated a petition and sent it to government officials, Senator George Malone responded with a letter cautioning against un-founded alarm and adding "it is not impossible to suppose that some of the 'scare' stories are Communist inspired."

On the weekly prime-time Walt Disney television show, an an-imated fairy with a magic wand urged youngsters to drink three glasses of milk each day. But airborne strontium-90 from nuclear tests was falling on pastures all over, migrating to cows and then to the milk supply and, finally, to people's bones. Radioactive isotopes from fallout were becoming inseparable from the human diet.

The more that work by expert scientists endangered us, the more we were informed that we needed those scientists to save us. Who better to protect Americans from the hazards of the nuclear industry and the terrifying potential of nuclear weapons than the best scientific minds serving the industry and developing the weapons?

In June 1957—the same month Nobel Prize–winning chemist Linus Pauling published an article estimating that ten thousand cases of leukemia had already occurred due to U.S. and Soviet nuclear testing—President Eisenhower proclaimed that the American detonations would result in nuclear warheads with much less radioactivity. Ike said that "we have reduced fallout from bombs by nine-tenths," and he pledged that the Nevada explosions would continue in order to "see how clean we can make them." The president spoke just after meeting with Edward Teller and other high-powered physicists. Eisenhower assured the country that the scientists and the U.S. nuclear test operations were working on the public's behalf. "They say: 'Give us four or five more years to test each step of our development and we will produce an absolutely clean bomb.'" But sheer atomic fantasy, however convenient, was wearing thin.

Many scientists actually opposed the aboveground nuclear blasts. Relying on dissenters with a range of technical expertise, Democratic nominee Adlai Stevenson had made an issue of fallout in the 1956 presidential campaign. During 1957—a year when the U.S. government set off thirty-two nuclear bombs over southern Nevada and the Pacific—Pauling spearheaded a global petition drive against nuclear testing; by January 1958 more than eleven thousand scientists in fifty countries had signed.

Clearly, the views and activities of scientists ran the gamut. But Washington was pumping billions of tax dollars into massive vehicles for scientific research. These huge federal outlays were imposing military priorities on American scientists without any need for a blatant government decree.

––––––––––

The book that I've remembered most vividly from my childhood, *David and the Phoenix*, was a selection of the Weekly Reader Children's Book Club in 1958. The story packed an emotional wallop, with themes that foreshadowed decades of conflicts involving science, careers, violence, and reverence for life.

It's summer, and David's family moves into a house with a wondrous mountain just behind the backyard. David, maybe ten years old, climbs the mountain and discovers a large, awesome bird. The Phoenix is glad to assist with the boy's education, which the erudite bird is quick to distinguish from schooling. ("Life is real, life is earnest. One must face it with a *practical* education.") Transported on the Phoenix's back, David goes to fascinating and mystical places. But there's danger lurking, as the Phoenix explains: "I had been here no more than three months when a Scientist was hot on my trail. A most disagreeable fellow, always sneaking about with binoculars, a camera, and, I fear, a gun."

Down from the mountain one night, David walks into the living room only to discover that his mother and father are hosting the Scientist, who is talking excitedly. "It's the discovery of the age," the honored guest is saying. "My name will be famous if I succeed in my plans."

The Scientist finally closes in—as it happens, on Phoenix's five-hundredth birthday—a day when, not quite knowing why, the fantastic bird has built a pyre. After David and Phoenix enjoy a lovely picnic on the mountainside, Phoenix sprinkles the pyre with cinnamon. And David realizes, with horror, what is about to happen. Averting his eyes, the child hears the scrape of a match, then crackling branches . . . indistinct time passes . . . and then, through a smoky haze, he sees the charred pile stir, and a magnificent young bird emerges. And then, from partway down the mountain, comes the sound of a man shouting. It's the Scientist, running up the trail and waving a rifle.

Paralyzed with fear, David remained on his knees as the Scientist reached an open place and threw the gun up to his shoulder. The bullet went whining by with an ugly hornet-noise, and the report of the gun echoed along the scarp.

"Fly, Phoenix!" David sobbed. A second bullet snarled at the bird, and spattered out little chips of rock from the inner wall of the ledge.

"Oh, fly, fly!" David jumped up and flung himself between the bird and the Scientist. "It's me!" he cried. "It's David!" The bird gazed at him closely, and a light flickered in its eye as though the name had reached out and almost, but not quite, touched an ancient memory. Hesitantly it stretched forth one wing, and with the tip of it lightly brushed David's forehead, leaving there a mark that burned coolly.

"*Get away from that bird, you little idiot!*" the Scientist shrieked. "*GET AWAY!*"

David ignored him. "Fly, Phoenix!" he cried, and he pushed the bird toward the edge.

Understanding dawned in the amber eyes at last. The bird, with one clear, defiant cry, leaped to an out-jutting boulder. The golden wings spread, the golden neck curved back, the golden talons pushed against the rock. The bird launched itself into the air and soared out over the valley, sparkling, flashing, shimmering; a flame, large as a sunburst, a meteor, a diamond, a star, diminishing at last to a speck of gold dust, which glimmered twice in the distance before it was gone altogether.

While many scientists climbed toward career peaks as fast as their brains would carry them, the continuation of life was in the crosshairs of very big guns. For the first time, weaponry at hand could bag the game with absolute finality: turning the current generations to ash all at once, with no one left to mourn or to carry on. The thermonuclear invention might end all death and life, courtesy of the most "advanced" science that money could buy.

The U.S. Treasury kept funneling billions into science with a doomsday twist. The trend had become evident soon after the

Second World War. In autumn 1946, speaking at a public-affairs forum in New York, atomic physicist Philip Morrison noted that the U.S. military was funding a hefty portion of scientific research. "Some schools," he said, "derive 90 percent of their research support from navy funds." Morrison saw where the juggernaut was headed: "The now amicable contracts will tighten up and the fine print will start to contain talk about results and specific weapon problems. And science itself will have been bought by war on the installment plan."

The purchase was apparent. As Morrison commented, "The physicist knows the situation is a wrong and dangerous one. He is impelled to go along because he really needs the money." By the time the century reached its midpoint, several dozen major universities held large nuclear contracts with the government.

In a lament that aired on NBC Radio in early 1950, the physics pioneer Leo Szilard—whose prewar work had made sustained chain reactions possible—raised a warning about the slippery slope to mass destruction. "In 1939 when we tried to persuade the government to take up the development of atomic energy, American public opinion was undivided on the issue that it is morally wrong and reprehensible to bomb cities and to kill women and children," he said. "During the war, almost imperceptibly, we started to use giant gasoline bombs against Japan, killing millions of women and children; finally we used the A-bomb. I believe there is a general uneasiness among the scientists. It is easy for them to agree that we cannot trust Russia, but they also ask themselves: To what extent can we trust ourselves?"

Such provocative questions went largely ignored. The decision to develop the hydrogen bomb followed a brief and secretive high-level debate that President Truman settled in 1950. Truman brushed off the physicists who counseled against going ahead with the "super bomb"—scientists were mere formula-crunchers with little political clout, unless their prestige and zeal helped propel Washington's top policymakers where they wanted to go. The same hierarchy that asserted its civilian control over the military also asserted its civilian authority over science, if only by dint of appropriations. A physicist with no budget might just as well be in a sandbox.

Truman rejected a somber report from the Atomic Energy Commission's advisory committee. (The chairman of the panel, J. Robert Oppenheimer, had become a national hero four years earlier for leading the secret effort to develop the atom bomb at the Los Alamos laboratory.) Assessing the hydrogen bomb, the report said: "It is clear that the use of this weapon would bring about the destruction of innumerable human lives; it is not a weapon which can be used exclusively for the destruction of material installations of military or semi-military purposes. Its use therefore carries much further than the atomic bomb itself the policy of exterminating civilian populations." A hydrogen bomb could top the destructive power of an atomic bomb by a factor of hundreds. At the fulcrum of the twentieth century, going ahead with H-bombs would catapult the world to the brink of full-blown nuclear holocaust.

The Los Alamos lab began joint work with the new Lawrence Livermore laboratory, which focused on the hydrogen bomb from the day its doors opened in 1952. Both labs operated under the aegis of the University of California; the academic affiliation served as a useful air freshener to cover the stench of Armageddon technology. Across the country a labyrinth of top-clearance facilities cranked out the collaborative work of academia, profit-driven contractors, and government agencies. Incalculable resources fueled the Bomb— the capital "B" would later fade as the presence of nuclear weapons became routine—an immutable fact of life.

"Delivery systems" could be faster and more elusive; "payloads" smaller and more powerful. In the early '50s, the first H-bombs were the size of large buildings, set off on Pacific islands far from American shores. News reports and Washington's political viewfinders abstracted into fuzziness the horrific realities of nuclear tests. Tropical locales of inestimable beauty, amid green dollops and sandy spits in the ocean, with names like Bikini and Eniwetok, vaporized in a split-atom second that flashed ultrabright, and then blotted out the sun. Repeatedly, a lacquer of radioactive isotopes settled onto a former paradise; thick, white fallout sometimes coated beaches, foliage, and the tops of palm trees. As the decade went on, cancer and birth defects began to afflict native islanders. Meanwhile, far away, Americans embraced risqué bathing suits known as bikinis.

Young people—dubbed "baby boomers," a phrase that both dramatized and trivialized them—were especially vulnerable to strontium-90 as their fast-growing bones absorbed the radioactive isotope along with calcium. The children who did as they were told by drinking plenty of milk ended up heightening the risks—not unlike their parents, who were essentially told to accept the bomb fallout without complaint.

Under the snappy rubric of "the nuclear age," the white-coated and loyal American scientist stood as an icon, revered as surely as the scientists of the enemy were assumed to be pernicious. And yet the mutual fallout, infiltrating dairy farms and mothers' breast milk and the bones of children, was a type of subversion that never preoccupied J. Edgar Hoover.

————

What was being suppressed might suddenly pop up like some kind of jack-in-the-box. Righteous pressure against disruptive or "un-American" threats was internal and also global, with a foreign policy based on containment. Control of space, inner and outer, was pivotal. What could not be controlled was liable to be condemned.

The '50s and early '60s are now commonly derided as unbearably rigid, but much in the era was new and stylish at the time. Suburbs boomed along with babies. Modern household gadgets and snazzier cars appeared with great commercial fanfare while millions of families, with a leg up from the GI Bill, climbed into some part of the vaguely defined middle class. The fresh and exciting technology called television did much to turn suburbia into the stuff of white-bread legends—with scant use for the less-sightly difficulties of the near-poor and destitute living in ghettos or rural areas where the TV lights didn't shine. On the surface, most kids lived in a placid time, while small screens showed entertaining images of sanitized life. One among many archetypes came from Betty Crocker cake-mix commercials, which were all over the tube; the close-ups of the icing could seem remarkable, even in black and white. Little girls who had toy ovens with little cake-mix boxes could make miniature layer cakes.

Every weekday from 1955 to 1965 the humdrum pathos of women known as housewives could be seen on *Queen for a Day*. The climax of each episode came as one of the competitors, often sobbing, stood with a magnificent bouquet of roses suddenly in her arms, overcome with joy. Splendid gifts of brand-new refrigerators and other consumer products, maybe even mink stoles, would elevate bleak lives into a stratosphere that America truly had to offer. The show pitted women's sufferings against each other; victory would be the just reward for the best, which was to say the worst, predicament. The final verdict came in the form of applause from the studio audience, measured by an on-screen meter that jumped with the decibels of apparent empathy and commiseration, one winner per program. Solutions were individual. *Queen for a Day* was a nationally televised ritual of charity, providing selective testimony to the goodness of society. Virtuous grief, if heartrending enough, could summon prizes, and the ecstatic weeping of a crowned recipient was vicarious pleasure for viewers across the country, who could see clearly America's bounty and generosity.

That televised spectacle was not entirely fathomable to the baby-boom generation, which found more instructive role-modeling from such media fare as *The Adventures of Spin and Marty* and Annette Funicello and other aspects of the *Mickey Mouse Club* show—far more profoundly prescriptive than descriptive. By example and inference, we learned how kids were supposed to be, and our being more that way made the media images seem more natural and realistic. It was a spiral of self-mystification, with the authoritative versions of childhood green-lighted by network executives, producers, and sponsors. Likewise with the sitcoms, which drew kids into a Potemkin refuge from whatever home life they experienced on the near side of the TV screen.

Dad was apt to be emotionally aloof in real life, but on television the daddies were endearingly quirky, occasionally stern, essentially lovable, and even mildly loving. Despite the canned laugh tracks, for kids this could be very serious—a substitute world with obvious advantages over the starker one around them. The chances of their parents measuring up to the moms and dads on *Ozzie and Harriet* or *Father Knows Best* were remote. As were, often, the real parents. Or at least they seemed real. Sometimes.

Father Knows Best aired on network television for almost ten years. The first episodes gained little momentum in 1954, but within a couple of years the show was one of the nation's leading prime-time psychodramas. It gave off warmth that simulated intimacy; for children at a huge demographic bulge, maybe no TV program was more influential as a family prototype.

But seventeen years after the shooting stopped, the actor who had played Bud, the only son on *Father Knows Best*, expressed remorse. "I'm ashamed I had any part of it," Billy Gray said. "People felt warmly about the show and that show did everybody a disservice." Gray had come to see the program as deceptive. "I felt that the show purported to be real life, and it wasn't. I regret that it was ever presented as a model to live by." And he added: "I think we were all well motivated but what we did was run a hoax. We weren't trying to, but that is what it was. Just a hoax."

———

In TV-land, as elsewhere, hoaxsters could earn a living, sometimes a very good one. There was no cabal. That was the system. Hoaxing was most of all about coaxing money out of pockets. And the proliferation of advertising on the increasingly powerful new medium was the essence of hoax. On television, hucksterism boomed through programs and commercials alike.

Mad Magazine was the only mass-distributed challenge to the saturating culture of hoax in the 1950s. While *Consumer Reports* tried to counteract advertising with factual evaluations of product quality, *Mad*'s satiric mission went for the jugular. The grinning young icon Alfred E. Neuman served as a zany alter ego for readers while the editors promoted slyly subversive sensibilities. For many kids, *Mad* was the first public source to acknowledge that respectables were lying to them on a regular basis—the first methodical exposure of absurd gaps between pretenses and realities. The professionals at work along Madison Avenue and Pennsylvania Avenue were frequent targets; so were more general patterns of conceits. For instance, in an era of new plastics widely regarded as virtuously antiseptic, a *Mad* cartoon spoofed such fixations: "Untouched by human hands," said a billboard outside a factory. Inside, chimpanzees were at the assembly line.

Symbolic of the shift into the 1960s was the election of a young president who had baby-boom children. John F. Kennedy arrived with pledges of renewal after campaigning with false claims that the USA was on the short end of a "missile gap" with the Soviet Union. He often emphasized science as the way to explore the new frontier on Earth and in space.

During the same autumn JFK won the presidency, John Hersey came out with *The Child Buyer*, a novel written in the form of a hearing before a state senate committee. "Excuse me, Mrs., but I wonder if you know what's at stake in this situation," a senator says to the mother of a ten-year-old genius being sought for purchase by the United Lymphomilloid corporation. "You realize the national defense is involved here."

"This is my boy," the mom replies. "This is my beautiful boy they want to take away from me."

A vice president of United Lymphomilloid, "in charge of materials procurement," testifies that "my duties have an extremely high national-defense rating." He adds: "When a commodity that you need falls in short supply, you have to get out and hustle. I buy brains. About eighteen months ago my company, United Lympho-

milloid of America, Incorporated, was faced with an extremely difficult problem, a project, a long-range government contract, fifty
years, highly specialized and top secret, and we needed some of the
best minds in the country . . ."

Soon, most of the lawmakers on the committee are impressed
with the importance of the proposed purchase for the nation. So
there's some consternation when the child buyer reports that he finally laid his proposition "squarely on the table"—and the boy's
answer was no.

Senator Skypack exclaims: "What the devil, couldn't you go
over his head and just buy him?"

The Child Buyer is a clever send-up, with humor far from light-
hearted. Fifteen years after Hersey did firsthand research for his
book *Hiroshima*, the Cold War had America by the throat. The child
buyer (whose name, as if anticipating a Bob Dylan song not to be
written for several more years, is Mr. Jones) tells the senate panel
that his quest is urgent, despite the fifty-year duration of the project. "As you know, we live in a cutthroat world," he says. "What appears as sweetness and light in your common television commercial
of a consumer product often masks a background of ruthless com-
petitive infighting. The gift-wrapped brickbat. Polite legal belly-
slitting. Banditry dressed in a tux. The more so with projects like
ours. A prospect of perfectly enormous profits is involved here. We
don't intend to lose out."

And what is the project for which the child will be bought? A
memorandum, released into the hearing record, details "the meth-
ods used by United Lymphomilloid to eliminate all conflict from
the inner lives of the purchased specimens and to ensure their uti-
lization of their innate equipment at maximum efficiency." First
comes solitary confinement for a period of weeks in "the Forgetting
Chamber." A second phase, called "Education and Desensitization in
Isolation," moves the process forward. Then comes a "Data-feeding
Period"; then major surgery that "consists of 'tying off' all five
senses"; then the last, long-term phase called "Productive Work."
Asked whether the project is too drastic, Mr. Jones dismisses the

question: "This method has produced mental prodigies such as man has never imagined possible. Using tests developed by company researchers, the firm has measured I.Q.'s of three fully trained specimens at 974, 989, and 1005 . . ."

It is the boy who brings a semblance of closure on the last day of the hearing. "I guess Mr. Jones is really the one who tipped the scales," the child explains. "He talked to me a long time this morning. He made me feel sure that a life dedicated to U. Lympho would at least be *interesting*. More interesting than anything that can happen to me now in school or at home. . . . Fascinating to be a specimen, truly fascinating. Do you suppose I really can develop an I.Q. of over a thousand?"

But, a senator asks, does the boy really think he can forget everything in the Forgetting Chamber?

"I was wondering about that this morning," the boy replies. "About forgetting. I've always had an idea that each memory was a kind of picture, an insubstantial picture. I've thought of it as suddenly coming into your mind when you need it, something you've seen, something you've heard, then it may stay awhile, or else it flies out, then maybe it comes back another time. I was wondering about the Forgetting Chamber. If all the pictures went out, if I forgot everything, where would they go? Just out into the air? Into the sky? Back home, around my bed, where my dreams stay?"

I went to the John Glenn parade in downtown Washington on February 26, 1962, a week after he'd become the first American to circle the globe in a space capsule. Glenn was a certified hero, and my school deemed the parade a valid excuse for an absence. To me, a fifth grader, that seemed like a good deal even when the weather turned out to be cold and rainy.

For the new and dazzling space age, America's astronauts served as valiant explorers who added to the élan of the Camelot mythos around the presidential family. The Kennedys were sexy, exciting, modern aristocrats who relied on deft wordsmiths to produce throbbing eloquent speeches about freedom and democracy. The bearing was American regal, melding the appeal of refined nobility and touch football. The media image was damn-near storybook. Few Americans, and very few young people of the era, were aware of the actual roles of JFK's vaunted new "special forces" dispatched to the Third World, where—below the media radar—they targeted labor-union organizers and other assorted foes of U.S.-backed oligarchies.

But a confrontation with the Soviet Union materialized that could not be ignored. Eight months after the Glenn parade, in tandem with Nikita Khrushchev, the president dragged the world to a nuclear precipice. In late October 1962, Kennedy went on national television and denounced "the Soviet military buildup on the island of Cuba," asserting that "a series of offensive missile sites is now in preparation on that imprisoned island." Speaking from the White House, the president said: "We will not prematurely or unnecessarily risk the costs of worldwide nuclear war in which even the fruits of victory would be ashes in our mouth—but neither will we shrink from that risk at any time it must be faced."

In our household, an elder half-heartedly piled cans of food and bottled water next to the ping-pong table in the basement. I didn't know enough to be very worried, but my parents seemed edgy. So did my teacher, who saw kids glancing at the clock on the classroom wall and commented that she knew we must be thinking about the U.S. ships scheduled to begin enforcing a naval quarantine around Cuba; actually I had been eager to get out to recess. At the time, most children didn't understand what came to be known as the Cuban Missile Crisis; it was mainly frightening in retrospect, when we realized that the last word could have been annihilation.

Early in the next autumn, President Kennedy signed the Limited Test Ban Treaty, which sent nuclear detonations underground. The treaty was an important public health measure against radioactive fallout. Meanwhile, the banishment of mushroom clouds made superpower preparations for blowing up the world less visible. The new limits did nothing to interfere with further development of nuclear arsenals.

· Kennedy liked to talk about vigor, and he epitomized it. Younger than Eisenhower by a full generation, witty, with a suave wife and two adorable kids, he was leading the way to open vistas. Store windows near Pennsylvania Avenue displayed souvenir plates and other Washington knickknacks that depicted the First Family—standard tourist paraphernalia, yet with a lot more pizzazz than what Dwight and Mamie had generated.

A few years after the Glenn parade, when I passed the same storefront windows along blocks just east of the White House, the JFK glamour had gone dusty, as if suspended in time, facing backward. I thought of a scene from *Great Expectations*. The Kennedy era already seemed like the room where Miss Havisham's wedding cake had turned to ghastly cobwebs; in Dickens' words, "as if a feast had been in preparation when the house and the clocks all stopped together."

The clocks all seemed to stop together on the afternoon of November 22, 1963. But after the assassination, the gist of the reputed best-and-brightest remained in top Cabinet positions. The distance from Dallas to the Gulf of Tonkin was scarcely eight months as the calendar flew. And soon America's awesome scientific capabilities were trained on a country where guerrilla fighters walked on the soles of sandals cut from old rubber tires.

2

INNOCENCE ON THE EVE
OF DESTRUCTION

One day, midway through the 1960s, NBC News correspondent Elie Abel spoke to a student assembly at Eastern Junior High School in suburban Maryland, a few blocks from an exit along the newly opened Beltway. He talked about the escalating war in Vietnam without a hint of challenge or skepticism. To my young ears, the take-home message was: this is happening, it's important, get used to it. At about the same time, in 1965, CBS viewers heard Walter Cronkite praise "the courageous decision that Communism's advance must be stopped in Asia and that guerrilla warfare as a means to a political end must be finally discouraged."

Around the time that Mr. Abel dropped by our school, I went with a friend to the Washington Coliseum for a concert. Our seats were in an upper balcony, far from the stage. All I remember, other than the singer's frizzy hair and guitar and harmonica in the spotlight, was the song with a refrain about how there was something happening but Mr. Jones didn't know what it was. I was in my fifteenth year, and I didn't know what it was either.

Bob Dylan wasn't getting much air play then. "Masters of War" and "With God on Our Side" were a long way from AM radio. But like millions of others who listened to songs on the hit parade, I often heard "Eve of Destruction," the only chilling tune on pop airwaves in the autumn of 1965. The song drew much of its power from what routinely went unspoken and unacknowledged. Barry McGuire's haunting voice gave the lyrics special resonance, and "Eve of Destruction" vibrated with specters usually examined in the privacy of one's mental home, if at all.

> Don't you understand what I'm tryin' to say
> Can't you feel the fears I'm feelin' today?
> If the button is pushed, there's no runnin' away
> There'll be no one to save, with the world in a grave

Orderly compartments aside, political "issues" and personal lives could be as close as strontium and our own bones. Fears were riveted on foreign enemies; in 1965 we of the baby-boom generation were not more than dimly aware of the dangers posed by the most widely esteemed leaders in our midst. During history lived as real time, "Eve of Destruction" was just ahead of the curving arc. "You don't believe in war/But what's that gun you're totin'?"

Those of us born after World War II were "postwar," but that was a misnomer. We were also prewar. During the 1960s alone, the Pentagon directly visited America's robust military expertise on Vietnam, the Dominican Republic, Laos, and Cambodia. We came of age not only in the tense superpower era of the Cold War but also within a warfare state.

The biggest war was happening in Vietnam, but it was more about the United States. (In Norman Mailer's novel titled *Why Are We in Vietnam?*, the word "Vietnam" would not appear until the last page.) America's most eminent foreign-policy thinkers were in sync with those who made the news and reported it, those who gave the largest campaign contributions and received them. The nation's powerhouses of cards showed signs of being more than a little shaky; after the Cuban Missile Crisis and the killing of JFK, just thirteen months apart, the usual pretenses of on-God's-footstool stability were farfetched; yet the dominant systems always regrouped to present images of transcendent solidity.

The decade's middle years coincided with a persistent craze for secret agents in movies and prime-time television. As one observer noted, "There was the shared enthusiasm for sadomasochistic spy thrillers—*The Man From U.N.C.L.E.*, *The Avengers*, the James Bond series, in all of which affectlessness is cultivated as a means to dignity, to be cool; in all of which freedom is blithely appropriated by the hero by the simple technique of not feeling compassion." Ultimately the secret agent was in control; that he represented the forces of good was to be assumed, no matter how icy his manner or deadly his actions. Any unscripted empathy, for the foreign enemy or even for the glamorous babe, would just get in the way.

Standard political rhetoric, from the White House and Congress or from reporters and commentators, kept affirming that the men at the helm of American power were profoundly trustworthy and the ship of state remained as dependably seaworthy as ever; the captains of industry and government were sailing onward with the blessed national grail on board, still the essential precious cargo loaded by the Founding Fathers almost two centuries earlier. Bottom line: The country was basically in good hands controlled by wise minds.

———

The year 1965 began on a reassuring set of political notes for most Americans, including—and perhaps especially—people with liberal outlooks. Lyndon Johnson's inaugural address came after his landslide defeat of someone who sounded like a reckless fanatic. The Johnson campaign had successfully portrayed Senator Barry Goldwater as an extremist, willing to speak casually about use of nuclear weapons. An LBJ commercial showed a girl counting petals on a daisy while the audio melded into a countdown for a missile launch and then a mushroom cloud, conveying the idea that the president—unlike his opponent—was a force for atomic sanity. President Johnson offered continuity, rationality, restraint. And his "Great Society" agenda lifted the sights of the country.

"In a land of great wealth," Johnson declared at his inauguration, "families must not live in hopeless poverty. In a land rich in harvest, children just must not go hungry. In a land of healing miracles, neighbors must not suffer and die unattended." The president voiced only a faint foreshadowing of the warfare that was to strangle the Great Society in its crib: "If American lives must end, and American treasure be spilled, in countries we barely know, that is the price that change has demanded of conviction and of our enduring covenant."

That such assuring words could come to mean almost anything—and virtually nothing—was a lesson that many attentive "baby boomers" would begin to learn during the last half of the decade. But getting wise to rhetorical appearances was usually a slow, intermittent process. And maybe no aspect of America's promise was more enticing, or ultimately more hollow, than the chimera of scientific deliverance. "Even now," Johnson proudly reminded the nation within the first minute of his inaugural speech, "a rocket moves toward Mars."

Top-notch scientists would discover how to prolong life, develop cures, and ease suffering. Science helped many people, and potentially could help many more at home and abroad. But efforts to extend those benefits were severely limited by the priorities of what President Eisenhower, in his farewell address, dubbed "the military-industrial complex." Less famously, in the same speech, he warned that "public policy could itself become the captive of a scientific-technological elite."

Scientists doing work with grisly applications had numerous ways to disclaim responsibility for the end use. One unsettling example was Wernher von Braun. In the words of NASA's official history, he was "well-known as the leader of what has been called the 'rocket team,' which developed the V-2 ballistic missile for the Nazis during World War II." For fifteen years after the war, von Braun and his German rocket team worked for the U.S. Army to develop ballistic missiles. "In 1960, his rocket development center transferred from the Army to the newly established NASA and received a mandate to build the giant Saturn rockets. Accordingly, von Braun became director of NASA's Marshall Space Flight Center and the chief architect of the Saturn V launch vehicle, the super-booster that would propel Americans to the Moon."

The renowned atomic scientist Edward Teller insisted, early in the nuclear age, that he and his colleagues should stick to making technical judgments. "The scientist is not responsible for the laws of nature," he commented. "It is his job to find out how these laws operate. It is the scientist's job to find the ways in which these laws can serve the human will." Robert Oppenheimer, who referred to devising the atom bomb as a "technically sweet problem," also said: "It is my judgment in these things that when you see something that is technically sweet, you go ahead and do it and you argue about what to do about it only after you have had your technical success."

Some American scientists, moving beyond the tunnel vision of their disciplines, tried to constrain or reverse ominous trends. But despite their efforts, the situation midway through the 1960s seemed to verify the prescience of Philip Morrison's warning two decades earlier that science itself would be "bought by war on the installment plan."

With nonviolent protests across the South pushing for enactment of federal laws against racial discrimination, the White House gave unprecedented support for civil rights and began an ambitious antipoverty program. But much of the momentum for domestic progress would be derailed, one way or another, by the Vietnam War. Two trains were on a collision course in the mid-1960s.

During this time, I began to think about the black maids walking from and to the bus stops where, in the late afternoons, they waited for the creaky, stinky buses of D.C. Transit that would take them far away from my suburban neighborhood. I knew that the maids were expected to do a lot for meager pay: dusting, vacuuming, cleaning toilets, and all the rest of it, in the new houses that had risen from empty tracts as suburbia took hold. In my own young way, I felt bad about the overburdened and underpaid women who left the neighborhood before nightfall.

———

When I was eight, the family moved to India. (My father had a job with the U.S. aid program.) During the next year and a half, I saw people so emaciated that their limbs reminded me of the dark brown pencils at school back in suburban Wilmington. On the streets, people begging for coins or sleeping on cement did not seem far from starvation; the most intense pleading came from ragged children and mothers with infants in their arms, thinner than thin.

I stared and had very little connection with what I saw. The beggars, the lethargic others were foreign to me. I had much more pressing concerns. For instance, I was into comic books—eager for Superman, Donald Duck, Mickey Mouse, and their pals in the cartoon menagerie—but I couldn't afford to buy nearly as many as I wanted. So in Calcutta's sprawling New Market, I made an arrangement at a rickety magazine stall where I could get high trade-in value from one stack of comics to the next. This worked out well until the day someone new—still a child himself—was staffing the stall when I arrived. The poor Bengali boy didn't have the foggiest notion what deal I'd worked out. Angrily, I demanded my fresh pile of comic books, and when I got no satisfaction I threw a fit.

A more frequent event was that I treated an Indian boy like a dog. Oneen was tall, on the very thin side of lanky. He had a quick smile. We were about the same age. In front of the apartment building where I lived, our routine went like this: I stood on pavement, lifted a racket, and hit a tennis ball down the street, and Oneen ran after the ball and brought it back to me. Then, I whacked at the ball and Oneen went running after it again. At the end of the session, I gave him the equivalent of a few cents. I took it for granted that the entire transaction was appropriate, and I probably figured that I was doing him a favor.

Being an American child gave me a sense of my place in the

world. I expected the apparently natural order of things to provide a continuum from one day and year to the next. I grew up feeling that I was entitled to comforts from privilege. What Oneen felt was beyond me.

It's easy to say that I was only nine years old when I swung my little racket in Calcutta. After all, childhood is self-absorbed. But shortfalls of empathy are chronic. Adults founder on human disconnects. And, looking back along the lines of tension between self-justification and self-reproach, we rarely do much with the belated empathy called remorse.

———

Stories from Dixie had already passed into the realm of truthful lore, archetypes of virulent racism. But I wasn't quite in the South, and there was much about the national character to be learned from living in a middle-class area so close to where the United States of America was headquartered. Many parents, including my father, worked for the government, and the proximity gradually put some human faces on those who helped to keep the federal machinery running. As long as I assumed the best of intentions from Uncle Sam, the flaws seemed only superficial or inadvertent.

The first place I ever protested was a segregated apartment complex in Maryland, near the D.C. border, named Summit Hills. Many of the picketers, black and white, wore buttons that proclaimed the group's name and demand with one word: "ACCESS." To me, picketing felt unfamiliar but not uncomfortable—a good thing to do.

Around then, the Federal Bureau of Investigation began to keep tabs on me. I can't say why. Only twenty-five words, including my name and childhood address, are legible on a heavily blacked-out page of an FBI memorandum (stamped "SECRET") that I obtained, decades later, via the Freedom of Information Act. The memo said that the FBI had received a report from a source on April 24, 1966. I was fourteen at the time. Maybe I rated because I'd been on that picket line for integration. If only the feds had been as diligent in tracking organized crime.

Fair housing was a big political issue statewide. Later in the year, I volunteered to work in the Maryland governor's race. The Democratic Party nominee was pandering to what was known at the time as the white backlash. (His campaign slogan: "Your Home Is Your Castle—Protect It.") So, during the general election campaign, I distributed flyers for the Republican nominee, who had a reputation as a moderate. He won. His name was Spiro Agnew.

What roiled the most in our all-white neighborhood during 1966 was racial tension. And "Eve of Destruction" had supplied a lyrical flashpoint for the social moment. One of my best friends was especially peeved at the lines "Hate your next-door neighbor/But don't forget to say grace." His family was both religious and hostile to black people. That couplet in the song wasn't precisely on target—local housing was so segregated that hatred usually focused on other neighborhoods—but the message was clear enough to move some people and anger others.

Compared to those tensions, the Vietnam War seemed distant to me that fall. But not for much longer. And unlike the controversies over civil rights, the disputes about the war indicated that the people in charge of our country—who spoke so eloquently about the need for visionary leadership and humane values—might be engaged in horrible wrongdoing.

––––––––––

Lenny Bruce wasn't a household name when he died of a morphine overdose in August 1966, but he was widely known and had even performed on network television. His nightclub bits, captured on record albums, satirized the zeal of many upstanding moralistic pillars. One of Bruce's favorite routines described a visit to New York by top holy men of Christianity and Judaism. They go to Saint Patrick's Cathedral: "Christ and Moses standing in the back of Saint Pat's. Confused, Christ is, at the grandeur of the interior, the baroque interior, the rococo baroque interior. His route took him through Spanish Harlem. He would wonder what fifty Puerto Ricans were doing living in one room. That stained glass window is worth nine grand! Hmmmmm . . ."

In what turned out to be his final performances, Bruce took to reciting (with a thick German accent) lines from a poem by the Trappist monk Thomas Merton—a meditation on the high-ranking Nazi official Adolf Eichmann. "My defense? I was a soldier. I saw the end of a conscientious day's effort. I watched through the port-holes. I saw every Jew burned and turned into soap. Do you people think yourselves better because you burned your enemies at long distances with missiles? Without ever seeing what you'd done to them?"

———————

After buying a hand-crank mimeograph machine and learning how to type stencils, I started a little neighborhood newspaper. Naturally I appointed myself editor-in-chief. In the summer of 1966 I wrote an article somewhat critical of the Vietnam War. ("By bombing North Vietnam, and now heavily populated areas around Hanoi and Haiphong, it is nearly impossible not to have a profound effect on the attitudes of the North Vietnamese civilians. Millions of these people live in fear, fear of United States bombers overhead. . . . By our actions, we are making negotiations impossible. . . . Since LBJ is in control, we hope that he is playing the right cards, for the stakes are much too high.") On April 15, 1967, I went to my first antiwar demonstration—the biggest ever in the country at that point, with a quarter-million or so people marching through steel-and-glass canyons of Manhattan. For me, the most memorable comment of the day was something I overheard an adult protester say at Penn Station as we waited for a train back to Washington: "Johnson will have to listen to us now."

At school I wanted to stay respectable. I was president of the sophomore class, my grades were good, and signs pointed to a strong record for college applications.

When I saw an acquaintance step out of bounds, I was careful not to follow suit. In the spring of 1968, near the end of my junior year, a provocative leaflet appeared at our high school. Under the head-line NAPALM A DOG?, it noted that "Napalm is used every day in Vietnam—on people." The school went into an uproar because the leaflet indicated that a dog would be burned alive in front of the main entrance. The student who concocted the leaflet was threat-ened with violent retribution by some students and then was sus-pended from school; a convoluted form of expulsion followed. Of course he never had any intention of napalming a dog.

I was assigned to write about the incident for the school paper. The faculty adviser warned me not to tilt in the offending student's favor, and I complied. After all, he had gone too far. Or so it seemed at the time.

3

REVULSION AND REVOLT

In 1968, "the largest building in Southeast Asia was the Infiltration Surveillance Center," science scholar Paul N. Edwards writes. It was a command headquarters for the U.S. Air Force at Nakhom Phanom in Thailand. "Inside the ISC vigilant technicians pored over banks of video displays, controlled by IBM 360/65 computers and connected to thousands of sensors strewn across the Ho Chi Minh Trail in southern Laos." The Pentagon called the ultramodern effort Operation Igloo White.

The sensors—shaped like twigs, jungle plants, and animal droppings—were designed to detect all kinds of human activity, such as the noises of truck engines, body heat, motion, even the scent of human urine. When they picked up a signal, it appeared on the ISC's display terminals hundreds of miles away as a moving white "worm" superimposed on a map grid. As soon as the ISC computers could calculate the worm's direction and rate of motion, coordinates were radioed to Phantom F-4 jets patrolling the night sky. The planes' navigation systems and computers automatically guided them to the "box," or map grid square, to be attacked. The ISC central computers were also able to control the release of bombs: the pilot might do no more than sit and watch as the invisible jungle below suddenly exploded into flames. In most cases no American ever actually saw the target at all.

The "worm" would then disappear from the screen at the ISC. This entire process normally took no more than five minutes.

Operation Igloo White ran from 1967 to 1972 at a cost ranging near $1 billion a year. Visiting reporters were dazzled by the high-tech, white-gloves-only scene inside the windowless center, where young soldiers sat at their displays in air-conditioned comfort, faces lit weirdly by the dim electric glow, directing the destruction of men and equipment as if playing a video game. As one technician put it: "We wired the Ho Chi Minh Trail like a drugstore pinball machine, and we plug it in every night."

The year Operation Igloo White began, Martin Luther King Jr. gave his first major speech about the war in Southeast Asia. "As I have walked among the desperate, rejected, and angry young men I have told them that Molotov cocktails and rifles would not solve their problems," he said on April 4, 1967, referring to his relations with increasingly militant black activists. "I have tried to offer them my deepest compassion while maintaining my conviction that social change comes most meaningfully through nonviolent action. But they asked—and rightly so—what about Vietnam? They asked if our own nation wasn't using massive doses of violence to solve its problems, to bring about the changes it wanted. Their questions hit home, and I knew that I could never again raise my voice against the violence of the oppressed in the ghettos without having first spoken clearly to the greatest purveyor of violence in the world today—my own government."

———

When I met Bill Higgs he was leaning over a mimeograph machine on the train chartered by Washington peace groups to the New York antiwar protest in mid-April '67. He spoke with a deep Southern drawl. Years earlier, Bill had been dangerously conspicuous as a young white attorney with the Mississippi Freedom Democratic Party struggling against the entrenched racist Dixiecrats of his home state. Once he told me that when he visited William Faulkner, the author said Bill reminded him of Quentin in *The Sound and the Fury*.

Now, the small row house that Bill rented in a poor black neighborhood in Northeast Washington, just a few blocks from the majestic Capitol, was a hotbed of informal soirees. Among his clients was the incendiary Black Power rhetorician H. Rap Brown, for whom a federal "antiriot" law was colloquially named. (Brown's most famous statement: "Violence is as American as apple pie.") Bill had done much of the research for the federal lawsuit *Hobson* v. *Hansen*, which in 1967 overturned the academic "tracking" system of de facto segregation in the D.C. public schools. He received scant public recognition or money for his work on the landmark case.

At his home, which looked shabby to my eyes, Bill always seemed to be talking strategy with visitors. And he was usually just one step, or less, ahead of creditors. With his tousled sandy hair, playful humor, and radical tenacity, Bill was a kind of avuncular counselor and coconspirator for young adults who were central to New Left organizing in the nation's capital during the late 1960s. He advised, cajoled, and urged more audacious action. Even during those fractious times, the only criticism I ever heard was that he kept running up bills without paying them, a negative trait to some of us who'd never faced a choice between financial solvency and doing potentially important political work. It was a dilemma that I would become very familiar with during the next decades.

Just before summer vacation in 1967, on the lawn of our high school, a few older students were scrutinizing maps of the Middle East at lunchtime. The news bulletins from a transistor radio sounded good: Israel was trouncing its enemies. Soon the Six Day War was history, and the occupation of Palestinian territories began.

I was glad about the Israeli triumph, and so was every other Jewish student I knew. The emotions stirred by the movie *Exodus* a few years earlier were consistent with adulation from relatives and media about the Jews whose perilous endeavors in Palestine made the desert bloom, as though no one of consequence had been living there before. Just about everything I'd ever heard about Arabs was negative.

The same fledgling movement that two months earlier had filled the streets of downtown Manhattan took no discernible position about Israel's new military hold on Arab lands. Few people in American antiwar groups voiced criticism of the stunning territorial gains (which included, for the first time in nineteen centuries, Jewish control over all of Jerusalem). Many who opposed the U.S. war in Southeast Asia were pleased with U.S. support for Israel. One factor was that numerous Jews were prominent in the movement. Most peace activists stayed away from Mideast issues—while some in the emerging New Left drew parallels between Vietnamese resistance and Palestinian resistance.

Such comparisons were anathema to future neoconservatives already moving rightward. Liberal writers like Norman Podhoretz, Midge Decter, and Irving Kristol voiced disgust with "black power," hippie sensibilities, psychedelic drugs, and other antiauthoritarian trends among the young. Expressions of solidarity with Vietnam's National Liberation Front and the Palestine Liberation Organization repelled many neocons-to-be, hastening their flight to the cold-warrior branch of the Democrats, and from there into the Republican Party.

The Six Day War fractured a foundation for cohesive activism to embrace the humanity of all who suffered from war and military occupation. Years would pass before I began to grasp what the progressive journalist I. F. Stone was talking about when he wrote that summer: "Both Israelis and Arabs in other words feel that only force can assure justice. A certain moral imbecility marks all ethnocentric movements. The Others are always either less than human, and thus their interests may be ignored, or more than human, and therefore so dangerous that it is right to destroy them."

The trees along the streets in our suburban neighborhood were still on the spindly side. Like the idealized lawns, our minds were supposed to stay carefully trimmed and edged—but cerebral and emotional reactions were clashing. I was supposed to learn how to be a professional, but I was losing enthusiasm for the mission. And if our bodies were not just vehicles for carrying around our brains, then why keep sensuality in check? What about human empathy, passion, anger? An internal battle escalated, centering on what to do with unauthorized feelings.

Partway through adolescence, I didn't know whether I was hitting a wall or getting over one. I felt partly trapped and partly freed. By the time Bob Dylan's *John Wesley Harding* came out at the start of 1968, I was stunned with elation and turmoil as I sat on a bench in a shopping plaza with the plain album in my hands. Old meanings were slipping away, new ones were not quite in focus. Ahead, the fine lines between the pursuits of self-awareness and self-indulgence could be thinner than gossamer. But going back did not seem like a live option; the linear jags of locksteps, represented by the previous generation, stood out as the epitome of a drag. Their daily routines banished vitality.

I identified totally with this passage from D. H. Lawrence: "It was as if dismalness had soaked through and through everything. The utter negation of the gladness of life, the utter absence of the instinct for shapely beauty which every bird and beast had, the utter death of the human intuitive faculty was appalling . . . . What could possibly become of such a people, a people in whom the living intuitive faculty was dead as nails, and only queer mechanical yells and uncanny will power remained?"

Faraway events seemed more and more connected to the "anti-life" atmosphere close to home. And suddenly the most powerful moral voice in the country was gone. After the murder of Martin Luther King on April 4, 1968, riots kept entire blocks of Washington burning for days. The president's calls for an end to that violence made me angry; by then I despised the war in Vietnam and the leaders who kept it going.

One afternoon in early summer, I went with my father to the national mall where remnants of the Poor People's Campaign—the maze of tents known as Resurrection City—were marooned a short walk from the Lincoln Memorial. The disappearance of King's leadership had been a terrible blow, and the encampment was sinking into deep mud from the rains, falling into a gloomy sinkhole of history.

I felt some of the moment's dreadful weight, but it was not mine to carry. I was turning seventeen, I was becoming disillusioned with the system, but I still did not want to run afoul of it. I wanted a bright future in sync with my right as a kid born into the middle-class at mid-century—the American Century. But at the same time, I was no longer sure I could have that future and really be myself.

———

A decade after *Sputnik*, the preoccupations of more and more "baby boomers" ran directly counter to the emphasis that had shifted the U.S. space program into overdrive. Society's crash course on a science trajectory was about learning and training to think in ways that would boost the quest for advanced technologies. But a lot of the new counterculture had to do with efforts to open doors of perception—feeling instead of just calculating—discovering and not just trying to solve intellectual puzzles. The poses of objectivity were losing their appeal for many who began to look at the customary straight-and-narrow path as a grim forced march.

"Around us are pseudo-events, to which we adjust with a false consciousness adapted to see these events as true and real, and even as beautiful," the radical psychiatrist R. D. Laing wrote in *The Politics of Experience*, a book that arrived in 1967 and quickly jolted a big readership. The tone was decidedly downbeat. "Our social realities are so ugly if seen in the light of exiled truth," Laing declared in the book's first paragraph, "and beauty is almost no longer possible if it is not a lie." *The Politics of Experience* became a clarion call for storming inner barricades and mounting a psychological insurrection.

The Politics of Experience took in the global and the intimate.

In order to rationalize our industrial-military complex, we have to destroy our capacity to see clearly any more what is in front of, and to imagine what is beyond, our noses. Long before a thermonuclear war can come about, we have had to lay waste our own sanity. We begin with the children. It is imperative to catch them in time. Without the most thorough and rapid brainwashing their dirty minds would see through our dirty tricks. Children are not yet fools, but we shall turn them into imbeciles like ourselves, with high I.Q.'s if possible. . . .

At this moment in history, we are all caught in the hell of frenetic passivity. We find ourselves threatened by extermination that will be reciprocal, that no one wishes, that everyone fears, that may just happen to us "because" no one knows how to stop it. There is one possibility of doing so if we can understand the structure of this alienation of ourselves from our experience, our experience from our deeds, our deeds from human authorship. Everyone will be carrying out orders. Where do they come from? Always from elsewhere. Is it still possible to reconstitute our destiny out of this hellish and inhuman fatality?

Not coincidentally, *The Politics of Experience* came on the scene about the same time as the Beatles album *Sgt. Pepper's Lonely Hearts Club Band*, released in June 1967. School was out, in more ways than one. At a party celebrating the end of the term, while the mind-blowing record filled the darkened room, I held a candle and peered at the lyrics on the back of the album cover. In their own ways, Laing and the Beatles encouraged personal subjectivity as wondrous and deserving of our passions. The rush was setting out to claim inner worlds as our own and disclaiming any desire to fit into deadening social patterns.

———

During the 1967 "summer of love," James Baldwin visited its symbolic center, and he later wrote: "The flower children were all up and down the Haight-Ashbury section of San Francisco—and they might have been everywhere else, too, but for the vigilance of the cops—with their long hair, their beads, their robes, their fancied resistance, and, in spite of a shrewd, hard skepticism as unnerving as it was unanswerable, really tormented by the hope of love. The fact that their uniforms and their jargon precisely represented the distances they had yet to cover before arriving at that maturity which makes love possible—or no longer possible—could not be considered their fault. They had been born into a society in which nothing was harder to achieve, in which perhaps nothing was more scorned and feared than the idea of the soul's maturity."

Baldwin continued:

> Their flowers had the validity, at least, of existing in direct challenge to the romance of the gun; their gentleness, however specious, was nevertheless a direct repudiation of the American adoration of violence. Yet they looked—alas—doomed. They seemed to sense their doom. They really were flower children, having opted out on the promises and possibilities offered them by the shining and now visibly perishing republic. I could not help feeling, watching them, knowing them to be idealistic, fragmented, and impotent, that, exactly as the Third Reich had had first to conquer the German opposition before getting around to the Jews, and then the rest of Europe, my republic, which, unhappily, I was beginning to think of as the Fourth Reich, would be forced to plow under the flower children—in all their variations—before getting around to the blacks and then the rest of the world.

Those words appeared in 1972, inside Baldwin's deeply pessimistic *No Name in the Street*, a book heavily burdened by pain from the assassination of Martin Luther King four years earlier. Baldwin was out of favor with the liberal white establishment and the media by the early '70s, for reasons similar to King's fall from such grace during his final year. (In a speech on the last day of April 1967, referring to Alabama's notorious Sheriff Clark, King said: "There is something strangely inconsistent about a nation and a press that would praise you when you say, 'Be nonviolent toward Jim Clark,' but will curse and damn you when you say, 'Be nonviolent toward little brown Vietnamese children.' There is something wrong with that press.")

No Name in the Street has many facets, and Baldwin's ruminations on his visit to Haight-Ashbury take up only a few paragraphs, yet over more than thirty years I've often remembered these words:

"They were in the streets in the hope of becoming whole. They had taken the first step—they had said, No. Whether or not they would be able to take the second step, the harder step—of saying, Yes, and then going for their own most private broke—was a question which much exercised my mind . . ."

The answers that meant the most would not come at any moment or in any season but over years and decades.

When the *Yellow Submarine* movie came out in 1968, I got stoned with a girlfriend and we were off to Pepperland; later, in the movie theater's dark parking lot, we made out (magically wetly, as novelist James Jones might have written), and every Blue Meany on the planet was far away. Barely seventeen, I was coming to believe that it was possible to do almost anything with enough desire. I wanted to write a book titled *No Compromise*.

The upheaval and awakening disproved a lot of what I had thought I knew about authorities, from school to home to police to the government. There was less and less to believe as believed before. I'd grown up figuring that prevalent rationality would stand the future in good stead. But the Vietnam War was something else, and gradually in my own mind I connected the suppression of political dissent with the throttling of sex and sensuality. No way did I want to participate in bludgeoning my own life or in accepting the war that continued at every moment. The "body counts," announced like ball scores on broadcast news reports, were attempts to quantify the achievements of madness.

No matter how much we were discussed, the young of our generation often felt close to invisible—treated as mere behavior. Meanwhile we were the first fully expendable batch of kids, in training to be ghosts; the glorified new "push-button world" might easily lead to a push-the-Button moment that would bring literal invisibility. Most of us came from a tamped-down environment of white monoculture. But inner worlds became important enough to be made visible and audible.

During the summer of 1968, when youthful rebellions shook the powerful from Paris to Chicago and beyond, a kinetic participant in the creative swirl known as the London Underground wrote in the preface of his book: "What has happened is that the pressure of restriction preceding nuclear suicide has precipitated a biological reflex compelling the leftist element in the young middle class to join with the delinquent element in the young working class for the reaffirmation of life by orgy and violence. What is happening is an evolutionary convulsion rather than a reformation. Young people are not correcting society. They are regurgitating it." The book was titled *Bomb Culture*.

The author, Jeff Nuttall, was almost a teenager when the future suddenly went radioactive in August 1945. By dropping atomic bombs on Hiroshima and Nagasaki, he wrote, "We had espoused an evil as great as the Nazi genocide, we had espoused the instrument for the termination of our benevolent institution, society, and our certain identity, human. We had espoused a monstrous uncertainty both of future and of morality."

The espousal had been of the most incontrovertible sort—not words but actions. The shift into a real-life nuclear theater, with the atomic bombings of Japan lifting the curtain, would give a different cast to the verities of patriotism, piety, and paternalism. From then on, life would always come with an obliterating sword of Nuclear Damocles overhead; whatever the pretenses of authority, from the household to the White House, the thread might break in an instant. Those who spoke of the future as a certainty were fakers. "No longer could teacher, magistrate, politician, don, or even loving parent, guide the young. Their membership of the H-bomb society automatically cancelled anything they might have to say on questions of right and wrong. Even Nature had come to mean poisoned stratosphere, contaminated rain, vegetables and milk that made men breed monsters . . ."

Generalizations may be riddled with exceptions even when valid.

(The holes in Swiss don't negate the cheese.) No doubt growing up in the nuclear age had no tangible effect on some kids, though—particularly in a culture that stuffs unpleasant feelings as a matter of course—we'd be foolish to assume that unexpressed distress doesn't exist. It takes an odd sort of credence to believe, as we've been encouraged to presume at least in public, that the constant threat of nuclear holocaust has only minor effects on human psyches. The actual effects are not matters we're prompted to ponder often while watching television or listening to the radio or reading newspapers and slick magazines. (Such a focus would hardly create an optimum media atmosphere for advertisements.) Major investors in the nuclear-destruction biz are not eager to subsidize public scrutiny of what the capabilities have meant for our emotional lives. Nor are government officeholders, or politicians with a chance to replace them, interested in speaking a lot more deeply than the polished veneer of platitudes that administer topical anesthetics for the nuclear-shadowed patient.

"At the point of the dropping of the bombs on Hiroshima and Nagasaki, the generations became divided in a very crucial way," Nuttall wrote.

> The people who had passed puberty at the time of the bomb found that they were incapable of conceiving of life *without* a future. Their patterns of habit had formed, the steady job, the pension, the mortgage, the insurance policy, personal savings, support and respect for the protection of the law, all the paraphernalia of constructive, secure family life. They had learned their game and it was the only game they knew. To acknowledge the truth of their predicament would be to abandon the whole pattern of their lives. They would therefore have to pretend, much as they had pretended about ecstasy not being there, and they proceeded to pretend as cheerfully as ever. . . .
>
> The people who had not yet reached puberty at the time of the bomb were incapable of conceiving of life *with* a future. They might not have had any direct preoccupation with the bomb. This depended largely on their sophistication. But they never knew a sense of future. . . . They pretended too, but they did not enter the

pretense at all cheerfully. In fact they entered the pretense reluctantly, in pain and confusion, in hostility which they increasingly
showed. Dad was a liar. He lied about the war and he lied about
sex. He lied about the bomb and he lied about the future.

Summer 1968:

Getting signatures in front of three-dollar movies. A petition for
the Eugene McCarthy antiwar presidential campaign. Taking clipboard along heeled-and-tied lines.

Off on side streets, men are on stoops, faded brick townhouses.
Another America.

"I was for Kennedy," the black man says. Wrinkles around seeing eyes. "Robert Kennedy."

"This man, McCarthy, wants to keep fighting for the same
things . . ."

He signs; he knows it won't do any good.

Sometime around the end of 1968, at a forum, I heard a national organizer from Students for a Democratic Society denounce the new
Beatles song "Revolution." Anyone who pulled away from the revolution then presumed to be in progress had sold out, the political
line went. In direct counterpoint, the Rolling Stones received acco-
lades for their "Street Fighting Man" song (on the sizzling *Beggar's
Banquet* album). Liberation News Service, under the control of a
doctrinaire faction—Leninist and now anti-Lennonist—threw its
editorial weight into the dispute. "LNS Backs Stones in Ideological
Rift with Beatles," a headline announced in one New York underground paper. That kind of dogmatism was a continuing hazard for
left-wing movements.

When Richard Nixon became president in January 1969, I was a
seventeen-year-old who wanted peace and love, social justice and

marijuana, by then common agenda items for increasing numbers of Americans. The day before Nixon raised his right hand and solemnly swore, I was in the "counter-inaugural" march down Pennsylvania Avenue. ("Tomorrow the old gray buildings will smile at another parade as it marches in the other direction, with soldiers and guns and military bands, thousands already uniform and uniformed," I scribbled in a notebook.) Standing next to me under a big tent while Phil Ochs sang "when I've got something to say, sir, I'm gonna say it now," a guy my age expressed disdain: We've been saying that for a long time, he complained impatiently.

High school looked more and more ridiculous. Early in the year I was a founder of the Montgomery County Student Alliance. We organized chapters at a dozen high schools and quickly made some headway with a list of demands, a widely publicized report titled "Wanted: A Humane Education," and a rally of six hundred students at a school-board meeting in March. "The public schools," I wrote in the report, "have critically negative and absolutely destructive effects on human beings and their curiosity, natural desire to learn, confidence, individuality, creativity, freedom of thought and self-respect. . . . Instead of the system's being built around the needs of the students, the students are being built around the needs of the system." Our twenty-four-point program included only one demand that could directly affect the U.S. government: "The providing of the names and addresses of senior boys to the armed forces must be ended."

The school routine was the antithesis of the changes that I was eager to be part of. During spring vacation I visited California for the first time; I loved the sunny mix of vibrant counterculture and leftist sensibilities. Flying back home left me close to tears when I wrote:

Chronology looms to challenge me; there is no beginning and no end, only now and always . . . On the jet plane it's 10:15 in San Francisco and dark, and less than five hours later six AM in Washington as we aboard the United craft race to meet the sun, the beauty When I get off the plane a uniformed sailor kisses his

wife hello, long ago I think they had said good-by, and there are a
lot of US uniformed people around waiting for their luggage A
soldier's son tugs at his father's dog tags, and puts them in his
mouth, his father puts them back underneath his uniform. . . . In
this strangling country the people are taught to rush away from
birth, and they rush If you work for the Government for twenty
years you get an especially good retirement pension . . .

At that point the FBI was more impressed with my involvement
in the Montgomery County Student Alliance than I was. One FBI
memo, dated March 20, 1969, said that a report on the high school
group was being distributed to various Bureau offices, the Secret
Service, "and interested military intelligence agencies." The memo
included my name on a list of "leads" for the FBI's Washington
field office to "review indices re following persons" and added that
"the majority of the above individuals are apparently the organizers
and leaders of the MCSA." Meanwhile, the FBI's Baltimore Divi-
sion was tasked to further investigate our activities and, "through
established sources, conduct investigations re high schools and individuals at these schools who have recently joined the MCSA."

An FBI report quoted the assertion from the Montgomery
County Student Alliance that the public school system "presently
inhibits students' individuality, creativity, and independent thinking." Evidently, independent thinking and action were seen as subversive tendencies. The FBI document also cited an article that ran
in the daily *Washington Star* under the headline "School Officials
Will Meet with Dissident Students." The federal sleuths went on to
note that I was a high school senior and that I "stated the MCSA is
working in conjunction with . . . an association of several underground newspapers in the county, and the MCSA has the backing of
Compeers, Inc., a social action and antipoverty group."

Compeers was the creation of Brint Dillingham, a portly activist
in his mid-twenties with an acerbic sense of humor. He was highly
principled and—when his mind was made up—unyielding. Always
supportive of student activism without ever being obtrusive, Com-

peers had recently rented a little bungalow, somewhat incongru-
ously set in the middle of Bethesda's downtown. We called the place
Freedom House (which may sound corny now but it didn't seem
that way then), and it served as a headquarters for the student alliance as well as for activities to support the farmworker grape boy-
cott, oppose police abuses, organize against the draft, and so forth. In
January a little offset press in the building churned out remarkable
quantities of leaflets for the counter-inaugural. During the months
that followed, Freedom House became a happening place. The more
that went on there, the more police cars circled the block, sometimes
shining bright lights into the building.

By late spring, Brint was facing the prospect of serious jail time
on "obscenity" charges because he'd challenged a county judge's
ban on an edition of the *Washington Free Press*. The offending
issue had included a cartoon that depicted a power-crazed judge
masturbating from the bench. When Brint heard about the ban, he
picked up a stack of newspapers and started selling them in front of
a police station. His impending trial and the overall atmosphere of
police harassment built up plenty of stress.

That spring I was at Freedom House a lot, especially after I quit
high school. Nixon had been president for a few months, and the
war was still going, horrific as ever. I testified at a county government hearing against police abuses. It was all merging together in
my mind: the war, social injustice, repressive cops. Police kept tight-
ening surveillance of Freedom House, even slipping inside to rum-
mage through desks. Across the street was a multistory parking
garage run by the county, and the cops seemed to use it as a staging
area. One night I went with a few acquaintances and spray-painted
the plastic faces of the parking meters—as it turned out, 179 of
them. And on a wall of the garage, I sprayed in big letters: "REVOLT
For Peace." Then I retreated, back toward Freedom House, before remembering that I'd dropped a paint can in the parking-garage elevator; the can might have my fingerprints on it, I thought, so I went to
retrieve it. A police car was on the scene.

I'd never been arrested before, and for me it turned out to be a big deal. Fork in the road; respectability went that-a-way. I don't know whether it was before or after the arrest when I sat on the porch of Freedom House, taking cards out of my wallet, including a press pass (from my part-time work for a mainstream weekly paper, the *Montgomery County Sentinel*), and pouring chocolate milk over my ID. Maybe I was crying; I can't quite remember. Call it whatever—identity crisis, breakdown, coming of age, clarity, or confusion—it was a turning point. But turning toward where? I scarcely had a clue.

The Freedom House existence didn't have much of a future. Many standoffs with police ensued, with nights of cat-and-mouse maneuvers through the suburban shopping district, and numerous arrests. As for my case, the county juvenile court—whether by chance or with a touch of melodrama—scheduled my trial for my eighteenth birthday. In the meantime I was smoking pot and listening to music and kind of letting my former life fall away. I'd been accepted to college, but I was losing interest in that scenario. My parents were suitably mortified on all counts. In a matter of months, I'd gone from got-it-together student to long-haired lawbreaker. From all appearances, I looked like a hippie dropout, and thought like one too.

The usual and respectable—most of all, the war on Vietnam— made no sense to me. About my actions that had led to my arrest, I was ambivalent. I reproached myself with the aphorism that "the first duty of a guerrilla is to not get caught." The best thing about the spray-painting escapade was that coverage in the *Washington Post* had prominently featured a photo of my "REVOLT For Peace" lettering on the garage wall; the accompanying story reported that the words were "painted in foot-high green and black letters." I looked at the picture in the paper and imagined people at the White House and the Pentagon seeing it. At least the message had gone through. And a lot of the extensive local news accounts of the conflicts between Freedom House adherents and police conveyed that these were affluent white kids freaking out and rebelling, in well-to-do Montgomery County of all places. The way I saw it, we were fighting against bogus socialization.

At my trial, on "destruction of public property" charges, I said that I'd been involved in the spray painting, and the judge ordered me to get a job and earn the money that would reimburse the county for the cost of replacing the plastic parking-meter faces. That added up to a bit more than six hundred dollars. During the next weeks I wandered barefoot for many miles on suburban sidewalks, and sometimes in Washington too.

One day in 1969, a biology professor from Harvard visited the Massachusetts Institute of Technology—the biggest military contractor in academia—and gave a speech that he called "A Generation in Search of a Future." The full text of the speech, by Nobel Prize–winner George Wald, appeared first in the *Boston Globe* and then other periodicals. "Our government has become preoccupied with death," Wald said, "with the business of killing and being killed."

While he denounced the Vietnam War, the focus of Wald's speech was nuclear weapons. "There is an entire semantics ready to deal with the sort of thing I am about to say," he told his audience. "It involves such phrases as 'Those are the facts of life.' No—these are the facts of death. I don't accept them, and I advise you not to accept them. We are under repeated pressure to accept things that are presented to us as settled—decisions that have been made." And Wald said:

> A few months ago, Senator Richard Russell, of Georgia, ended a speech in the Senate with the words "If we have to start over again with another Adam and Eve, I want them to be Americans; and I want them on this continent and not in Europe." That was a United States senator making a patriotic speech. Well, here is a Nobel laureate who thinks that those words are criminally insane. . . .
>
> I think I know what is bothering the students. I think that

what we are up against is a generation that is by no means sure that it has a future.

I am growing old, and my future, so to speak, is already behind me. But there are those students of mine, who are in my mind always, and there are my children, the youngest of them now seven and nine, whose future is infinitely more precious to me than my own. So it isn't just their generation; it's mine, too. We're all in it together. . . .

Unless we can be surer than we now are that this generation has a future, nothing else matters. It's not good enough to give it tender, loving care, to supply it with breakfast foods, to buy it expensive educations. Those things don't mean anything unless this generation has a future. And we're not sure that it does.

I don't think that there are problems of youth, or student problems. All the real problems I know about are grown-up problems.

Perhaps you will think me altogether absurd, or "academic," or hopelessly innocent—that is, until you think of the alternatives—if I say, as I do to you now: We have to get rid of those nuclear weapons. There is nothing worth having that can be obtained by nuclear war—nothing material or ideological—no tradition that it can defend. It is utterly self-defeating. Those atomic bombs represent an unusable weapon. The only use for an atomic bomb is to keep somebody else from using one. It can give us no protection—only the doubtful satisfaction of retaliation. Nuclear weapons offer us nothing but a balance of terror, and a balance of terror is still terror.

We have to get rid of those atomic weapons, here and everywhere. We cannot live with them.

I think we've reached a point of great decision, not just for our nation, not only for all humanity, but for life upon the Earth. I tell my students, with a feeling of pride that I hope they will share, that the carbon, nitrogen, and oxygen that make up ninety-nine percent of our living substance were cooked in the deep interiors of earlier generations of dying stars. Gathered up from the ends of the universe, over billions of years, eventually they came to form, in part, the substance of our sun, its planets, and ourselves.

While Wald spoke, the Apollo 9 manned spacecraft was orbiting the Earth in the second day of a ten-day mission to test rendezvous maneuvers between a lunar module and the command ship. Two and a half months later, in late May, Apollo 10 would evaluate the module in a flight that brought it to within fifty-thousand feet of the Moon. And the climax would come in July.

4

TO THE MOON
AND TO WOODSTOCK

On a timeline, as it turned out, *Sputnik* went into orbit midway between the obliteration of Hiroshima and the celebration of the first moonwalk. In space, the dozen years from the first Soviet satellite to the Apollo 11 man-on-the-Moon mission spanned from American humiliation to triumph.

The two most memorable accomplishments of the 1960s for American aerospace were the moonwalk and the high-tech bombing that, among other benchmarks, had already turned vast expanses of Southeast Asia into cratered wastelands. From 238,000 miles away or a few thousand feet above the ground, Uncle Sam's dominance of space and air was dazzling—presumably the leading edge in the hands of the good. The same patriotic persona taking a giant step for mankind on the Moon was calling in nonstop air strikes on planet Earth.

———

A few days after my eighteenth birthday, I went to the local draft board and registered. For my file I submitted a big green leaf from a tree outside the office (the symbolism made perfect sense to me). It was the only evidence I provided in support of my unpersuasive request for conscientious objector status. Several weeks later, when my neatly typed draft card arrived in the mail, it included a ten-digit Selective Service Number and explained on the back, under the rubber-stamped date August 18, 1969: "The law requires you to have this certificate in your personal possession at all times and to surrender it upon entering active duty in the Armed Forces. The law requires you to notify your local board in writing within 10 days after it occurs, (1) of every change in your address, physical condition and occupational (including student), marital, family, dependency and military status, and (2) of any other fact which might change your classification." I thought the people running the Selective Service System were out of their minds.

At about that time I took a liking to Beethoven's *Eroica* symphony in much the same way that a couple of months earlier I'd stood on the roof of Freedom House listening to the foghorns and organ riffs on the Steve Miller Band's *Sailor* album; I imagined sailing through the seas of cement, above the harshness of the concrete.

A lot of people seemed to have plans for me. Rather than get with the program, I flew standby to San Francisco.

––––––––––

We saw butterflies turn into bombers, and we weren't dreaming. The 1960s had evolved into a competition between American excesses, with none—no matter how mind-blowing the psychedelic drugs or wondrous the sex or amazing the music festivals—able to overcome or undermine what the Pentagon was doing in Southeast Asia. As journalist Michael Herr observed in Vietnam: "We took space back quickly, expensively, with total panic and close to maximum brutality. Our machine was devastating. And versatile. It could do everything but stop." At the same time that Woodstock became an instant media legend in mid-August 1969, melodic yearning for peace was up against the cold steel of America's war machinery. The gathering of 400,000 young people at an upstate New York farm implicitly—and, for the most part, ineffectually—rejected the war and the assumptions fueling it. Jimi Hendrix's rendition of "The Star-Spangled Banner" was an apt soundtrack for U.S. foreign policy.

In 1969, Fred Branfman was a humanitarian aid volunteer in Laos when he discovered that his country was taking the lives of peasants there by the thousands. More than thirty-five years later, he described what in essence would ring true for me and many other Americans:

> Believing so deeply in America, I felt particularly betrayed when I realized beyond any serious doubt that my leaders—and the generation that spawned them—were selfish hypocrites and murderers. I experienced the undeniable fact that my government was prepared to send me to fight and possibly die for a clearly unjust war as the deepest possible *personal* betrayal. . . . I think this strong feeling of being abandoned and betrayed by our elders is the key to understanding the sixties, and what has occurred since. I believe my generation, which grew up deeply believing in American values, was thrown into a moral abyss from which we still have not emerged. I think this has had disastrous effects upon American politics, culture, and civilization.

Raymond Mungo cofounded Liberation News Service in the autumn of 1967 to serve "underground" newspapers around the country. More than a hundred of those papers carried the coverage that LNS provided on its first major story—the "confrontation with the war-makers" at the Pentagon on October 21, 1967. A few seasons later, looking back at the events of that Saturday, Mungo wrote: "Between 100,000 and 250,000 persons marched on the war factory to announce their disapproval of mass murder in Vietnam; some 660 were arrested, myself included, by federal marshals who did not hesitate to break the bones and crack the skulls of the most gentle people, in pursuit of 'lawnorder'; although many an OMMMM Shantih failed to elevate the Pentagon building, they raised the spirits of a cold and lonely multitude on the Pentagon lawn, and in foreign lands afar; several of those jailed are still in jail, or in St. Elizabeth's Hospital for the mentally disturbed, today, as a result of their experience; but most of us are still around, and still refusing to cooperate with that war, which is still going on."

In the chaotic collectivity of Liberation News Service's early months, Mungo recalled, there was no unifying ideology, just a shared general outlook. "I guess we all agreed on some basic issues—the war is wrong, the draft is an abomination and a slavery, abortions are sometimes necessary and should be legal, universities are an impossible bore, LSD is Good and Good For You, etc., etc.— and I realize that marijuana, that precious weed, was our universal common denominator." As it turned out, a thin weed.

By summer 1968, about nine months after the launch of LNS, differences between two factions were afflicting the news service. Ugly verbal conflicts escalated when the office relocated from Washington to Manhattan. Soon the Mungo countercultural faction pulled off a surreptitious move of everything in the office to farmhouses in Massachusetts—but hours later the hardliners tracked down Mungo's faction and physically assaulted some of its leaders.

A year after the news service began, Ray Mungo was living with some close friends on a farm they'd bought in Vermont. When he finished writing *Famous Long Ago: My Life and Hard Times with Liberation News Service* in August 1969, he was twenty-three years old. Much of the book, particularly its closing chapters, can be read as the work of someone struggling with the aftermath of recent traumas. Violence repeatedly punctuates the story—the massive violence of a far-off war in Southeast Asia, the nearby violence of police and jails, the crossfire that erupted in Washington and many other cities immediately after the killing of Martin Luther King, the violence adopted by some in the antiwar movement as the war continued to escalate, and the night of beatings when LNS came unglued.

Mungo did not just retreat from active political engagement. Though he was among those "still refusing to cooperate with that war," now his refusal was decidedly passive. Or, as he saw it and phrased it in his book, "we came over to the New Age." But that "New Age" existed no more tangibly or foreseeably than "the Revolution" that Mungo had grown to distrust and even loathe. Many others made similar jumps for the mythic New Age destination; the country's leading war-makers would not mind such ineffectual noncooperation.

Nearing his book's end, Ray Mungo summed up: "I no longer have *any* kind of program to save the world, let alone nineteenth-century Marxism, except perhaps to pay attention to trees. I wish everybody would pay as much attention to trees as I do, but since everybody won't listen, I'll just go my solitary way and strive to enjoy what may well be the last days of this beautiful but deteriorating planet."

For what he called the Invocation page of his book, Mungo chose a biblical quote, "all is vanity and a striving after wind." And a short poem from a loved one on the farm:

> God help us,
> refugees in winter dress
> skating home on thin ice
> from the Apocalypse

Millions of "baby boomers" were to live much of their adult lives on the rebound from unresolved traumas. Whether in our teens or later, we came to realize that institutions we'd trusted should not be trusted. Sooner or later, many in our generation who went to Vietnam saw through the deception, and so did huge numbers of relatives and friends. Disillusionment festered as evidence mounted that forces of authority were willing to jail, beat up, and even shoot people for visibly objecting to the war and social injustice.

Some black activists, facing methodical violence from police and the FBI, answered in kind. The Black Panthers evolved into a paramilitary organization, riven with factions and agents provocateurs. Guns emerged as a central symbol on both sides, and the big guns were on one side. Government bullets killed the inspirational young

Panther leader Fred Hampton in his bed, George Jackson in prison, and many others.

Across the United States, the short end of the system's economic stick continued to crush lives with the casual routine of a heel on a soda can. Virtue went unrewarded as the morally compelling movement for civil rights hit a wall of the moneyed status quo (epitomized by the barriers of corporate power that stymied Martin Luther King's campaign for economic justice in Chicago during summer 1966). While Jim Crow was fading into history at last, the impoverishing rule of Jim Dough showed every sign of perpetual resilience, from Southern deltas to Northern ghettos and barrios.

Meanwhile, the paths of what we called "the movement" were altering many lives. For some, the dizzying changes came at a steep price. Profuse creative energies went into Students for a Democratic Society, with hundreds of chapters organizing to challenge the war, racism, and economic injustice. Many SDS activists were flexible and committed to a far-reaching vision of participatory democracy. But during 1968 and 1969 the national leadership of SDS mostly degenerated into top-this dogmatism and vanguard sloganeering, often accompanied by adrenaline for dishing out retribution to the war machine.

I drove with friends to an SDS regional convention in Lexington, Kentucky, in early 1968. Not quite seventeen, I couldn't make much sense out of the ideological factions and power maneuvers at the plenary sessions. Understandable arguments flared over whether to shun the "bourgeois" antiwar candidacies of Eugene McCarthy and Robert Kennedy, but much of the discussion seemed highly theoretical—and rhetorical. On the last day of the gathering, a few delegates passed out a satirical mimeographed list of Marxist buzz phrases alongside numerals. They proceeded to mock the debate by shouting out sequences of numbers.

During that period I became acquainted with Cathy Wilkerson, a dynamic SDS organizer who was a few years older. She spoke to an extracurricular group at my high school, and we talked when our paths crossed at movement events in Washington. Cathy made a big impression on me. She was passionate about radical social change. And, from what I could tell, the continuation of the Vietnam War made her sick at heart. By the end of 1969 she was helping to form the Weather Underground; in March 1970 an accident blew up the Manhattan townhouse where she and some comrades were building bombs. They wanted to engage in armed struggle. But the war industry understood violence, and I believe preferred it at home to the nonviolent militancy that King had consistently urged.

For many young people, the violence in the streets (mostly inflicted *on* rather than *by* protesters) and myriad other forms of war-related conflicts were enlivening yet also disturbing. Confrontations could be catalysts for personal growth, but they also could take an emotional toll. And consciously or not, large numbers of the young went into retreat. For some it was far from surrender; they regrouped, found more solid personal ground, reengaged politically to be part of progressive social change over the long haul. For others, political involvement faded away.

A big variable was drugs. Of course some, notably heroin and amphetamines, were unalloyed disasters. But the drugs often hailed as positive catalysts—pot, mescaline, LSD, psilocybin—were, as time went on, called upon to carry a much heavier load than they could possibly bear. Onto these illicit substances we projected many or (at the urging of the likes of Timothy Leary) even most of our hopes for personal happiness, social change, world peace—in a word, liberation. The romanticism attached to psychedelic drugs ran the gamut from fanciful to ludicrous. In late 1967, Jeff Nuttall noted: "The drugs, whilst accelerating our strategy, could create a vacuum as desolate as any H-bomb crater. . . . It's clearly necessary now to get firm hold of the fact that the nature of vision is human not chemical."

There was no way to change our past—individual or national—

with any drugs known or unknown. And the present could not be severed from the past, no matter how much we wished or claimed otherwise. The shortcuts available for spiritual or political change were limited. But Leary and others staked their public identities on pitching psychedelics as the absolute key to the joyous castle. The most extreme of the psychevangelists displayed signs of megalomania, egged on by media coverage. They did a lot of harm when people fell for the pitch.

Sooner or later, marijuana and psychedelic drugs wore thin. Contrary to hype about intrinsic qualities, they were in some senses akin to the color of water. No matter how much they satisfied thirst for wonder and joy, the drugs still could not change the aggregate realities of self or society by loaded fiat. We might trust our own feelings more—as opposed to what had deadened us at home, in school, on the streets, with other people, even in our most personal of hearts—but cannabis and the rest could not enable us to shed our pasts, much less overcome the political economy of suppression and war. No hashish high or acid trip could possibly substitute for real and enduring change: inside a person or in the wider world.

The downsides of the "drug culture" included police, court labyrinths, jails, good drugs spiked with bad, dealers who functioned as thugs. But as time went on, the most common problems with the mind-expanding drugs had to do with how they were overused and oversold. We might sneer at advice like "Nothing to excess"—what did Aristotle have to offer compared to the pithy "Turn on, tune in, drop out"? And when we saw a poster with William Blake's insight that "The road to excess leads to the palace of wisdom," we figured that he, and we, knew what he was talking about. (At the time I didn't see the full quote: "The road to excess leads to the palace of wisdom . . . for we never know what is enough until we know what is more than enough.") We cherry-picked Thoreau, so less was not more; feasting on a bit of subjectivity could revive us, but gluttony beckoned. If getting stoned a few times a week was delightful, why not three times a day? If a tab of acid opened doors of perception, then a higher dose might carry us through the jambs.

Combinations of various elements—political, social, psychological, pharmacological—had ways of spinning out. To whatever extent young people landed on their feet or their heads, the external and internal disarray that many faced was difficult to resolve. But pacific resolution was sometimes offered as the reachable destination of the counterculture path. Even some of the most eloquent prophetic voices greatly over-pitched the package, tying it all up neatly with sex, drugs, and enlightenment.

Speaking in November 1966 at a church in Boston, poet Allen Ginsberg said:

> What satisfaction is now possible for the young? Only the satisfaction of their Desire—love, the body, and orgy: the satisfaction of a peaceful natural community where they can circulate and explore Persons, cities, and the nature of the planet—the satisfaction of encouraged self-awareness, and the satiety and cessation of desire, anger, grasping, craving. . . .
>
> I am in effect setting up moral codes and standards which include drugs, orgy, music and primitive magic as worship rituals—educational tools which are supposedly contrary to our cultural mores; and I am proposing these standards to you respectable ministers, once and for all, that you endorse publicly the private desire and knowledge of mankind in America, so to inspire the young.

"No one pointed out to Ginsberg that the quick and only way to that peace beyond 'desire, anger, grasping, craving,' is to cut your throat," Jeff Nuttall commented, "that anyone who has no appetite for stress has no appetite for life on human terms, desires merely life on cosmic terms, desires death."

Nuttall had been part of the surrealist anti-Bomb activist artist scene in Britain for the better part of two decades by the time he sat down to write a conclusion of sorts for his book *Bomb Culture* in November 1967. He was a poet, a painter, a jazz musician, and he'd been deeply involved in campaigns against nuclear weapons. Now he wrote: "I want to say that drugs are an excellent strategy against society but a poor alternative to it."

The subtitle of *What the Dormouse Said*—a book by *New York Times* cyber-technology reporter John Markoff— states that "the '60s counterculture shaped the personal computer industry." The only graphic on the cover is a peace symbol. Inside, the book makes a strong case that many of the techno-visionaries of the 1960s and 1970s were personally antiwar and partial to marijuana, LSD, torn jeans, sandals, sexual exploration, progressive politics, and community activism. Based in Berkeley, San Francisco, and especially the South Bay vicinity of Stanford University, they were seeing beyond the old mainframe/terminal assumptions: glimpsing and then helping to make possible the personal computer and the Internet.

By 1960 the orchards and pastures of what became known as Silicon Valley "were giving way to tract homes for the waves of engineers and scientists who were arriving in the area," Markoff recounts. "*Sputnik* had shocked the nation out of its complacency, and Santa Clara County was quickly becoming an important aerospace and technology center." The Pentagon and NASA paid for much of the cutting-edge work there. Many of the innovators who pushed computer science forward were young men who opposed the Vietnam War and chose to fill jobs with military contractors that would exempt them from conscription. At the seminal Stanford Research Institute, a crucial outfit for the era's computer advances, a lot of the incoming funds purchased help for American warfare in Southeast Asia.

The utility of a silicon chip was on a steep climb. "Computer speed and capacity would continue to increase while costs fell and the size of computer shrank," Markoff writes. "It was a straightforward insight, but for those who made the leap it was the mind-expanding equivalent of taking a psychedelic drug." The analogy is apt, and not only because plenty of computer pioneers were turning on and tripping. (In response to an hour-long demonstration of the new "oNLine System" at the Stanford Research Institute, a few years after his Merry Prankster bus toured the country in 1964, writer Ken Kesey commented: "It's the next thing after acid.") Over time, faith in a drug or a technology could seem like a shortcut to self-realization.

A popular psychedelic poster in the late '60s—"Better Living Through Chemistry"—mocked and appropriated DuPont's motto. By the end of the twentieth century, there was no need to print a "Better Living Through Technology" poster; everyone but a complete dunderhead understood that. But there was no profound drug fix, and there would be no profound techno fix. In ways unacknowledged by fervent users, consumer digital technologies were new "drugs," legal this time, onto which we could project hopes with a kind of binary fundamentalism. Digital technology, like God and psychedelic drugs before it, would get credit for what humans could achieve. Yet the defining variable would not be God or drugs or technology. For better or worse, it would be human.

Along the way, the same drugs and technologies adored as forces for enlightenment and liberation could, and would, be quite compatible with the warfare state. In the case of the emergent Silicon Valley and its vibrant young innovators, Markoff's reporting turned up numerous examples. Here's one: "Sandy Miranda, a self-styled 'child of the sixties' . . . could feel the vibe in the [Stanford Research Institute] Augment Group the moment she arrived for her first interview. . . . People were barefoot, and she could smell pot. The Augment researchers looked like a bunch of hippies. *Whoa, I could fit in here,* she thought to herself. It was a different world. Office parties consisted of grabbing sleeping bags at the end of the day, driving to the beach, dropping acid, and spending the night." This milieu was enjoyed by employees whose jobs included such activities as training upper-tier air force officers on how to use the latest computer systems to improve operations manuals for ICBMs with nuclear weapons.

I wasn't in very good shape when I got off a plane at San Francisco Airport. The summer of 1969 had left me fatigued, probably malnourished, and not quite able to get a grip. I looked up an older exschoolmate and settled into a small house in Marin County. *Abbey Road* had just come out, and I listened to it over and over, along with the Led Zeppelin album that featured a big dirigible on the cover. And I wrote nonlinear articles, getting a couple published in San Francisco's weekly *Good Times* newspaper.

Out of money, I was rapidly wearing out my welcome at the house. Soon I got a message from a *Washington Post* education reporter who happened to see one of my spacey essays in *Good Times*. The result was a big article in the *Post*, chronicling my transformation from student reform leader in suburban Maryland to alienated refugee in California, some kind of momentarily newsworthy Zeitgeist example. For my part, I didn't feel like I had anything to hide, and even if I couldn't say where I was headed, at least I knew what I'd rejected. The *Post* article, however, was not well received in my current household. The coverage might "bring down heat," I was told. Besides, I was behind on my rent. What ensued was the reasonable suggestion that I vacate the premises, pronto.

I checked bulletin boards for rides and caught one to Albuquerque, where Bill Higgs was helping to defend a Mexican-American insurrectionist. Reies Tijerina had led a raid on a New Mexico courthouse to demand enforcement of centuries-old Spanish land grants that gave title to Mexicans deprived of their homes. Bill was welcoming, as always. I accompanied him on a long, hot, dry ride to Las Cruces. There, and back in Albuquerque, I ate pine nuts and listened to strategy meetings around kitchen tables.

My parents called to let me know that the judge had read the *Post* article and was furious. Why the hell was I in California when I was supposed to be in Maryland, working to pay my fine? Soon I was back in Montgomery County, under threat of jail. I started looking for work.

The county was offering jobs in leaf-raking crews, and for a short time that's how I spent my days. Now, looking at what I wrote back then, I feel that time has stood still for millions of people, their lives going by in such thankless work.

The locker room smells vaguely like a gym class. Sweat; cement floors; we wait for the man with the clipboard.

Our yellow truck is full of rakes and old grass. We hop in, seven or eight of us; we're called work crew no. 2.

"Goddamn it's early," a young black guy says as the motor starts up. "Too cold to go chasin' some motherfuckin' leaves." The truck turns onto Colesville Road; up behind us come some early commuters, windows rolled up.

"Well, m'friend, two-thirty-nine an hour sounds like pretty good money to me," a voice from farther into the truck goes. The man talking has a weatherbeaten older black face; the frames of his glasses are a thick brown with a little orange too. "Let's see, that's what, eighteen dollars a day . . ."

The truck swings onto a side street; we never know where we're going, we just hope the truck keeps moving.

"I can dig this," Jack, the young black man, says, "getting paid for sittin' on my ass." He's sitting right across from me next to the open back of the truck; we look out at the houses. "Like the dudes that live out here."

"Yeah, but they been educated on how ta sit," someone drawls.

The man with the orange-brown frames is counting on his fingers. "Yes-sir," he says, "we'll be getting nineteen dollars a day for this, nineteen-twelve, I think . . ."

"You're forgetting about taxes," somebody says.

When the truck stops and the engine quits we jump out.

"Work your way down the street and around the corner," the foreman says, pointing down the street and around the corner. He's wearing an orange WWI kind of pilot hat with orange fur flaps that look almost fluorescent.

We all have rakes; we stand in front of the curb and start clearing the strips of county lawns in front of houses. You don't have to really walk around on the grass, you just stand along the edge of the street and toss your rake four feet or so onto the lawn and pull the leaves back over the curb. There are lots of leaves, brown and yellow and crispy as your rake scoops and drags them over the grass and dumps them into the gutter. Every once in a while a leaf-sucking truck comes up behind us and swallows the snaky brown line of leaves we've left behind along the curb.

"Motherfuckin' cocksuckin' leaves," Jack mutters. The leaves soon begin swimming in front of your eyes, tumbling; they swirl where you're shoving them, rolling over each other into jumbled cylinders growing larger under your rake.

Lots of leaves. The foreman comes up behind driving the truck.

"Be back in a few minutes," he says. "Keep going up to the next street and around the corner."

The truck grates a gear and turns the corner. We lean on our rake handles.

"How'd you like to live in a house like that," says the older man with orange/brown glasses. "Some house to live in."

We're standing in front of an elaborate-looking white colonial home with pillars behind a spacious carpet-mowed lawn, lots of shrubs and an arc half-circle driveway.

"Yeah. Sheeeeeeet," Jack murmurs.

"Yessir," the orange/brown framed man says. "That's some mansion."

While I was in the midst of my leaf-raking stint, the editor of the *Sentinel* graciously offered me a full-time job—despite my recent notoriety—at the weekly paper's wage floor of $2.50 per hour. I was a passable reporter on general assignment, and my responsibilities also included editing the Business Page and the Religion Page. Every week I'd get a jigsaw diagram of the advertising for those pages, and I filled the remaining space with headlines, articles, and photos. The five reporters in the newsroom (which Bob Woodward would later grace for a year on his way up to the *Post*) banged away at manual typewriters and rearranged paragraphs with scissors and glue pots; we typed the copy on newsprint sheets of paper, to be marked up with fat blunt pencils before typesetting. To me, the most meaningful story I wrote was about a guy just a little older than me; he'd been denied conscientious objector status, and he was about to begin a lengthy prison term for refusing to go into the military.

I felt fairly anesthetized during my five months on the *Sentinel* payroll that fall and winter. The "Chicago Eight" trial was underway, the huge November 15 antiwar rally happened on the Washington Mall (with a turnout first estimated by police at a quarter million, later revised to 600,000 based on photo counts), and the war seemed unstoppable. I was in a nine-to-five grind, living with my parents, eating hamburgers at lunch, gaining weight, and eager to leave. At the first wisps of spring 1970, when a letter arrived from the county court saying that I'd paid all of my fine and was off probation, I gave notice and packed. In April, driving west through Pennsylvania, I heard news reports about the first Earth Day.

The Greening of America, by Charles Reich, caused a sensation in 1970 when a portion appeared in *The New Yorker*. Soon afterward the book became a much-debated bestseller.

Reich, a teacher at Yale University Law School, hit the timing just right. The book's portentous cover showcased a big-type summary: "There is a revolution coming. It will not be like revolutions of the past. It will originate with the individual and with culture, and it will change the political structure only as its final act. It will not require violence to succeed, and it cannot be successfully resisted by violence. This is the revolution of the new generation."

I liked that kind of theme. After all, I was part of "the new generation" and damn proud of it, in the way that Jefferson Airplane, on a track of the *Volunteers* album, sang the phrase "and young"—vibrating proudly, some might say narcissistically, but in any event also beautifully. Reich's book condemned the war, praised hippies to the skies, denounced the overcapitalized Corporate State, panned the rigidity of schools, lauded the sensuality that marijuana was aiding, and dismissed as pathetically venal the liberalism that we scorned as the best-and-brightest vehicle that had driven the country to war in Vietnam.

At the time, I scarcely picked up on the fact that *The Greening of America* was purposely nonpolitical. Its crux was personal and social liberation—in a word, "consciousness," which "plays the key role in the shaping of society." And so, "The revolution must be cultural. For culture controls the economic and political machine, not vice versa." Under that dreamy scenario, culture would be a silver bullet, able to bring down the otherwise intractable death machine.

Meanwhile, Reich voiced disdain for the usual struggles toward reform. "The political activists have had their day and have been given their chance," he wrote. "They ask for still more activism, still more dedication, still more self-sacrifice, believing more of the same bad medicine is needed, saying their cure has not yet been tested. It is time to realize that this form of activism merely affirms the State. Must we wait for fascism before we realize that political activism has failed?" The verdict of recent history was supposedly clear: "The great error of our times has been the belief in structural or institutional solutions. The enemy is within each of us; so long as that is true, one structure is as bad as another."

The benefits of hindsight enable us to see the youthful and vicarious hubris in *The Greening of America* that combined with group delusion to make flimsy assumptions seem plausible. Reich was twice my age but we were both taken with—and taken in by—a profound social moment. His book was trying to turn a few snapshots into a full-blown motion picture, with more than a little wishful thinking thrown in: The zipless luck of the new generation would ignite wisdom that had arrived by almost spontaneous combustion within a pressure cooker of affluence, alienation, plastics, and a war started by liberals. They were trying to foist onto the latest generation the retrograde consciousness of New Deal holdovers in league with modern technocrats. And the Vietnam War was the final wake-up call. "The whole edifice of the Corporate State is built on tranquilizers and sleeping pills; it should not have done the one thing that might shake the sleeper awake."

Towering above the nineteenth century's "Consciousness I" and the corporate liberal constraints of "Consciousness II," the author told readers, was "Consciousness III"—with "liberation" as the foundation. "It comes into being the moment the individual frees himself from automatic acceptance of the imperatives of society and the false consciousness which society imposes." And after the shedding of that false consciousness, the horizon would be rosy: "The new generation cannot be pacified or bought off, because it rejects false consciousness and false satisfactions, and the Corporate State is incapable of producing anything that will satisfy real needs. When the society does begin to satisfy real needs, that will not be pacification, it will be revolution."

The optimism came from the belief that "the whole Corporate State rests upon nothing but consciousness. When consciousness changes, its soldiers will refuse to fight, its police will rebel, its bureaucrats will stop their work, its jailers will open the bars. Nothing can stop the power of consciousness." The upbeat assessment soared toward the preposterous: "By the standards of history, the transformation of America has been incredibly, unbelievably swift. And the change to Consciousness III is not, so far as we know, reversible. Once a person reaches Consciousness III, there is no returning to a lower consciousness."

The idea that "consciousness"—or, for that matter, culture—can fundamentally change as swiftly as hats was to cause enormous confusion, shallow posturing, and bitter disappointment in the 1970s and beyond.

By the start of the '70s, many people had come to see modern Americana as close to formulaic: Not much open feeling equaled not much vibrant life. And the dysfunction went from tongue to ears; if you couldn't really find your own voice then you couldn't really hear anyone else's, either. The failures of expression and comprehension were circular. Numbing at home facilitated imposing deadly routines across town or on the other side of the planet in Southeast Asia. The proof was in patterns that kept crushing lives, on the installment plan or with instant firepower; the policies of violence refuted the noble words.

5

WAR ON THE HOME FRONT

May 1970:

Telegraph Avenue smells of CS tear gas, acrid smoke wafting across the streets, empty except for people holding vinegared rags and handkerchiefs to their faces, regrouping on the sidewalks. Boards cover store windows; white Berkeley unmarked police cars zipping around corners are the only autos moving through the streets, with gas-masked police crammed inside. Across Bancroft, a dozen cops are wearing riot helmets and clutching fat two-foot clubs, standing like alert journeymen batters on deck at the edge of the campus. Suddenly several canisters arch across the street, exploding thick gray gas as they land with loud coughs on the pavement, on both sides; got to decide which way to run, quick; resolving not to breathe, turning to the right, I'm running past the nearest steaming canister, back to Telegraph, and the CS gas violently insists it has entered my system; eyes are burning, all at once it seems impossible to breathe; the chemicals are doing as the manufacturers must have guaranteed, I'm choking, the gas inside grudges every thin gasp of oxygen it can't block; stomach is trying to vomit nothing. Gasping for breath, breathe please . . . slowly yes . . . Eyes start to open, standing in a store doorway; gradually air is coming back, wheezing down Telegraph; a medic is squirting a white liquid into my eyes and handing me a vinegar-soaked cloth, and then he's gone; the trash cans are on fire.

————————

I had arrived back in Berkeley just in time for the aftermath of the U.S. invasion of Cambodia. I'd buy gas for my '63 Fury in one-dollar increments, and when not camping up in the hills off Derby Street behind a school for the deaf, I was renting a room at a fraying place called the Cal Hotel that must have been among the seediest of the city. Some very sweet people were living there, trying to eke out a sort of subsistence; one was a middle-aged man who used to wrap his head with a black scarf and liked to joke about people mistaking him for Muddy Waters; he'd go down to the Marina and catch fish. I had a little pack-up portable stereo with me, and some records, and a guy named Bob and I used to hang out in my room and listen. We were about the same age, easily close in immediate interests yet worlds apart; he had come out of a ghetto, with bleak prospects. The beauty of blues offered rhythms of heart and breath, reconnecting pulse and voice. One of the albums we listened to was *Fathers and Sons*—with Muddy Waters, Otis Spann, Mike Bloomfield, Paul Butterfield—released the previous summer. Near the end of the first track, "All Aboard," Waters summed up:

> I worked *hard* all my *life*
> Now I'm gettin' *push*ed around

One time I knocked on the door of the guy who kept being mistaken for Muddy Waters and asked him for the few dollars I'd lent. He walked me across the small room to a dresser where some coins were spread out, then picked up a smattering of quarters, nickels, dimes, and put them in my hand, till only copper was left on the dresser. "Always leave yourself a few pennies," he said, almost cheerfully.

The poverty was grotesque, and so was the war far away. By then, a kind of rage had set in for me. Nearly forty years later I can't say it has dissipated in the slightest. The poverty is grotesque, and so is the war far away.

———————

After several weeks in Berkeley, I drove up the coast to Portland, where my higher learning would start at Reed College in early fall. For the summer I moved into a room in a house that Reed students had been renting on busy Belmont Street. Downstairs was a jewelry shop owned by one of the students; he and his girlfriend made rings, bracelets, chokers, and broaches. Another woman living in the house specialized in macramé, or maybe batik; her boyfriend was away for the summer, working as a lumberjack. The main collective activities in the house involved eating meals with plenty of brown rice, drinking wine, smoking pot, and listening to soft lyrical hippie music.

During that summer, when I was in the newly instituted draft lottery, the number drawn for my birth date was 365; that got me off the hook for conscription under any foreseeable circumstances short of World War III, in which case it would all be moot anyway. I noticed that if I'd been born just two days after my actual birthday, my draft number would have been 001.

———————

Countless pundits, for years already, had taken to bemoaning the "quagmire" in Vietnam. Scratch the surface and the country's pre-occupation was mostly about what the war was like for America; the despair was mainly about us; the tragic picture was mostly framed around our own kind—suffering wounds and sometimes dying in a place where the U.S. military was bogged down.

We called it the Vietnam War, while Vietnamese people would naturally enough call it the American War. Decades later, as a figure of American speech, people would use phrases like "during Viet-nam," almost as though Vietnam ceased to exist after the U.S. mili-tary finally left the "quagmire."

———

During 1970 the tone of the country shifted. That spring, hundreds of college campuses had shut down in an antiwar frenzy spurred by the Cambodia invasion and the shootings of students at Kent State and Jackson State. Yet, in the fall the campuses reopened in a largely quiescent mood. Despite the best efforts of many, the peace movement—and all it seemed to imply about who we were or might become—finished the year visibly depleted. American troop levels were dropping in Vietnam, and the draft's impact began to ease; over the next few years, much more of the USA's warfare would be high tech from the air.

Psychedelia started to decorate mass-media products. In the early 1970s, I saw bright-colored billboards done up in unmistakable Peter Max style, advertising "Super Jobs in the Air Force," while B-52s were still dropping enormous loads of explosives on Vietnam. It was a mistake to underestimate the flexibility of institutions we reviled.

We took our own symbols (long hair, rock music, roach clips, radical rhetoric) too seriously; and when they proved insubstantial under pressure, so did the psychological fortresses constructed with them. We may have deeply felt our desires—to stop a war, shatter rigid body armor, reject oppressive gender roles, challenge injustices based on race and class—but it was all too tempting, and easy, to gravitate toward icons of discontent, symbols that could then be imitated and co-opted by marketers and politicians. The finger pointing at the Moon was not the Moon.

———

Portland's favorite nickname was "the Rose City." Less floridly, it had been dubbed "the biggest small town in America." The city was laid back, and fairly traditional except for some dissenting enclaves. The annual Rose Festival was an occasion for U.S. Navy ships to dock ceremoniously in the Willamette River downtown—and for a few hearty activists to stand on drawbridges, slowing the arrival of the little armada before they were dragged off to paddy wagons. In the industrial section along the east side of the Willamette, I took note of a sign that said: "Anything Will Sell If You Box It Well."

Oregon's Wayne Morse was one of only two senators to vote against the Gulf of Tonkin Resolution that opened the floodgates for the war on Vietnam in August 1964. The state's dominant newspaper, the *Oregonian*, went after Morse with a vengeance because of his strong position for peace. He'd been a premature antimilitarist. In February 1968, while skipping classes as a high school junior, I'd seen Morse up close at a hearing of the Senate Foreign Relations Committee. I still remember the way afternoon light came through the Venetian blinds in the small room while Morse let loose with his sandpapery voice. A transcript of the hearing has preserved Morse's declaration that he did not "intend to put the blood of this war on my hands." And he spoke prophecy: "We're going to become guilty, in my judgment, of being the greatest threat to the peace of the world. It's an ugly reality, and we Americans don't like to face up to it." He went down to defeat in '68 in a close election that mostly turned on his opposition to the war.

Slowly, I got to know activists around Portland. I couldn't persuade members of the local chapter of Business Executives Move For Vietnam Peace to protest at a speech in the city by superbanker David Rockefeller—a strong supporter of the Vietnam War and an advocate of "enlightened self-interest," whose Chase Manhattan loans had long shored up the apartheid regime in South Africa as well as many other dictatorships. I wrote a flyer that denounced "the Chase Manhattan Bank's financial support for the brutally cruel, totalitarian, barbaric and inhuman oppression of the people of South Africa, Greece, South Vietnam, Spain, Rhodesia and Latin America." It was a partial list.

In the Hilton Hotel downtown, at a banquet set to hear Rockefeller's speech, I went through the large room, handing out the leaflet during dessert. I got it into the hands of quite a few diners before security guards hauled me out and took me to a little room, where I was told to go away and never come back.

The Vietnam War continued for years even after opinion polls showed that most Americans were opposed. In November 1971 the liberal magazine *Saturday Review* featured an article by Peter Schrag that pointed out: "The American majority is against the war. To oppose it involves no risk: the only risk lies in trying to stop it."

In 1972, *Voices From the Plain of Jars* came out—words and drawings from children and adults in a book subtitled "Life Under an Air War." Published by Harper & Row, it gained some circulation at the time, but three decades later was difficult to find even in library systems. Online, a bookseller offered an apt description: "This little-known book is the work of one American volunteer outraged by the secret bombing of Laos by his own country. The book is composed of the translated essays of the people who lived under the bombing. . . . This is the story of the first society to be totally destroyed by aircraft."

In 2006, I asked the outraged American volunteer Fred Branfman for an overview of his long-ago experiences in Laos—a country targeted by ideological cold warriors in Washington. "At the age of twenty-seven, a moral abyss suddenly opened before me," Branfman replied. "I was shocked to the core of my being as I found myself interviewing Laotian peasants, among the most decent, human and kind people on Earth, who described living underground for years on end, while they saw countless fellow villagers and family members burned alive by napalm, suffocated by five-hundred-pound bombs, and shredded by antipersonnel bombs dropped by my country, the United States. Even more shocking was the realization that the bombing was continuing apace, and that a few hundred miles away Laotians alive today would be dead by the morrow."

The "moral abyss" opened for Branfman in early September 1969 when he visited a Buddhist pagoda in the center of Vientiane, the Laotian capital:

> Every single villager that day, and every one of the more than two thousand refugees I was to interview in the next fifteen months, told essentially the same story. The bombing began in mid-1964, gradually escalated, until in late 1968 the planes were coming every day, raining down death and destruction, and destroying whole villages and, eventually, the whole society that had existed for the previous seven hundred years on the Plain of Jars. And, they made it clear, most of the bombing was from American jets. They knew the difference between the small, propeller-driven aircraft of the Royal Lao Air Force (many of which, I later discovered, were piloted by U.S.-trained Thais), which were relatively few in number, and the enormous numbers of jets which dropped huge bombs upon them day after day, month after month, year after year.

Branfman's discoveries led him to scrutinize U.S. policy: "I soon learned that a tiny handful of American leaders, a U.S. executive branch led by Lyndon Johnson, Richard Nixon, and Henry Kissinger, had taken it upon themselves—without even informing let alone consulting the U.S. Congress or public—to massively bomb Laos and murder tens of thousands of subsistence-level, innocent Laotian civilians who did not even know where America was let alone commit an offense against it. The targets of U.S. bombing were almost entirely civilian villages inhabited by peasants, mainly old people and children who could not survive in the forest. The other side's soldiers moved through the heavily forested regions in Laos and were mostly untouched by the bombing."

———

From an Oval Office tape, April 25, 1972, during a conversation between President Nixon, White House press secretary Ron Ziegler, and Henry Kissinger:

PRESIDENT: "How many did we kill in Laos?"

ZIEGLER: "Maybe ten thousand—fifteen?"

KISSINGER: "In the Laotian thing, we killed about ten, fifteen . . ."

———————

From an Oval Office tape, May 4, 1972: "I'll see that the United States does not lose," the president said while conferring with aides Al Haig, John Connally, and Kissinger. "I'm putting it quite bluntly. I'll be quite precise. South Vietnam may lose. But the United States *cannot* lose. Which means, basically, I have made the decision. Whatever happens to South Vietnam, we are going to *cream* North Vietnam. . . . For once, we've got to use the maximum power of this country . . . against this *shit-ass* little country: to win the war. We can't use the word, 'win.' But others can."

———————

A few months later, in August 1972, several thousand people went to Miami Beach to protest and disrupt the Republican National Convention renominating President Nixon. We vowed to blockade the amphitheater and force Nixon to give his acceptance speech to an empty convention hall. It didn't work out that way, but we tried.

One of the first speakers I heard was longtime activist Dave Dellinger. "It is as bad as it seems," he said. "We must achieve a breakthrough in understanding reality."

The final night of the convention brought plenty of troops along with lots of tear gas and mace. The protests got little media attention; after all, to hear the mainstream press tell it, the Vietnam War had been winding down. About a thousand people were arrested for nonviolently blockading the streets near the convention hall; we went to jail, and Nixon made his acceptance speech.

Afterward, in a booklet titled *In the Belly of the Dinosaurs*, I wrote about what happened in Miami Beach during those few days. Some of the words now seem frozen in amber, from long ago yet still current: "There was a slide show through the dark. Pictures of warfare inflicted this second . . . humans burned by the phosphorous of our own lies . . . flesh burned and torn past death . . ." At the bottom of the page was an illustration of planes over a village and bombs falling on buildings, with the caption "Drawing by Laotian Refugee."

Two pages later was a paragraph pasted in from one of the many leaflets that circulated at the demonstrations that week. Next to a photo of a round object was the headline GUAVA BOMB and a few sentences: "If you were in Indochina, and this round bomb about the size of a baseball exploded near you, you'd be riddled with pellets. (American ingenuity has 'improved' the original bomb by substituting plastic pellets for steel balls. Medical X-rays can't detect the plastic ones.) Guava bombs are anti-personnel bombs designed to kill and maim people. They do little damage to structures. Millions have been dropped on Indochina, some with delayed action fuses that can make them explode anytime—even when a child is nearby."

By mid-1972, U.S. troop levels in Vietnam were way down—to around seventy thousand—almost half a million lower than three years earlier. Fewer Americans were dying, and the carnage in Vietnam was fading as a front-burner issue in U.S. politics. Nixon's withdrawal strategy had changed the focus of media coverage. In a 1969 memo, the executive producer of ABC's evening news, Av Westin, wrote: "I have asked our Vietnam staff to alter the focus of their coverage from combat pieces to interpretive ones, pegged to the eventual pull-out of the American forces. This point should be stressed for all hands." In a telex to the network's Saigon bureau, Westin gave the news of his decree to the correspondents: "I think the time has come to shift some of our focus from the battlefield, or more specifically American military involvement with the enemy, to themes and stories under the general heading 'We Are on Our Way Out of Vietnam.'"

The killing had gone more technological; from 1969 to 1972 the U.S. government dropped 3.5 million tons of bombs on Vietnam, a total higher than all the bombing in the previous five years. The combination of withdrawing U.S. troops and stepping up the bombardment was anything but a coincidence; the latest in military science would make it possible to, in Nixon's private words, "use the maximum power of this country" against a *"shit-ass* little country."

Less than two months after Nixon's landslide reelection, he delivered on his confidential pledge to *"cream* North Vietnam," ordering eleven days and nights of almost round-the-clock sorties (Christmas was an off day) that dropped twenty thousand tons of bombs on North Vietnam. In the process, B-52s reached the city of Hanoi for the first time. During that week and a half, Pentagon Papers whistleblower Daniel Ellsberg later noted, the U.S. government dropped "the explosive equivalent of the Nagasaki A-bomb."

In the early '70s, I started Out of the Ashes Press, a short-shoestring effort that published brief softcover books. The first authors were me and the taboo-defying Northwest poet Walt Curtis; we'd sell our books in the streets and bars for a dollar or two. Also I began to send out little collections of poems and bursts of prose to editors of underground papers and alternative magazines. As much as meager finances allowed, I'd bring stacks of stuffed envelopes to the post office counter, sending them the cheapest way possible.

Many years later, I learned that the FBI was monitoring my paltry mailouts of mimeographed poetry and polemics. The agency held back some of the surveillance records that mentioned me, but it released fourteen pages, heavily blacked out with magic marker. One of the FBI memos said:

On 5/31/73, a third knowledgeable source in a position to have information of this type stated Post Office Box 42384, the mailing address of "Out of the Ashes Flash Food Service," was rented 1/5/71 by NORMAN SOLOMON, 3132 S.E. Gladstone, Portland, Oregon. Source stated SOLOMON sent out large quantities of anti-establishment literature. SOLOMON, a white male, born 7/7/51 at Washington, D.C., is the subject of PDfile 100-

13484 captioned "NORMAN (NMN) SOLOMON, SUBVER-
SIVE MATTER, 00: Portland." Portland is conducting intensive
investigation of SOLOMON to determine adherence to RU
[Revolutionary Union] ideology and activity.

The date of that memorandum, sent to "Director, FBI" from the
Bureau's Portland office, was August 13, 1973. Five weeks later, another memo ("Subject: NORMAN SOLOMON, SUBVERSIVE
MATTER") said that the Portland office "will determine subject's
activities." On January 14, 1974, a follow-up memo concluded:
"Subject is not known to be a member of any New Left organization and has been described as a pampheteer [sic]." The memo
added: "No association has been established between subject and
known leaders of the New Left movement at Portland, Oregon. In
view of the above, it is recommended that this case be closed."

That sort of trivial and wasteful surveillance was a tiny facet of
the FBI's COINTELPRO operations that violated the constitutional
rights of huge numbers of politically active Americans—and sometimes damaged or destroyed their lives—at the behest of the warfare state.

6

REGROUPING IN THE '70s

The downturn of the antiwar movement during the early 1970s overlapped with the emergence of many grassroots organizations; some would endure, grow, or morph into larger-scale projects. Most of the significant changes happened well below the mass-media radar, which did little to track nonprofit food co-ops, health clinics, community radio stations, art collectives, legal cooperatives, rank-and-file union caucuses, and other decentralized efforts that responded to urgent issues and needs.

Feminism's "second wave" was in its first years, repudiating sexism and the romanticization of violence, both personal and political. Gay rights activism began to reframe sexual orientation in contexts of human rights and universal love. Some new laws were chipping away at institutionalized racial bias. Welfare recipients made headway in organizing for their rights. Concern about ecology sank roots in many communities; battles for cleaning up polluted air and waterways, for preventing new environmental disasters, for public power and against nuclear power, became ongoing campaigns. In diluted form, progressive social changes seeped into some schools, civic groups, and even workplaces; those trends were rarely front-page news, but long-term effects were tangible.

The spreading counterculture took many shapes. Visible changes were apt to be minor, along the lines of the gradual mainstreaming of massage or yoga or tofu. Meanwhile, the era brought plenty of boundary-pushing and challenges to automatic pilot. At Portland's noncommercial KBOO Radio, the station manager told me about an encounter that left him nonplussed: When a young volunteer came by for a tape recorder, the manager asked why she didn't say "thank you." She responded, "Thank you is a fucked concept."

Sexual freedom was sometimes promoted as a vital way to transcend individual and social problems. But what more and better sex did for society as a whole—or, say, for ending the war underway—was murky at best. Despite the mercifully short-lived antidraft slogan "Girls say yes to boys who say no," countless females said yes to males who, reluctantly or fervently, said yes to war. And warriors, battlefield or armchair, could be as focused on sex as anyone. The idea of making love as an antiwar statement was pushed about as far as it could go, and laudably so, by Yoko Ono and John Lennon. But plenty of sex enthusiasts, ranging from grunt soldier to president, avidly explored their sexual freedom and also participated in military slaughter.

It turns out that society can keep moving in the direction of more sexual liberty without in the least impinging on its war functions. We'd seen the wisdom of urging people to make love not war. We didn't see how easy it would be to make love *and* war.

My well-meaning parents, living in suburbia on the opposite coast, were unhappy when I dropped out of college. Even while going through a middle-class version of financial crisis, they had come up with a semester of hefty tuition and were more than willing to do so again. But I hadn't been much tempted to stay enrolled; in the lingo of the time, the classes seemed "irrelevant."

I read and reread *King Lear*, with no mystery why the play held such an attraction for me. The authority figure is a blowhard whose insanity evolves from subtle to full blown—as the loyal Gloucester observes, "'Tis the time's plague when madmen lead the blind"— dispensing favors and withdrawing them on the basis of fealty from his offspring. It was apparent to me, early in the 1970s, that the game was going to be played in roughly that way for "baby boomers" in America. Obedience, or at least sufficient lack of resistance, would be rewarded. Those who opted out might benefit from relative independence, but they'd pay for ostracism from the mainstream.

In my adaptation titled *King Lethal* (which never got closer to Broadway than an Oregon community radio production), the three daughters are named Gonericia, Rulie, and Joyeux. Their dad, Lethal, enters the first act saying things like:

> Order must bless order, lest kingdoms fail.
> So, this crown's benefits I shall soon assign,
> To prevent future unpleasant mind.

A dithering earl, Humpty of St. Paul, says things like "Yes indeed. Oh, and Hail to the Chief." And, aside: "Though my eyes see a wrong, my voice has learned/To substitute equivocation for resonance."

When Joyeux's turn comes to suck up to father, she says:

> My love cannot caress what wrong you do,
> The blood you spill, corrupt coffers you fill—
> Amid obese, poor hungry and in need;
> After the soldiers you prod, humans bleed.

Of course the errant daughter's dowry instantly plummets, and her most powerful suitor, the King of Sacramento, instantly loses interest. But the Duke of Berkeley sings a different iambic tune:

> Young Joyeux, you are most rich, being poor;
> Poverty in coin but not in spirit.
> Thee and thy virtues I seize upon, with the time.
> Thy dowerless daughter, king, who you discard,
> Is our true queen, essence of our Berkeley.
> All the riches in Sacramento sties
> Could not buy up her soul's most honest cries.
> Though you, Joyeux, may now be called "unkind,"
> Real joy will come without a whoresome mind.

Act 3 ends with the liberal Humpty passing out just after a belated lament that his soul went bankrupt: "To have curried favor with gold calves, while/Victims of my broad-based prudence cry and die!"

And, of course, there is the Fool, who speaks a prophecy ere he goes:

> When poor sit in jail, while rich go free;
> When children learn to fear father's knee;
> When ruling gangsters praise the law;
> In city faces you'll find no thaw.
> When every stomach is full and pleased;
> And tension and distress is eased;
> When abuse of human beings is shunned,
> As life over death finds public fund;
> When dry green land is found by the dove
> And joy proclaimed in open love:
> Then confusion will reign with the clash
> 'Tween feeling and cash.
> Then the simple fact will not seem ached,
> That beneath our clothes we all are naked.

When King Lethal finally keels over, Humpty's son gets the last lines:

> The debt to his madness we must repay;
> Speak what we feel, not what we "ought" to say.
> Age is not wisdom, freedom not for sale;
> The future is ours, to free it or fail.

———

One of my friends seemed to be an intrepid pioneer of psychedelic drugs. As the milieu got more cosmic, he provided in-depth descriptions of his mind-expansive trips. He became especially fond of telling—and retelling—about the time his ego died; he talked about the trip so much that I began to wonder.

Like numerous others, I bought *Be Here Now* by Baba Ram Dass, formerly "Dr. Richard Alpert, Ph.D." Physically square—but psy-

chologically anything but!—the book was the author's account of
his "internal journey" that transformed him from an affluent
Harvard psychologist into, by the mid-1960s, a renowned psychedelic avatar, into, by the early 1970s, a full-blown mystic providing
transcendent tales of gurus, dharmas, chakras, and sadhanas. When
I heard Ram Dass speak inside a large auditorium filled with fans, in
1973, he was impressive. I remembered *Be Here Now* as a very
good book for another thirty years or so, until I picked it up again
in 2006. The book derided the pretensions of the author's discarded
"Richard Alpert" persona, but in retrospect "Baba Ram Dass" didn't
seem any less driven to making extraordinary self-indulged claims
of knowing life's deepest meanings. *Be Here Now* had virtues but,
almost immediately, more was less; the book might have been more
valuable if the huge type that dominated most of its pages simply
repeated the book's most valuable words: Be here now.

In 1974, with the Vietnam War purportedly over, Washington kept
funneling large amounts of military aid to the government in
South Vietnam. I wrote to Robert Packwood—the man who had de-
feated Wayne Morse—asking him to vote against U.S. assistance to
the Saigon regime because of the widespread torture being inflicted
on political prisoners held in small "tiger cages." A letter came back
from Senator Packwood saying that he was concerned but would
not oppose the aid. After putting together a leaflet that displayed his
letter next to a picture of tiger-cage prisoners with grotesquely de-
formed legs, I went to a reception for the senator at a church building near the University of Oregon campus in Eugene. As soon as
Packwood saw the leaflet, he cut short his appearance and made an
abrupt exit.

By the time the last helicopter fled the roof of the U.S. Embassy in
Saigon—immediately renamed Ho Chi Minh City—in late April
1975, America's defeat in Vietnam was history. So was a lot else.

And in the West, many would-be revolutionaries felt awash in dissatisfaction. "Men always want history to go as fast as life," a woman said in the European film *Jonah Who Will Be 25 in the Year 2000*. "It doesn't work that way." Young adults in the 1976 movie were feeling an acute loss of possibilities, several years after being inspired by the social upheavals of the late 1960s. Outward events had failed to keep pace with the timelines of their hopes.

Since then, the slowness of lived history has not been as disappointing as its overall trajectory, grim at any speed. America's economic order has become more dog-eat-dog. War efforts are routine. And many who found such developments ominous also found them tolerable enough to do little or nothing in opposition; if history could not keep up with an individual's preferred storyline, then history would probably be set aside to more or less fend for itself. At a personal level, that could easily seem rational; at a social level, it was somewhere between evasive and suicidal. While history would surely have profound effects on our lives, there was no assurance that our lives could have positive effects on history—but the only way to change the course was to try.

———————

I hadn't paid much attention while plans to build the Trojan nuclear power plant—just a few dozen miles from Portland—cleared hurdles for licensing from state and federal agencies in the early 1970s. Oregon enjoyed a reputation for protecting the environment, but antinuclear activists didn't get very far with regulators or the public before Trojan began generating electricity in 1976. By then, about one hundred commercial nuclear power reactors were operating in the country, and President Gerald Ford was urging that the number be doubled.

Ford was in sync with every other post-Hiroshima president. National leaders kept touting nuclear fission as a cheap and safe energy source, proving that the split atom could be made into an indisputable force for human progress. President Dwight Eisenhower, speaking to the U.N. General Assembly in 1953, had proclaimed the realism of atoms for peace. "The United States knows that peaceful power from atomic energy is no dream of the future," he said. "That capability, already proved, is here—now—today. Who can doubt, if the entire body of the world's scientists and engineers had adequate amounts of fissionable material with which to test and develop their ideas, that this capability would rapidly be transformed into universal, efficient, and economic usage." Eisenhower pledged the determination of the United States "to help solve the fearful atomic dilemma—to devote its entire heart and mind to find the way by which the miraculous inventiveness of man shall not be dedicated to his death, but consecrated to his life."

Trojan drew a regional spotlight to nuclear power. Supporters— including the editorial writers at the mighty *Oregonian*—were often derisive about opponents, likening them to Luddites with irrational hostility to technological advances. But when I read reports from the Union of Concerned Scientists, nuclear power reactors hardly seemed to qualify as appropriate technology. The results of a plausible accident could be catastrophic. And even best-case scenarios involved generating huge quantities of nuclear waste that would be deadly for millennia.

Like many other people, I'd spoken against Trojan at a final round of hearings run by government officials as they approved the startup of the 1,130-megawatt plant—the biggest light-water nuclear reactor in the country. Trojan's backers were triumphant and hailed it as a model for building twenty more nuclear power plants in the Pacific Northwest. But the year after Trojan went on line, I got involved in direct action because of an example provided by activists in New England who set off "Seabrook fever."

A grassroots campaign against the Seabrook nuclear power plant, under construction in New Hampshire, grew so large that a demonstration at the site in early May of 1977 resulted in more than one thousand arrests for nonviolent civil disobedience. I talked with some antinuclear activists in the Portland area about initiating similar protests at Trojan, and they thought it made sense. And so, in early summer, at a Portland news conference, we announced the

formation of the Trojan Decommissioning Alliance and our intention of nonviolently shutting down the nuclear plant.

Leaving the news conference, I envisioned just a few of us being
hauled away in front of Trojan. After all, we only had weeks to organize the whole effort from scratch. But a strong response came from
around Oregon and southwest Washington. Soon we were immersed
in meetings that involved hundreds of people at an old church in
Portland. We held "nonviolence training" sessions and clustered into
"affinity groups"—enabling close communication and mutual support while lessening the hazards of infiltration by provocateurs.

In Gandhian fashion, we wrote letters to state officials, explaining
our intentions and asking to meet with them. (Tensions were likely
to be especially high because our "occupation" at Trojan would be
the first time that anyone had tried to pull off such an action at an
operating nuclear power plant.) At a meeting in Salem, the state police chief seemed to be trying to figure out whether we were lunatics
or merely audacious. Either way, he appeared to be worried.

The Trojan Decommissioning Alliance operated by consensus.
At large meetings, that could be very cumbersome—and frustrat-
ing—but the result was usually greater unity and a feeling that
everyone's concerns had been heard. That made a big difference
when we marched under the shadow of Trojan's cooling tower and
blockaded the main gates on the first Saturday in August.

"Protesters Vow to Close Trojan N-Plant," said the banner headline across the top of the front page of the Sunday *Oregonian*. The
story said that the nuclear plant's main owner, Portland General
Electric, apparently "was willing to wage a war of nerves with the
protesters."

We stayed in front of the gates through a second night. And
then, as the *Oregonian* reported under another front-page banner
headline:

Oregon state police Monday arrested eighty-four demonstrators at the Trojan nuclear power plant, ending a thirty-eight-hour
sit-in against nuclear power in Oregon.

Organizers of the protest, which began Saturday on the 32nd

anniversary of the bombing of Hiroshima, Japan, promised more "occupations" of the plant in the future.

. As about seventy-five officers moved in at 6 A.M., the protesters locked arms and chanted "We shall not be moved" and "No nukes, close it down."

A second occupation happened in November at the same spot. This time, 122 people blocked the gates. And this time, the police didn't wait long to drag us off.

In mid-December, preparing to face the first batch of trespass charges in a courtroom, we told the media that we would "put Trojan on trial." A range of experts in science, medicine, nuclear engineering, and biostatistics testified for the defendants. We offered a "choice of evils" defense—also known as "necessity" or "competing harms"—arguing that the threat of nuclear power outweighed the wrong of trespassing, just as one might disregard a "No Trespassing" sign to save an imperiled child. The jury, drawn from the heavily pronuclear rural area around Trojan, deliberated for almost five hours and then came back with a not guilty verdict.

"A District Court jury last night acquitted ninety-six persons who were charged with criminally trespassing on the grounds of a nuclear power plant in a demonstration," the *New York Times* reported.

> The defendants argued in the week-long trial that the Trojan nuclear power plant in Rainier, Ore., constituted an "imminent danger" to the public. An Oregon "choice of evils" law allows certain illegal acts when they are committed for the purpose of preventing a danger to the public.
>
> After five days of testimony from experts on nuclear energy, Columbia County District Judge James Mason instructed the jury to decide whether officials of the Portland General Electric Company, which owns the power plant, had the authority to order the demonstrators away from the site forty-five miles northwest of Portland.
>
> The jury decided that they did not, but the judge stopped them short of calling the plant an "imminent danger."
>
> The verdict is likely to "create some enthusiasm" among op-

ponents of nuclear power plants, according to Steven Loy, director
of public information for the utility. But he said that if further
demonstrations took place at the Trojan plant, the company
would again press charges.

The Columbia County District Attorney, Martin A. Sells, who
prosecuted the case, has suggested that trespassing on the
grounds of a nuclear power plant be made a felony.

We were elated by the trial. It turned out to be the last time the
DA went along with allowing extensive testimony on dangers of
nuclear power. After a guilty verdict for the second batch of cases,
the Trojan Decommissioning Alliance redoubled its media outreach
to challenge the usual arguments for nuclear energy. And planning
got underway for daily waves of blockades at Trojan over a four-day
period in early August 1978. When the time came, the protests resulted in the largest mass jailings in Oregon that anyone could remember; 272 people arrested at Trojan's gates were dispersed to jails
in seven counties.

The *Oregonian*'s evangelically pronuclear editorial board was
on the defensive even before early spring 1979, when the accident at
the Three Mile Island nuclear power plant nearly made a large portion of central Pennsylvania uninhabitable. In Oregon, the public
debate no longer revolved around a far-along scenario for building
another nuke; instead, the fiercest dispute centered on whether
Trojan should remain open as the state's only nuclear power plant.
(The process was slow, but Oregon became a state without any nuclear power when a series of radioactive leaks forced the permanent
closure of Trojan in 1992.)

Along with shifting the terms of the region's debate in an antinuclear direction, the Trojan Decommissioning Alliance campaign
taught a lot of us how to organize nonviolent direct action. As a participant, I saw with my own eyes that people could embrace
Gandhian principles along with participatory decision-making—
and that it was possible to change history, not because of the heroic
actions of a few but with cooperative activism involving thousands
of determined people.

And I learned about fallacies of rhetorical efforts by Truman, Eisenhower, and every president since to exalt nuclear power as removable from the ominous shadow of nuclear arsenals. The civilian and military nuclear industries shared the same fuel cycle, from uranium mining and enrichment to reactors and atomic waste. For decades the radiation safety standards trumpeted by the nuclear-power industry and medical authorities came from skewed interpretations of Hiroshima and Nagasaki data that fit snugly with claims from the Pentagon. And the export of nuclear-power technologies to developing countries would provide the essential ingredients for the proliferation of nuclear weapons. "The peaceful atom" had always been a myth.

A thirty-day jail sentence, for civil disobedience at Trojan, gave me a look at life on the incarcerated side of class divides. The initial stint was in the "holding tank" of the courthouse in downtown Portland. Each day, the cells got more crowded as the newly arrested clientele jammed into the spaces behind old bars. The atmosphere was gritty, smelly, peeling-paint metallic, noisy, and chaotic—quite a contrast to the genteel courtrooms and public offices of the justice system. Patrolling a narrow walkway that spanned the outside of the cells, jail employees kept tabs, shouted out names, and rolled carts of food. A nurse came by, offering aspirin while rebuffing pleas for stronger medication. On Sunday afternoon, a TV we could watch through the bars showed an old black-and-white movie set during the French Revolution. Toward the end, Marie Antoinette was in a prison tower, weeping. The man next to me said, with evident satisfaction, "You gonna *die*, you motherfuckin' bitch."

For many in the baby-boom generation, a lot of introversion seemed to happen as the 1970s went on. Art was profuse, and so were artisans. We made and appreciated all kinds of music. Plenty of us played guitars. We learned how to make jewelry and sand candles, became proficient at a multitude of crafts. We cooked healthy food and gardened, organically of course. We helped worthy causes. Meanwhile, in electoral arenas, conservative politicians and their backers were finding out how to refashion and swing the political ropes. They had their eyes on state power and moved toward grabbing it. We had much better songs. They learned how to gain more pull with the government and jerk it rightward.

Overall, for increasing numbers of young Americans, intense alienation gave way to the belief that the Vietnam War could well have been an aberration. It was a comforting thought—the nightmarish era had been a real-life very bad dream, out of character with the basic decency of the United States and its government. The shadings of perceptions were spread along a wide spectrum, but the trend was evident over the course of the decade. For many who had grown hostile to the lethal arrogance of power in the Oval Office, the transition to peace and a less bellicose presence in the White House was reassuring. Gradually, an oppositional stance was likely to seem less appropriate and less practical as longer-term horizons came into view.

7

AGENCIES OF ANNIHILATION

Several years after Nixon resigned the presidency, Jimmy Carter was in the White House and Democrats controlled Congress. In 1978, when I began to visit nuclear weapons facilities, the government's top officials were supposed liberals, people of reputed restraint.

I'd heard and read about the vast Hanford Nuclear Reservation along the Columbia River in eastern Washington, but for many years—though I was living downriver—it held little interest for me. I knew the place had to do with nuclear weapons, and they seemed nearly as intractable as the sun itself, here to stay. But my participation in the movement to stop nuclear power eventually made me wonder what was going on at the site, which had provided the plutonium for the atomic bomb dropped on Nagasaki. I made some appointments and headed upriver.

The manager of Hanford's technical operations, Franklin Standerfer, had chosen an oil painting of roses in a vase to adorn the wall behind his desk. Affable, handsome, moderately reserved, he supervised the department in charge of supplying plutonium. When I pressed him on the need to keep making more of it, he replied: "We don't say, 'Why do you want that much material?' That's not our job. The president makes that decision." The U.S. government's Hanford public relations director, Tom Bauman, spoke up then. "It's like if you're raising chickens," he said, "you don't ask why people want the eggs."

Almost nonexistent in 1940, the adjoining cities of Richland, Pasco, and Kennewick contained a hundred thousand people by the time of my visit. In fiscal year 1979 the federal government was spending more than half a billion dollars on nuclear projects at Hanford. The residents of Tri-Cities expressed no interest in biting the hand that fed. To me, it resembled the one gripping Dr. Strangelove's chair.

Rockwell International—the conglomerate responsible for handling forty million gallons of high-level atomic waste and other assorted nuclear garbage at Hanford—had offices in the Federal Building downtown. My guide from the company was a "public relations specialist" who confided that atomic work ran in the family; she dropped the name of the nuclear chemist who led the team that first isolated plutonium. ("My husband used to work with Glenn Seaborg, whom you may have heard of.") She was driving a new gray car with "U.S. Government, For Official Use Only" stenciled on the doors.

We visited the man some people at Hanford were calling the smartest nuclear waste expert in the world. His name was Raul Deju, and he managed Rockwell's thirty-million-dollars-a-year basalt rock-drilling project to evaluate possibilities for disposal of atomic waste. (PR problems included the news that 115,000 gallons of high-level nuclear waste had seeped into the ground at Hanford during two months in 1973.) Physically, Deju was a small guy in a suit with very wide shoulders. He told me that "the approach we're taking is a systems analysis approach." When I asked Deju if he ever felt any moral dilemmas about his role in programs for nuclear waste that was genetically dangerous and would remain deadly for 250,000 years, he leaned back in his chair behind the big desk and waved a hand. Suddenly he was almost smiling, as if the question had sparked some fond memories. "I used to teach that kind of stuff, and I used to have a ball with it," Deju said. He waited for the next question.

Not far away was Columbia High School, which called its athletic teams "The Bombers" and featured a mushroom-cloud emblem on banners, stickers, and pennants. The school seal, inlaid in the linoleum at the main entrance, was the shape of an unexploded bomb. Sitting in his office, Principal John G. Nash smiled confidently when I asked about the symbolism. "The kids have been around it their whole lives," he replied. "There's no fear whatsoever. Our kids look at the symbol of the atomic bomb as something that has been good for humanity, for energy and other purposes." I walked around the school and paused to watch several cheerleaders practicing in front of a trophy case; above it a banner read "Bomber Football—AAA District Champs '77."

Back home I read from Thomas Merton: "It is the sane ones, the well-adapted ones, who can without qualms and without nausea aim the missiles and press the buttons that will initiate the great festival of destruction that they, *the sane ones*, have prepared."

During 1979 and 1980, I interviewed veterans who had been U.S. Marines sent to clean up rubble near ground zero in Nagasaki a few weeks after the A-bomb fell. Many atomic vets suffered from radiation-linked illnesses, and they—or their widows—wanted the Veterans Administration to recognize their claims as service connected.

I visited Sheridan Clapp in an Oregon hospital. The bombing of Nagasaki was supposedly for protection of soldiers like him. But ever since he arrived in Nagasaki with orders to clean up amid officially "safe" amounts of radiation, Clapp's life was never the same. Thirty-three years later, he was in a crowded VA hospital, battling an extremely rare blood disease—a severe lack of blood coagulant "Factor VIII." No more than a hundred cases had been reported worldwide in the previous three decades. On April 20, 1979, Clapp picked up a blunt pencil and wrote a letter that mentioned plutonium and ended with the words: "Stop these people. Sincerely, Sheridan Clapp." He died five weeks later.

I also met Harry Coppola, one of a dozen Marine machine gun-
ners sent into Nagasaki around September 20, 1945, as an early
squad of MPs. Harry was suffering, and I do mean suffering, from
multiple myeloma bone marrow cancer when I got to know him in
mid-1979 after writing an article about the Nagasaki veterans for
The Progressive magazine. We were part of a Capitol Hill news conference, sponsored by Congresswoman Pat Schroeder, that released
the story and launched some appreciable coverage in the *New York
Times* and other media outlets.

Harry Coppola became famous. He was well aware of the irony
that only his proximity to death enabled him to gain media attention.
In his hotel room near the Capitol, he told me about plans to write a
book; the title, he said, would be *The Nuke Is Killing Me*. Later that
summer, Harry visited Japan for the first time in thirty-four years.
He stood with tens of thousands of Japanese people in Hiroshima and
Nagasaki, at ceremonies marking the atom-bomb attacks. Scores of
Japanese reporters followed him around the country for ten days. In
the United States, *CBS Evening News* began its August 6 coverage of
Hiroshima Day with a filmed report about him.

The journey to Japan—the nuclear disarmament rallies he addressed, the outpourings of affection from his hosts, the visits to
hospitals filled with A-bomb victims—changed Harry. At the age of
fifty-nine, in the throes of an increasingly painful terminal disease,
he came to see his plight as much more than one man's isolated ordeal. History and chance cast him as a living—and dying—symbol
refuting the illusion that the effects of a nuclear weapon can be
confined to its intended victims.

On September 23, 1979—exactly thirty-four years after Marine
occupation troops entered Nagasaki—Harry was at the gates of the
White House with Virginia Ralph, whose husband Harold Joseph
Ralph (another Marine veteran of the Nagasaki bomb cleanup) died
of multiple myeloma in 1978. They presented a White House official
with petitions signed by several dozen veterans and widows of the
Nagasaki cleanup. That afternoon, at a press conference, Harry cut
loose. The *Chicago Sun-Times* described his presentation this way:

A cancer-ridden ex-Marine who said he has eight months to live blasted the Veterans Administration Monday as "a bunch of bastards . . . looking out for their jobs" in denying him and other former servicemen compensation for disability they say was caused by atomic radiation exposure thirty-four years ago. . . . "The VA don't want to know nothing," Coppola said. "They're a bunch of bastards, pardon the expression. They've got beautiful jobs, living high on the hog. They're just looking out for their own jobs. They don't want to say this is service-connected." Coppola said he was "broke" after having spent "$29,000 out of my own pocket so far" for medical treatments, which involve monthly hospital admissions for blood transfusions. "I need three pints," Coppola said. "That's 512 bucks and I've got to come up with the cash every month or the hospital won't take me in."

Two months later, Harry made his last trip to Washington. This time he spoke more softly; yet he was more combative, his words hard-edged. He looked terrible, his cheeks pale gray, his eyes subdued. Along with his deepened cynicism—about the government and the nuclear industry—there was idealism as he talked of the need to avoid radiation-caused suffering, fully aware that his own was past the point of survival. "Sometimes I feel like I'm in hell," he said, describing the pain searing his bones. After many transfusions, his body would not tolerate the allergens in new blood; even the mixed blessing of chemotherapy had become too dangerous. He was left with the feeling "It's like someone cut your leg off."

We had dinner. Harry ate a steak. "That rabbit food you eat," he said, serious and kidding, "a person can't live on it." We talked about the press coverage and the importance of getting his experiences and viewpoint out to the public. "This," he said, "is the only thing keeping me alive." A reporter from the *Washington Post* had come to his hotel for an interview. The next day, he stood in front of dozens of reporters in a building near the Supreme Court and described officials refusing to admit radiation effects as "bloodsuckers."

Waiting for a plane at National Airport, we talked about the media, organizing strategies, the weather in Florida, corporate con-

trol of the government—familiar topics between us—but there
was an engulfing sadness as the airport clocks moved, and we fell
silent, uneasy, suddenly awkward, too much to say and words not
coming. The last time I'd seen him off, as he was boarding the plane,
Harry had said: "I'll keep fighting till my last breath." This time
there was no need to say it. We said good-bye.

———————

Much of the media coverage was sympathetic and even high quality. An exception was *60 Minutes* on CBS; the segment was produced by Joseph Wershba, one of the legendary "Murrow's Boys,"
but his warm tones on the phone came before an aired report that
gave key facts short shrift; at one point, Harry was shown on screen
while a voiceover described such atomic veterans as confused. In
any event, whatever the quality of the news coverage, it all had a
way of evaporating. An official in Washington commented that the
public's memory of nuclear stories had a half-life of thirty days; and
though his apparent pleasure at the thought made me angry, he
probably overstated the duration in most cases.

    After Harry died, I went to a meeting at the National Academy of
Sciences in Washington. Around a long conference table were seated
uniformed officers from the Pentagon, who had a big stake in low-
balling the health effects of atomic radiation. Those military officials
were allowed to play an improper role in what was supposed to be a
rigorous scientific look at the health problems of U.S. soldiers who'd
been sent into the core areas of Hiroshima and Nagasaki. Later, the
National Academy of Sciences put out a report saying there was no
evidence of a radiation link. The Pentagon-NAS partners didn't seem
concerned about too much scrutiny of their report. *Science* magazine
belittled it as a whitewash. But by then the national media attention
had receded from atomic veterans; it was that half-life thing.

———————

During its final two years, the Carter administration stepped up
military spending and slashed budgets for domestic social programs.

(The swerve rightward was sufficient to cause Ted Kennedy to make a brief, and at times notably inarticulate, move to challenge the incumbent for the 1980 Democratic presidential nomination.) Carter provided more goodies for the Pentagon, including an intense public-relations offensive for new weapons systems. The concept of "arms control" had been redefined as a thermonuclear equivalent of tree-pruning; arsenals could be trimmed to propagate new, "modernizing" growth. Within the mechanisms of the political economy (in other words, who got paid how much for doing what), it all made sense, like a finely tuned and immaculately engineered vehicle purring quite nicely, heading toward a cliff.

Jimmy Carter was in his fourth year as president when I received permission to visit the nuclear test site in the windswept desert of southern Nevada. By then, more than five hundred atomic bombs had exploded there during three decades, first in the air and then underground. I couldn't help being in awe of a place that was practicing for the end of the world. The quality control was for nuclear obliteration. Tunnel vision was not a hazard of the activities; it was integral, essential.

Amid the large pockmarks of the arid site, where craters gave off the appearance of a moonscape, dreadful clarity mixed with the euphemisms. The "reliability" of the "devices" would assure the designed "yield." When I visited, in February 1980, the nuclear detonations were continuing at a rate of one every three weeks, ranging up to 150 kilotons each. (The bomb that destroyed Hiroshima was thirteen kilotons.)

The Energy Department's deputy manager of the test site, Troy Wade, a thin man with a goatee, was wearing a sports jacket when he greeted me. "Weapons designers, the physicists who design the things, are a special breed of people," he said. "They can do other things, but it would be a great loss to the government."

The site's director of public relations, David G. Jackson, chimed in: "Any scientist, or professional of any kind—a doctor, a lawyer, a writer—you have to stay up with the state of the art. You have to maintain that challenge." A flat-out ban on all nuclear tests, then being hotly debated, would pose a problem of how "you keep the really top people interested," Jackson went on. "Could you keep them challenged without allowing them to conduct experiments from time to time?—to allow them to practice their trade, if you will." Jackson was well-practiced in his own trade; he'd been doing public relations work for the U.S. government at the Nevada Test Site for ten years by then.

I was twenty-eight, and I'd interviewed enough PR flacks to not be taken aback by almost anything they said. But I wasn't quite prepared for the avuncular fellow named Raymond Guido who was sitting behind an austere desk. He'd been working for a long time as a nuclear-bomb designer for the Lawrence Livermore Laboratory. With a bald head and thick-framed glasses and ready smile, Guido looked a bit like Phil Silvers. "You do bring your personal pride into an operation, into a profession, when you're working for an organization that has a national reputation, has the prestige that goes along with what I think we have at Livermore and I believe we have at Los Alamos," he said.

Jackson chose that moment to interject: "Kind of like being on the New York Yankees. I mean, you know, there's being a pro and then there's being a Pittsburgh Steeler."

"I could never, in the twenty-two years that I've been working at the laboratory, think of much of the things we do as routine," Guido continued. "I really think it's very exciting. It offers a special kind of opportunity for people who have some technical skills." Like the boy in Hersey's *Child Buyer* novel, he would not be bored. Guido was speaking into my tape recorder:

> You don't do very many of the same things over again. There are so many new features that get introduced, and in most of today's concepts there's differences in the measurements that people want to make, from a technical standpoint, to be able to say, "yes, this indeed is satisfying the requirements." There's always challenge and there's always excitement. And that, I think, exists right from the cradle to the grave routine, really—from the start of the ideas back at a physicist's planning level in the laboratory,

maybe consulting with people who are looking at the military re-
quirements, to the completion of the concept, to design, to fabri-
cation, to building the systems out here, to building the diagnos-
tics for the particular systems, safety systems, putting it all down
hole.

Clearly scientists like Raymond Guido got quite a bang out of
what happened "down hole," the climax of all their labors. The official story was that the entire nuclear weapons assembly line made
us safer and a successful test explosion offered the final assurance.
But one old hand at nuclear testing asked me to turn off my tape
recorder; after I had done so, he said: "No head of state, in the world,
has ever seen a nuclear bomb explosion. To me, that's scary. I don't
think anyone who has ever seen a nuclear explosion has ever not
asked the question *My God, what have we done?*"

Before I left the test site that day, Wade and Jackson took me to
a massive canyon left by a hydrogen-bomb explosion code named
Sedan. The cone-shaped crater was several hundred feet deep and a
quarter of a mile across. I still have a photo of the two Department
of Energy professionals, standing in front of the abyss.

———

Days later, I drove from Nevada to St. George, Utah. There, on East
Tabernacle Street, a seventy-three-year-old woman named Irma
Thomas sat in her living room, downwind of the nuclear test site.
Family photos covered a wall. In a heavily Mormon community
where smoking was rare, thirty-one cancer victims were on her list
of people who lived within a one-block radius. "We're not numbers, we're not statistics, we're human beings," she said. And:
"They couldn't pay anyone for the loss of a child. I hope they realize that." And: "We accepted all this. It was our government and we
accepted it."

———

While researching one of the Energy Department's key sites, I
stumbled on a major story. When I reported it for Pacific News

Service in mid-October 1981, the Sunday newspaper in San Francisco and the *Toronto Star* printed my article, which began this way:

> Seven years ago, government scientists working on the U.S. nuclear weapons program discovered that an explosive substance used in warhead construction was so unstable that it exploded half the times it was dropped from a height of less than a foot.
>
> Three years after that discovery three workers at the Pantex nuclear weapons assembly plant near Amarillo, Texas, were killed when a worker accidentally detonated the substance during normal machining procedures. After the accident, which caused $2.5 million in damage and hurled debris more than 320 feet, use of the plastic-bonded explosive was halted in 1977.
>
> However, the substance, known as LX-09, remains in hundreds of nuclear warheads today, posing what some experts believe is a very serious threat of accidental detonation and possible plutonium contamination of port cities in the United States and Europe.
>
> Maj. Gen. William Hoover, the Energy Department's director of military application, confirmed that "several hundred" nuclear warheads presently deployed on Poseidon submarines contain the volatile explosive.
>
> Hoover said the government has no safety concerns about the LX-09 warheads. He said it was only "a coincidence" that a special program was undertaken about one year after the fatal accident to gradually replace the Poseidon warheads with ones that do not contain LX-09. Removal of the warheads is scheduled to take about six years.

The article went on to quote official laboratory documents and scientists who expressed concern. If the LX-09 went off, it wouldn't cause nuclear fission, but it could widely disperse plutonium in port cities where the Poseidon subs routinely docked. A top expert on radiation effects said that such an event "could be a quite serious problem from a public health standpoint."

The story caused a stir in Britain; seventy-eight members of Parliament called for an official investigation after coverage appeared in several English and Scottish newspapers. (In addition to ports in South Carolina and Connecticut, the Poseidon subs carrying nuclear warheads with LX-09 routinely docked at Holy Loch, Scotland, where a missile-loading accident had recently occurred.) British media outlets were much more willing than their American counterparts to pursue the story.

Looking back, the most striking thing about the whole episode was the reaction from the Pentagon. While I put the finishing touches on my article at the Center for Investigative Reporting office, I received an early-morning call from a general I'd interviewed. He was phoning to emphasize, in reassuring tones, that all of those nuclear warheads currently on Poseidon submarines would work as designed if the order came to launch a nuclear attack.

—————

I was becoming impatient with my investigative journalism. What did it mean to cause little scandals? Why be content with trying to slightly mitigate the activities of those who, in Thomas Merton's words, "can without qualms and without nausea aim the missiles and press the buttons"? The nuclear-weapons conveyor belt kept moving.

At the same time, the country was undergoing a big upsurge of concern and protest that peaked on June 12, 1982, when nearly one million people rallied against nuclear arms in Manhattan's Central Park. Public unease was threatening to destabilize the nuclear confidence game. But the Reagan administration plunged ahead with new nuclear weaponry, and few on Capitol Hill did much to interfere. While the nuclear-freeze movement was at its height, congressional leaders did not dispute the gist of the sentiments behind this statement from right-wing icon Phyllis Schlafly: "The atomic bomb is a marvelous gift that was given to our country by a wise God."

While the United States and the Soviet Union aimed thousands of nuclear missiles on hair-trigger alert, tensions were spiking upward—and deployment of new weaponry wasn't the only reason. The Reagan administration was making incredibly cavalier noises about nuclear war, as *Los Angeles Times* reporter Robert Scheer wrote:

Very late one autumn night in 1981, Thomas K. Jones, the man Ronald Reagan had appointed Deputy Under Secretary of Defense for Research and Engineering, Strategic and Theater Nuclear Forces, told me that the United States could fully recover from an all-out nuclear war with the Soviet Union in just two to four years. T.K., as he prefers to be known, added that nuclear war was not nearly as devastating as we had been led to believe. He said, "If there are enough shovels to go around, everybody's going to make it." The shovels were for digging holes in the ground, which would be covered somehow or other with a couple of doors and with three feet of dirt thrown on top, thereby providing adequate fallout shelters for the millions who had been evacuated from America's cities to the countryside. "It's the dirt that does it," he said.

What is truly astounding about my conversation with T.K. is not simply that one highly placed official in the Reagan administration is so horribly innocent of the effects of nuclear war. More frightening is that T. K. Jones's views are all too typical of the thinking of those at the core of the Reagan administration, as I have discovered through hundreds of hours of interviews with the men who are now running our government. The only difference is that T.K. was more outspoken than the others.

During a mike check before his weekly radio address, President Reagan was apparently unaware that his words would reach the public when he said: "My fellow Americans, I am pleased to tell you today that I've signed legislation that will outlaw Russia forever. We begin bombing in five minutes." The reckless jest came years after Reagan's alarming rhetoric and policies had spurred many Americans into antinuclear activism.

In the fall of 1983, a made-for-TV movie—dramatizing the effects of nuclear war on some Kansas residents—generated enormous debate before it aired. *The Day After* was hardly as horrifying as black-and-white footage shot thirty-eight years earlier in Hiroshima and Nagasaki, but it conveyed an important message to 100 million American viewers on a Sunday evening: belief in "surviving" nuclear warfare was a delusion. However, the broadcast disappointed those hoping that it would set off a powerful clamor for an end to the nuclear arms race. The film proved to be a political dud.

Two months after *The Day After* appeared on America's TV screens, President Reagan gave a nod to widespread emotions when he declared in his State of the Union address: "A nuclear war cannot be won and must never be fought." Members of Congress responded with thunderous applause, but few opposed huge military outlays in subsequent budgets—including line items to keep developing nuclear weaponry. Fears and platitudes encouraged by *The Day After* turned out to be fully compatible with continuing buildups. The film addressed whether we could survive a nuclear war. It said nothing about how we could prevent one.

———

In June 1982—exactly fifteen years after the Six Day War—the Israeli army invaded Lebanon. Later that summer, in the house where I lived, a woman sat at the breakfast table reading a newspaper and sobbing. The paper was filled with reports on the massacres of many hundreds of Palestinians at the Sabra and Shatila refugee camps near Beirut. She was crying not only because of the grisly news but also because she felt powerless to do anything about it. Criticizing Israel's invasion would be too hazardous for the local chapter of the pacifist organization that employed her. No matter how unfounded, the accusation of anti-Semitism didn't even need to be hurled in order to be preemptively effective.

Slow to respond, I waited until mid-August to write about the invasion in an op-ed piece, which the *Chicago Sun-Times* distributed on its wire service:

> As the war was dragging on, our personal and national evasions grew more pronounced. While West Beirut became rubble under methodical pounding from Israeli jets and artillery, disturbing questions loomed larger for Americans whose taxes were subsidizing Israel's military actions. . . . What Israel is doing in Lebanon is terribly wrong. This reality is difficult for Jews to face. Yet, along with people of all faiths and nationalities, we must face

it. . . . I was born six years after the Nazi concentration camps shut down. Tremors of the Holocaust reverberated during the earliest family conversations in my memory. Had my parents been teenagers in Berlin or Warsaw, instead of New York, they would have probably lost their lives in death camps. Israel, as a Jewish homeland, was to be a refuge to protect Jews from oppression and mass murder. In time, it has also become a strategic beachhead in the Middle East for U.S. government policymakers eager to exert military leverage in the region.

After twenty-five more years of American evasions and taxpayer subsidies for Israel's government, U.S. policy in the Middle East could be further measured in rubble, carnage, and rage.

When I visited a center for peace activism near the home port of Trident submarines, west of Seattle, several people walked to the fence of the base. Standing there, an organizer commented that if we were really in touch with the reality of the nuclear weapons aboard the Trident subs, we would be climbing over the fence in protest.

On August 6, 1983, my friend Charles Gray and his wife Dorothy Granada began a fast for disarmament, saying they wouldn't eat again without "a break in the momentum of the nuclear arms race." More than five weeks went by without food, and they almost died.

Specially marked trains—painted white to reduce heat buildup— began to appear on the Oregon and Washington sides of the Columbia River. They were carrying nuclear warheads for deployment. In response, impromptu trainspotting became a coordinated activity; before long, people were on the tracks in front of the trains at various spots along the way.

On February 24, 1984, in Portland, one of the "white trains" halted for two and a half hours because more than fifty people kept getting in the way. Squads of police repeatedly dragged us off the tracks in a Union Pacific railway yard. Thirty-five arrests were necessary before the nuclear warheads on the seventeen-car train could continue their trip to Trident submarines. Each sub was going to carry twenty-four missiles. Each missile carried eight 100-kiloton nuclear warheads. With a range of at least four thousand miles, the missiles' satellite-guided accuracy made them ideal for first-strike use with extraordinary silo-busting precision.

Union Pacific and the DA's office wanted to avoid a jury trial in Portland. They dropped the charges. But the white trains kept coming through the area, and I was glad to be among the people who returned to the tracks. During a ten-day stay at a county jail in October 1984, I wrote about why we were trying to obstruct nuclear weapons deployment:

> In Franz Kafka's classic novel *The Trial*, a man spends many years in front of an open door. He badly wants to walk through it, but his fears prevent him from doing so.
>
> In contrast, several dozen Oregon residents stepped through an existential door last summer when a white train, specially designed to carry nuclear warheads, passed through neighboring Vancouver, Washington. The law warned against this step, but we took it anyway. The train stopped for forty-eight minutes— until we were removed from the tracks and placed under arrest.
>
> So this fall our cases went to trial. Like the presidents and executives and police officers who had preceded him, the judge sought to define the parameters of reality. When we objected, he grew impatient. "I have ruled," he said, again and again.
>
> Such social dynamics have much to do with humanity's current proximity to nuclear holocaust. Figureheads for institutional hierarchies proclaim their versions of reality, in the full expectation that we will follow, lockstep, behind. Never mind that we are all headed toward nuclearized oblivion. It has been duly authorized.
>
> "They said they spent hours looking for some way to acquit the defendants, but jurors in the so-called 'white train trial' decided they had to convict them," a local newspaper reported after the jury's eight hours of deliberation. The U.S. Supreme Court

"has said juries can disregard the law," the account added. "But jurors cannot be told that ahead of time."

In a very real sense, obedience is "the system"—whether in the form of staying off the tracks as a white train approaches, falling silent when a judge wishes to hear no more, or voting "guilty" because of the judge's instructions rather than voting "not guilty" because of one's conscience. Most of all, the system is agreement to restrain one's disquiet to a whimper as the world prepares to end with a bang.

Judges rule, politicians debate, pundits comment, and people vote. So far the door of life has remained ajar. But nuclear war threatens to slam it shut, forever, in a few instants of global terror.

Kafka's doorkeeper, an authority at long last indulging in candor, informs the protagonist that it was fear rather than realism which kept the threshold from being crossed. "No one but you could gain admittance through this door, since this door was intended for you. I am now going to shut it."

When nuclear weaponry reaches its designed conclusion, we will hear no such words. Instead there would be a blinding flash (reputedly brighter than a thousand suns) and then, before long, extinction. Such an ending depends on people's failure to empower themselves as active guardians of life on this planet.

In the meantime, reasons not to take action are many. They are often "good" reasons. The better, singular, reason to take action usually remains undiscovered or suppressed within ourselves.

For now, human possibilities for assertive action continue to drown in a sea of conditioned obedience. Recently I have noticed the ambivalence of frail compassion before the deluge: in a police officer who whispers "thank you" on behalf of his family while he drags someone off tracks so that the white train can continue its mega-death journey; in the young prosecuting attorney who seems a bit embarrassed to be just following orders; in the courthouse guard who quietly hands Tootsie Rolls to defendants handcuffed to each other; in the hardline judge who momentarily seems drawn into the profound truth of a defendant's weeping on the witness stand about the fearsome fate of the Earth.

But most of all, orders were followed. That is how the tracks from the Pantex nuclear warhead assembly plant in Amarillo, Texas, to the Trident submarine base at Bangor, Washington, remain clear of interference from human bodies. That is how tacit agreement to obey makes probable the collective death of the human species.

Testifying in Clark County District Court a few weeks ago, one of the white train defendants spoke of growing up with the knowledge that some of his relatives perished in the Holocaust after being transported in sealed railway cars. He wondered aloud whether some might still be alive if concerned citizens had gotten onto the tracks between those trains and the death camps. "Objection!" the prosecutor exclaimed. "Sustained—not relevant," said the judge.

Yet any nuclear war would dwarf all past barbaric cruelties. Trains carrying Trident nuclear warheads—for missiles of unparalleled long-range accuracy suited for first-strike use—are transporting death technology many orders of magnitude beyond even the Nazi gas chambers and ovens.

Obedience is easier to fault in other societies of other times. But here in the United States, in 1984, fear of authority is an extremely powerful force sustaining the rush to nuclear annihilation. In final instants of global incineration, many will regret that their internalized, socialized fears kept them from defending life while it was still an open possibility.

The door remains open. People in authority are preparing to shut it. They want us to stay out of the way.

———

Those words expressed my outlook after exactly one-third of a century on the planet. And it didn't get any rosier when, a few weeks later, President Reagan won reelection.

Walter Mondale's loss was grim; he seemed less crazed and less reckless. Yet the Democratic candidate was no bargain. Typically, after one primary victory, Mondale had proclaimed that people who cast ballots for him "voted to end this insane nuclear arms race, so that our children can have a future"—but he continued to back every major nuclear weapons system in the doomsday pipeline. Two weeks before the 1984 presidential election, Mondale steadfastly declared in a debate with the incumbent: "I support the air-launch cruise missile, ground-launch missile, Pershing missile, the Trident submarine, the D-5 submarine, the Stealth technology, the Midgetman—we have a whole range of technology."

By then much of the language accompanying nuclear-freeze advocacy had been hijacked. According to a *Los Angeles Times* poll, 62 percent of delegates to the Republican National Convention said they supported a freeze on nuclear-weapons testing, production, and deployment—results the National Freeze Campaign organizers applauded. Yet those delegates joined in renominating Reagan by acclamation.

Mondale, like Carter in his presidential farewell address, could seem heartfelt as he deplored the escalating spiral of nuclear arsenals. And even the Reagan administration was grasping the power of soothing rhetoric to ease nuclear fears.

8

COLD WAR SEQUEL

By the time Election Day 1984 arrived, I was starting a new job at the national office of an interfaith pacifist organization, the Fellowship of Reconciliation. The match fell short of ideal—my faith was not religious and I didn't quite consider myself a pacifist—but I admired FOR's longstanding commitment to nonviolent activism for peace and social justice. For several years I'd been immersed in organizing civil disobedience and other protests against nuclear power, weapons production, and nuclear bombs, a process that sometimes mobilized what Gandhi called *satyagraha*: a Sanskrit word for a force derived from truth, love, and nonviolence. Time and again I saw effective use of nonviolent direct action, and FOR was in that tradition. Plus, the job of "disarmament director" came with a decent salary (the first in my life) and a real budget for national organizing.

The FOR headquarters was a pastoral mansion, nicknamed Shadowcliff, on the Hudson River in the town of Nyack, New York. My office was along a narrow hallway with a warren feel. Twenty-five or so people worked in the building, mostly longtime employees. Soon I was getting the impression that, whatever FOR's past glories, the current leadership had become too preoccupied with direct-mail fundraising pitches to the nationwide membership. I didn't doubt the sincerity, but the entrepreneurial push seemed to be more zealous than the activism.

Still, there was a lot of meaningful work to do. Some of my focus was local. I helped organize actions at the West Point Military Academy, just up the Hudson. One day in October 1985, I went with area residents to hand out flyers between the gray stone buildings. Shortly before Thanksgiving, a rally with a "die in"—reportedly the first peace demonstration at West Point in seven years— generated some regional publicity. At the war-glorifying West Point Museum, sixteen of us were arrested for civil disobedience. Near the main gate, rally speakers included a former Marine, Ron Kovic, the Vietnam War veteran who wrote *Born on the Fourth of July*. Ron spoke from his wheelchair. He went out of his way to denounce Sylvester Stallone's *Rambo*, then in vogue. "I saw that same type of movie when I was growing up on Long Island," he said. "But that time it starred John Wayne. . . . Take a look at me. I'm a living reminder of the Americans who went without question. War is sitting in a wheelchair for the rest of your life. . . . I'm here to tell the men and women of West Point that I don't want what happened to my generation to happen to them."

A local newspaper reported that the West Point cadets "reacted with an indifferent politeness." One cadet said: "They told us we really shouldn't get involved with the demonstrators. That's part of our professionalism—not to get involved in politics. Also, we just got out of a military science test."

————

Soon after I got to the Fellowship of Reconciliation, the Nobel Peace Prize–winner Adolfo Perez Esquivel visited and spoke to the staff. As a human-rights activist in Argentina, he'd been imprisoned and tortured by the military junta. He was working tirelessly, as usual, on behalf of political prisoners and the poor. When FOR staff members solemnly asked him philosophical questions about nonviolence, he bluntly replied that he and his comrades in Latin America were much too busy to engage in such a theoretical discourse.

I worked on a project for human rights in Chile, then a dozen years into the Pinochet dictatorship. The U.S.-backed regime had recently unleashed a new wave of repression in response to protests surging in Chilean streets. It seemed a pivotal time. I arranged for a meeting on February 25, 1985, between Perez Esquivel and the U.S. ambassador to the United Nations, Jeane Kirkpatrick, primarily to discuss Chile. It was grim to sit in the well-appointed office of the ghoulish intellectual Kirkpatrick and see her ultracivilized pretensions while the U.S. government enabled atrocities in the hemisphere— from Chile to El Salvador, Nicaragua, and Guatemala—as she spoke.

A story in the *New York Times* the next morning led off by reporting that Adolfo Perez Esquivel had met with Ambassador Kirkpatrick "to express concern about rights violations in Chile and elsewhere in Latin America." It went on: "Speaking through an interpreter at a news conference before the meeting, Mr. Perez Esquivel called the Chilean regime of Gen. Augusto Pinochet 'one of the bloodiest dictatorships in Latin America.' He said repression in Chile had intensified. 'For this reason, it is incomprehensible that the Reagan administration holds that the situation has improved,' he said."

Other Chile-related media work that year involved the father of Charles Horman, a U.S. citizen killed by the incoming junta at the time of the U.S.-supported coup in September 1973. I visited with Edward Horman at his apartment in Manhattan, unable to quite shake the image of him as portrayed by Jack Lemmon in the film *Missing*. Sad as that movie was, visiting with the murdered young man's father was a lot sadder.

I'd met Ben Linder when he was getting involved in the civil disobedience campaign to close the Trojan nuclear plant. At the age of seventeen, he had a gentle disposition and a sweet smile. Ten years later he was murdered with bullets from his own government.

With a degree in civil engineering, Ben had traveled to Nicaragua in 1983 to work on small-scale electrical projects. His salary amounted to thirteen dollars a month. "He brought electricity to clinics to keep vaccines cold, to light schoolhouses and to light farmhouses," recalled a friend who visited him. Ben was working at a rural hydroelectric project when he died on April 28, 1987, at the hands of Contra guerillas fighting to overthrow the elected Sandinista government. The Contras—termed "freedom fighters" and "the moral equivalent of our Founding Fathers" by President Reagan—were increasingly using terror tactics and disrupting the already destitute Nicaraguan economy. Contras purposely targeted health-care workers, teachers, clergy, and engineers who were helping peasants to overcome grinding poverty.

Ben became the first volunteer from the United States to share the fates of thousands of Nicaraguan civilians murdered by the Contras. His death came while a new infusion of U.S. aid was supplying the Contra forces with more weapons and ammunition. In mourning, John Linder said: "The U.S. government killed my brother. The Contras killed my brother. Ronald Reagan says he is a Contra. My brother's death was not an accident. His death was policy."

Meanwhile, former Contra leader Edgar Chamorro said: "The Central Intelligence Agency is very much in control of the Contras. The CIA is sending a message to those in the international community who provide political support for Nicaragua that they are no longer safe there. The CIA and the Contras are killing the best, the people who want the best for Nicaragua." Ben Linder was one of those people; that's why he died, shot at close range, execution-style.

The night before his burial in the Nicaraguan countryside northeast of Managua, a thousand or so people gathered to light candles at dusk in front of the Federal Building in downtown Portland. Together we listened to speeches, we sang, and we cried.

Many months afterward, looking through a bus window, I saw Ben's father walking near downtown, alone. And I thought again of Edward Horman.

———

When I first visited the Soviet Union, in the summer of 1985, Mikhail Gorbachev had recently come to power, and glimmers of a political opening (*glasnost*) were visible. My three-week trip made me think hard about how Soviets and Americans viewed each other. In a Leningrad hotel, looking into a full-length mirror, I remembered that U.S. nuclear missiles were pointed at the city where I stood.

At a place called Piskaryovskoye Cemetery, about 470,000 people who died from the siege of Leningrad during World War II were buried in mass graves. More than forty years later, the manicured rows of earthen mounds seemed to tremble. At the memorial wall, next to me a teenage Russian girl cried.

At the time, the Soviet Union had just begun a unilateral moratorium on nuclear bomb testing. The U.S. government, however, kept setting off nuclear warheads under the Nevada desert floor. The White House disputed what any careful reader of *Scientific American* knew: Existing technology could easily monitor a ban on underground nuclear explosions.

American news reports and editorials—from such outlets as *CBS Evening News*, the *New York Times* and the *Washington Post*—heaped scorn on the Soviet initiative, labeling it propaganda. The derisive media coverage assisted President Reagan as he continued to rebuff Gorbachev's one-sided moratorium. (It was to continue, unreciprocated, for nineteen months.)

Someone deeply upset about the situation was Anthony Guarisco, who had witnessed A-bomb tests at Bikini in 1946 as a young navy seaman. Forty years later, he was the director of the Alliance of Atomic Veterans. For Anthony, the Soviet suspension of nuclear bomb testing was a dream come true; the American refusal to respond in kind was a nightmare.

Anthony and I decided to try a new tactic. In early 1986, we made an appointment to discuss the matter with the U.S. ambassador in Moscow, then went on the long trip from the United States—hoping to help boost pressure on the Reagan administration to join in the nuclear test moratorium. On a very cold February afternoon, we rode a subway to the stop near the U.S. Embassy.

The conversation with Ambassador Arthur Hartman was polite

as he sat behind his desk, but tensions rose after half an hour when Anthony and I said that we wanted to stay at the embassy for a while to do work for an end to nuclear testing. "You don't understand," the tall silver-haired envoy said as he stood up. "This meeting is over."

The ambassador suggested that we sit in an adjoining reception area. So Anthony and I took seats in the ninth-floor waiting room, next to magazines and a courtesy telephone. I called the Moscow bureau of the Associated Press and explained that we would like to "stay here and fast a few days" as a "presence for the disarmament movement." I had the phone numbers of many other news organizations in my pocket, but within minutes the phone's dial tone was gone.

An embassy official arrived to say that we could come back the next day and visit the first-floor consulate area. That sounded like an easy way to get rid of us. Soon, the official was back with four U.S. Marines, and he urged us to leave the building. I didn't want to go, and neither did Anthony. Two of the Marines picked me up, and another one led Anthony to the elevator after he explained that he had a spinal condition. The Marines brought us through the embassy's front door and left us on the sidewalk on Tchaikovsky Street.

Reporters from a few media outlets appeared, mildly curious. They asked us some questions. Hours later, the Associated Press reported: "Two American peace activists tried to stage a sit-in inside the U.S. Embassy but were evicted by Marine guards who carried one of them out in an over-the-shoulder fireman's grip." The *Chicago Tribune* said that we were "urging President Reagan to accept the Kremlin's offer to ban nuclear tests." The short dispatches ran in some U.S. newspapers, but the story had no traction.

Like the earlier protest at West Point, the sit-in at the embassy in Moscow did not please my supervisors at the Fellowship of Reconciliation, who worried aloud that such actions would make future dialogue with West Point cadets or the ambassador more diffi-

cult. After eighteen months at FOR, the mismatch of my employ-
ment was evident. The organization showed me the door, and I
gladly walked through it.

I wanted to return to the USSR. Russian culture was compelling,
but the main reasons for my interest had to do with relations between the two nuclear-armed superpowers. I studied Russian and
raised money for a long visit. At last I got back to Moscow in September 1987.

Though I wrote articles saying that Gorbachev's *glasnost* was
for real, I certainly didn't see that the Soviet Union was nearing col-
lapse. Occasionally I'd go to news conferences—as when Secretary
of State George Shultz visited Moscow for nuclear-arms talks—but
the official events weren't very informative. Mostly I liked to wan-
der the city with the help of its fast and cheap subways. The capital
of America's archrival seemed culturally rich, economically strapped,
and intellectually complex.

My application for a journalist visa was in limbo at the Soviet
Foreign Ministry, so the government required that I stay in a hotel
for foreigners, at a steep rate. And transmitting my articles back to
the United States was a challenge. From the Soviet Union, postal
mail could take months, and international phone calls were prohib-
itively expensive. As a freelancer I had no access to a telex machine.
So, every week I'd ride a train to Helsinki, where I air-mailed pieces
to op-ed editors. Some of the articles appeared in the *Chicago
Tribune*, the *Cleveland Plain Dealer*, *Newsday*, and the Minneapolis *Star Tribune*. Logistics aside, when I sat down to write, the
distances between the USSR and the USA seemed longer than any
words could stretch.

November 1987:

Snow is inexplicably falling from a blue sky above Novodevichi
Cemetery, onto hundreds of elaborate headstones for Soviet writers,
artists, scholars, and Communist Party officials. When I arrive at the
tomb of Nikita Khrushchev, dozens of people are in front of the

sculpture there. I still can't account for the snowflakes out of the blue. An elderly man steps from the crowd and places a handful of flowers on Khrushchev's grave. I think of Siberia, imagining how old the man might have been thirty years ago when, soon after emerging as the new Kremlin leader, Khrushchev saw to it that at least seven million political prisoners could leave the Stalin-era labor camps and return home. A few of them might be among those stepping out of this crowd now to place flowers on Khrushchev's grave, more than sixteen years after his death. These gestures of tribute, almost private, seem unorganized.

Under the cloudless Moscow sky, I'm left to ponder how failures of moral nerve so often cause human lives to be twisted and crushed. In my luggage is a recent essay by an *Izvestia* political commentator, Aleksandr Bovin, who wrote: "Some pages from the past which we pass over in silence take their revenge in the form of repetitions of that past. The fact is that today, too, we have not everywhere broken through the barrier of half-truths." He added: "Let us then muster our courage and see to it that the moment of truth should not be merely a fleeting instant, but should become an integral part of our life—both when we reflect on the past and when we take stock of the present." Later, I read the words over again, as if looking in a faraway mirror, this time thinking about the United States.

———

Often I went to Red Square, where special decorations were going up for ceremonies to mark the seventieth anniversary of the Revolution. It wasn't hard to strike up a conversation. My Russian language skills were rudimentary at best, but young Soviet citizens tended to be especially sociable, and many spoke some English.

When a man in his early twenties referred to me as "a capitalist," I objected.

"Do you have a credit card?" he asked.

I had to admit it.

"Then you're a capitalist," he said.

'A few times I went to the Foreign Ministry and tried to get my visa application unstuck. At a meeting with an official there, I was eager enough for rapport that I suppressed my taste buds' aversion to coffee and drank the intense Russian brew he offered. Although I enjoyed the aesthetics of the old Soviet trains running between Moscow and Helsinki, the frequent travel wore thin. I often felt lonely. My application for a journalist visa seemed to be sinking into a bog of pseudo-red bureaucracy. Finally, around Thanksgiving, I returned to the United States.

———

Back in Portland, my girlfriend told me that she'd found a new man. My travels to Russia had done a lot to undermine our three-year relationship. But losing it was a terrible experience. Time crawled; each day and night was an extended ordeal. I had no idea what to do next. I listened to Brahms as never before.

After a few months of slowly bouncing back, I took a long train trip to a small town near the Colorado River, where Anthony Guarisco picked me up. Two years had passed since we'd been tossed out of the embassy in Moscow.

Anthony was struggling with medical problems related to his military service. Meanwhile, he tried to keep the Alliance of Atomic Veterans going. His house in the western Arizona desert served as a makeshift headquarters; mail from veterans and their relatives kept arriving—with endless stories of illness and anguish. Letters and documents, typed and handwritten, routinely included the code name of one nuclear test series or another. The pair of atomic detonations that Anthony saw at Bikini in 1946 was *Operation Crossroads*. Later, at Eniwetok, came *Sandstone* and *Greenhouse*. The nuclear testing in Nevada featured names like *Ranger*, *Buster-Jangle*, *Tumbler-Snapper*, and *Upshot-Knothole*. Those operations had a nice ring to them in press coverage.

Anthony's lobbying role on Capitol Hill had diminished. He'd been working for federal legislation that would give some financial relief to survivors of nuclear tests. But Anthony also wanted a halt to the entire nuclear juggernaut, and he made that clear when testifying at a Senate hearing. The clarity didn't go over well with some previously warm lawmakers and staffers. But Anthony had seen atomic bombs go off, and the half-life of his memory was more than adequate.

———

The next winter I moved to a small town in the mountains near Santa Cruz, California. My intention was to concentrate on writing. George H. W. Bush had just been elected president, and it looked like Reaganism would outlast Reagan. Soon I was working on a book about media bias with Martin Lee, the first editor of *Extra!*, the magazine published by the media watch group FAIR. (Since its beginnings in the mid-1980s, I've been an associate of FAIR—a scrappy organization that combines in-depth research with incisive analysis to challenge media bias.) I never set out to be a media critic, but my efforts in the realms of journalism and activism had led me there.

The hardcover edition of our book, *Unreliable Sources*, arrived on shelves a few days before Iraqi troops invaded Kuwait on August 2, 1990. Media spin for American military intervention began almost immediately. Early the next year, during the Gulf War, grainy TV videos of the air assault caused elation on the U.S. side of the missiles.

Michael Deaver, a former PR whiz for President Reagan, voiced admiration. "If you were going to hire a public relations firm to do the media relations for an international event," he said, "it couldn't be done any better than this is being done." CBS correspondent Charles Osgood called the bombing of Iraq "a marvel," and his network colleague Jim Stewart extolled "two days of almost picture-perfect assaults." *Time* magazine defined "collateral damage" this way—"a term meaning dead or wounded civilians who should have picked a safer neighborhood." The rising civilian death toll was of little or no media consequence. Days after gory pictures showed the remains of children burned alive when a missile hit a Baghdad shelter, NBC's *Today Show* host Katie Couric told viewers that Operation Desert Storm "was virtually flawless."

After the truce, it was a minor story when the Associated Press cited sources inside the U.S. military estimating that the six-week war had killed a hundred thousand Iraqi people. At the Pentagon, the chairman of the Joint Chiefs of Staff, Colin Powell, fielded a reporter's question about those deaths. Powell said: "It's really not a number I'm terribly interested in."

There was plenty of material for the new preface that Martin and I wrote for the paperback edition of *Unreliable Sources.* "Coverage of the Gulf crisis showed that U.S. news media primarily reflect the opinions of official Washington, thereby shaping public opinion," we concluded. "American journalism surrendered to the U.S. government long before Iraqi forces did on the battlefield."

One afternoon in early 1991, I sat drinking carbonated water with Grace Slick. It was the first time we met; I'd recently sent her a letter suggesting that she write an autobiography. Back in 1969, when Jefferson Airplane was at its zenith and I saw her in concert, I would have given a lot to be able to sit with her and talk. Now, looking out on the sparkling San Francisco Bay, she was irreverent, witty, environmentally concerned, enthusiastic about animal rights . . . and somehow struggling to be on the mend. She was "in recovery"— recuperating, as if some great violence had been done to her, by others and by herself. Her confusion was so bad for much of the '70s and '80s, Slick told me, that she'd been "a sellout slug," performing empty songs for the big bucks they could bring. As we spoke, the Gulf War was raging, and our conversation was shrouded by a profound loss of collective power to respond appropriately to the distant carnage. Days later, on the phone, I listened in full agreement as she railed against the pro-war bombast pouring out of Washington through the TV channels.

Eight months after the Gulf War ended, when I crossed the Allenby Bridge from Jordan into the West Bank, I spoke with a nineteen-year-old border guard who was carrying a machine gun. The young man told me that he'd emigrated from Brooklyn to Israel a few months earlier. He said that the Palestinians should get out of his country.

In East Jerusalem, I saw Israeli soldiers brandishing rifle butts at elderly women in a queue. Some in the line reminded me of my grandmothers, only these women were Arab.

9

SLICK TORCH

Twenty-five years after *The Greening of America* made a big splash, I interviewed its author. Charles Reich was on tour with a new book (*Opposing the System*), his first in two decades. Gone were the reveries about the transcendent power of clothes, music, consciousness, revolutionary youth, and the potential for individual liberation. Gone, too, were the claims that meaningful structural change would come only as a final step after people got their heads and culture together.

The year was 1995, Reich was sixty-seven, I was forty-four, and his new book made perfect sense to me as he excoriated the melded power of huge corporations and American government. Unfortunately, the new book was as ignored as *The Greening of America* had been ballyhooed; no high-profile excerpt in *The New Yorker* or any other magazine, scant publicity, and not even faint controversy. Few media outlets bothered to review *Opposing the System*; the notable exception, the *New York Times*, trashed the book. Evidently its truths were more threatening to what Reich had called "the Corporate State" and (in his new book) "the System"—"a merger of governmental, corporate, and media power into a managerial entity more powerful by reason of technology, organization, and control of livelihood than any previously known form of rule."

Charles Reich circa 1970 would have been contemptuous or patronizing toward Charles Reich circa 1995, dismissing him as a throwback to old-style liberalism with a program to retread the

New Deal. But in 1995, the current Charles Reich astutely noted that "we deny and repress the fact of corporate governmental power," and he pointed out: "There will be no relief from either economic insecurity or human breakdown until we recognize that uncontrolled economic forces create conflict, not well-being."

In sharp contrast to his flat assertion a quarter century earlier that "the whole Corporate State rests upon nothing but consciousness," Reich now emphasized the egregious imbalances of financial power: "It is economic deprivation that comes first, dysfunctional behavior second, in the true cause-and-effect sequence." He saw a much fuller social context for the yearning and euphoria that had animated *The Greening of America* and the era that it had celebrated to excess. Far wiser in 1995, he wrote: "Most of the important things in life, the things we truly desire, such as love, joy, and beauty, lie in a realm beyond the economic. What we do not recognize is how economics has become the destroyer of our hopes. It is economic tyranny that cuts off our view of a better future."

September 25, 1995:

Several dozen reporters and photographers are packed into the room, bright with TV lights. The mayor steps to the microphones with a formal welcome for Colin Powell, who strides to the podium. He looks very executive in a black pinstriped suit, a crisp pastel blue shirt, a tasteful burgundy tie. From the start, the former chairman of the Joint Chiefs of Staff gives off authoritative confidence.

Powell, on tour for his new autobiography, is considering a run for president. Here in San Francisco, like everywhere else, he's big news. Journalists are asking easy questions. He discusses race, then talks about next year's presidential campaign, then launches into an explanation for why so many Americans are now extremely proud of the military—"the superb performance of the armed forces of the United States in recent conflicts, beginning with the, I think, Panama invasion, and then through Desert Shield and Storm"— but a voice breaks in from the back of the room.

"You didn't tell the truth about the war in the Gulf, General."

The loud voice is coming from a middle-aged man in a wheelchair.

Powell tries to ignore him, but the man persists, shouting about civilian dead in Panama and Iraq. Finally, Powell acknowledges the interruption. "Hi, Ron," he says, "how are you? Excuse me, let me answer one question if I may."

"But why don't you tell them, why don't you tell them why—"

"The fact of the matter is—I think the American people are reflecting on me the glory that really belongs to those troops," Powell says. "What you're seeing is a reflection on me of what those young men and women have done in Panama, in Desert Storm, in a number of other places . . ."

Beneath Powell's amplified voice, Vietnam veteran Ron Kovic can be heard only in snippets: ". . . 150,000 people . . . the bombing . . ."

". . . So it's very, it's very rewarding to see this change in attitude toward the military. It's not just Colin Powell, rock star. It's all of those wonderful men and women who do such a great job."

Later, after Powell leaves, I see a small knot of journalists around Ron, who's on a tear: "I want the American people to know what the general hid from the American public during the Gulf War. They hid the casualties. They hid the horror. They hid the violence. We don't need any more violence in our country. We need leaders who represent cooperation. We need leadership that represents peace. We need leaders that understand the tragedy of using violence in solving our problems. . . . Did Colin Powell really learn the lessons of the Vietnam War? Did he learn that the war was immoral? I think that he learned another lesson. He learned to be more violent, to be more ruthless. And I've come as a counterbalance to that today. I've come as an alternative voice. . . . I came down today because I just can't allow this to continue—this honeymoon, this love affair with someone who was part of a policy which hurt so many human beings."

In the middle of the 1990s, when a Republican majority swept into Congress, the new House speaker Newt Gingrich said that the Heri-

tage Foundation "is without question the most far-reaching conservative organization in the country in the war of ideas." Heritage
was proficient at hiring right-wing writers, commentators, and out-
of-office politicians, giving them titles like "senior fellow" and "distinguished scholar," and promoting them with a relentless public-
relations juggernaut.

One day in 1996 I went to the spacious headquarters of the
Heritage Foundation near the Capitol and interviewed the men
running its PR operation. The organization's annual budget was almost $30 million, and much of it went to prodigious media outreach
and other publicity efforts. Heritage constantly flooded the media
with messages favored by its wealthy conservative donors and corporate backers.

Leaving the interview, I thought about the need for progressive
infrastructure to do such media work on a national scale. There was
no way to raise $30 million, but I figured that even a fraction of that
amount could fund a consortium drawing on the expertise of literally thousands of academics, researchers, and activists who were
routinely shut out of news media. So, I applied for grants to launch
a nonprofit organization called the Institute for Public Accuracy.
Seed money materialized, and in late 1997 the Institute opened a
small office in San Francisco. The next spring, an IPA media office
got underway in the National Press Building in Washington—and
soon we were sending out news releases to several thousand reporters, editors, and talk-show producers across the country.

I had no way of knowing that a decade later, the Institute for
Public Accuracy would be going strong. But I did have a hunch that
a staff of just a few people, committed to doing media outreach for
progressive voices, could have a tangible effect on what Americans
might see, hear, and read in news media. Of course the playing field
remained badly tilted in favor of big-money interests. But we made
inroads by offering journalists a range of experts available for
timely interviews. While churning out a couple of hundred news releases per year via email and fax, we established a regular way of
challenging the dominant media messages. And there was always a

massive amount to challenge as the country's media machinery kept spinning for economic privilege, corporate power, and war.

———

"The hidden hand of the market will never work without a hidden fist," Thomas Friedman wrote approvingly in one of his explaining-the-world bestsellers. "McDonald's cannot flourish without McDonnell Douglas, the designer of the U.S. Air Force F-15. And the hidden fist that keeps the world safe for Silicon Valley's technologies to flourish is called the U.S. Army, Air Force, Navy and Marine Corps."

Those words appeared in Friedman's book *The Lexus and the Olive Tree*, but the passage first surfaced (with a few tweaks of syntax) in the *New York Times Magazine* on March 28, 1999, near the end of a long piece adapted from the book. Filling almost the entire cover of the magazine was a red-white-and-blue fist, with the caption "What The World Needs Now" and a smaller-type explanation: "For globalism to work, America can't be afraid to act like the almighty superpower that it is."

The clenched graphic could be seen as the "hidden fist" that "the hidden hand of the market will never work without." While the cover story's patriotic fist was intended as a symbol of the globe's need for multifaceted American power, the military facet had been unleashed just as the magazine went to press. By the time the star-spangled cover reached Sunday breakfast tables, NATO air attacks on Yugoslavia were underway; the U.S.-led bombing campaign would last for seventy-eight straight days.

Writing columns and appearing on broadcast networks to assess the warfare, Tom Friedman could not contain his enthusiasm. (The man was widely viewed as a liberal, whatever that meant, and "the liberal media"—whatever *that* meant—provided Friedman with many platforms that often seemed to double as pedestals.) Interviewers at ABC, PBS, and NPR ranged from deferential to fawning as they solicited his wisdom on the latest from Yugoslavia. Even when he lamented the political constraints on the military options of the nineteen-member NATO alliance, Friedman was upbeat. "While there are many obvious downsides to war-from-15,000-feet," he wrote after bombs had been falling for more than four weeks, "it does have one great strength—its sustainability. NATO can carry on this sort of air war for a long, long time. The Serbs need to remember that." So, Friedman explained,

> if NATO's only strength is that it can bomb forever, then it has to get every ounce out of that. Let's at least have a real air war. The idea that people are still holding rock concerts in Belgrade, or going out for Sunday merry-go-round rides, while their fellow Serbs are "cleansing" Kosovo, is outrageous. It should be lights out in Belgrade: every power grid, water pipe, bridge, road and war-related factory has to be targeted.
>
> Like it or not, we are at war with the Serbian nation (the Serbs certainly think so), and the stakes have to be very clear: Every week you ravage Kosovo is another decade we will set your country back by pulverizing you. You want 1950? We can do 1950. You want 1389? We can do 1389 too.

The convenience marbled through such punditry is so routine that eyebrows rarely go up. The chirpy line "Let's at least have a real air war," for instance, addressed American readers for whom, with rare exceptions, the "real air war" would be no more real than a media spectacle, with all the consequences falling on others very far away. As for rock concerts and merry-go-rounds, we could recall—if memory were to venture into unauthorized zones—that any number of such amusements went full throttle in the United States during the Vietnam War, and also for that matter during all subsequent U.S. wars including the one that Friedman was currently engaged in cheering on. If the idea of civilians trying to continue with normal daily life while their government committed lethal crimes was "outrageous" enough to justify inflicting "a merciless air war"—as Friedman urged later in the same column—would someone have been justified in bombing the United States during its slaughter of countless innocents in Southeast Asia? Or during its active support for dictators and death squads in Latin

America? For that matter, Friedman could hardly be unaware that for several weeks already American firepower had been maiming and killing Serb civilians with weaponry that included cluster bombs. As I write these words, in 2006, news accounts today are matter-of-factly mentioning that a few more Iraqi children have been killed by some of the latest U.S. air strikes; meanwhile, of course, not a single concert or merry-go-round has stopped in the United States of America.

When righteousness moved Friedman to call for "lights out in Belgrade," he was urging a war crime. The urban power grids and water pipes he yearned to see destroyed were essential to infants, the elderly, the frail and infirm inside places like hospitals and nursing homes. Targeting such grids and pipes would seem like barbarism to Americans if the missiles were incoming. Any ambiguity of the matter would probably be dispelled by a vow to keep bombing the country until it was set back fifty years or, if necessary, six centuries. But Friedman's enthusiasm was similar to that of many other prominent American commentators who also greeted the bombing of Yugoslavia with something close to exhilaration.

The final paragraph of Thomas Friedman's column in the *New York Times* on April 23, 1999, began with a punchy sentence: "Give war a chance." It was a witticism that seemed to delight Friedman. He repeated it, in print and on national television, as the bombing of Yugoslavia continued. A tone of sadism could be discerned.

Three weeks into the bombing of Yugoslavia, I got a call from a producer at CNN, inviting me to participate in a live show about media coverage of the war. I ironed a shirt, grabbed a tie, and dashed to the car in front of my house on the Northern California coast. Minutes after racing across the Golden Gate Bridge, I made it to the studio in time for the satellite feed.

Looking into the blank dark lens of a camera, I heard the host's voice in my earpiece: "Norman Solomon, rate for us how the coverage has been so far in this adventure that we have in Yugoslavia."

"I would rate the fourth estate as functioning more like a fourth branch of government," I said. "We just saw this Pentagon briefing in the last half hour, where the Pentagon officials did their thing, which was video games trying to depict the dropping of 2,000-pound bombs as though it was just some kind of blip on screens. But we also saw the press corps in that room—in the Pentagon—beamed around the world, not posing even softball questions—I would call them beach-ball questions—in which the press corps uses, adopts, internalizes, and puts out into the world similar assumptions and terminologies used by the military."

I took a quick breath and went on: "Now generals are going to talk in terms of 'collateral damage,' 'degrade,' 'bombing campaign,' 'air campaign,' to try to use euphemisms, to turn this into something where Americans can distance from the destruction being wrought in our name with our tax dollars. But all those phrases I just mentioned were used by reporters without any reference to the underlying meanings underneath those euphemisms. So I would have to rate the journalists of this country very poor in covering this war, and frankly it dovetails with the strategy that has been implemented by the White House and the State Department and the Pentagon."

Moments later the host, Roger Cossack, turned to a *New York Times* reporter in another studio. "Judith Miller," he began, "Norman Solomon says that the press has become an ally of NATO in what is being accomplished in Yugoslavia. Do you agree or disagree?"

"I couldn't disagree more," Miller replied. "I mean, I think that what we've just seen is one small part of the day's coverage, which is a Pentagon briefing. I mean, if you look at, certainly, my newspaper, you see reports from all over the world, not just from the Pentagon briefing room. And I think that, if anything, this was a war that was kind of prompted by public outrage to the pictures that were shown on CNN, to the stories that were told in the *New York Times* and other papers."

In a minute the third guest, NPR news analyst Daniel Schorr, joined the discussion: "May I agree with my friend, Judy? Hello, Judy."

"Hi, Daniel."

"Let me say this," Schorr continued. "During the Vietnam War, we used to get briefings, which came to be known as 'the five o'clock follies,' about body counts—grossly exaggerated—about successes that weren't there. What happened was we got a whole generation of journalists, starting, say, with people like David Halberstam, Peter Arnett, who say, 'Let me go out there and see what's happening.' The result of that was the Pentagon's ability to lull the public may have collapsed, maybe forever as a result of the fact that a reporter said, 'They're lying to you. They're lying to you. Let's show you what's actually happening here.' . . . The fact that the reporters can't get everywhere in Yugoslavia right now makes it more difficult, but even after the Gulf War, with all of the smart bombs you heard about, later we heard that most of the bombs were dumb and that most of the Patriots didn't find their target. In the end, they can say what they want. We'll catch up with them."

To me, the discussion had veered into the familiar fog of American journalists praising their own supposedly intrepid persistence. I broke in: "Let me say that there's always an excuse that journalists use when they attach themselves to the basic assumptions of the Pentagon and the war planners and in this case the war makers. You can have tactical debates until you're blue in the face—and we have plenty of those—but the reality is that certain pictures get on television through the prompting and the urging and the showcasing of the Pentagon and the White House and certain pictures don't get on." Later, I added: "I think the problem is selectivity. All of the suffering that's being depicted that the Albanian-Kosovars have gone through is very newsworthy. So is the suffering of the Kurds in Turkey. But we are not seeing those pictures, we're not seeing those pictures, we're not hearing journalists raise that to a high-profile issue, precisely because Turkey is a part of NATO."

The host then asked: "Judith Miller, are we seeing enough of . . . the damage that is being caused in Belgrade to the Serbs? Have we seen enough of that?"

"I think we have," Miller replied. "I think we've seen a lot of it, and I thought we saw a lot of it from Baghdad, when American bombers were dropping payloads and bombs, and we didn't call it 'collateral damage.' Those terms are used in quotation marks. We don't use those euphemisms for war—which is ugly—and I think the media are showing as much of it as they possibly can. But the issue is, all forms of suffering are not equal, I'm sorry. It seems to me that Americans are being told that this bombing was brought about by Mr. Milosevic's refusal to accept a political settlement that had been agreed upon by everyone except him, and that is what has caused the bombing, and therefore the ethnic cleansing and the pictures that you see are not comparable in terms of a political calculation to the bombs that are falling, because the leader of that country will not accept the Rambouillet accord that could have prevented this violence. It is a huge problem for the world."

If a commercial break hadn't intruded then, I would have talked about that "Rambouillet accord"—the Clinton administration's purported formula for a prewar diplomatic solution to the Kosovo crisis. The White House had, with virtually no U.S. media coverage, slipped poison-pill demands into the Rambouillet ultimatum presented to Serbian leader Slobodan Milosevic in early 1999. Under the Appendix B provisions of the Rambouillet text, NATO troops would have basically had the run of Yugoslavia. (During a deep-background confidential briefing for journalists at the Rambouillet talks in France, shortly before the air war began, a senior State Department official said that the U.S. government saw a need to bomb Serbia and "deliberately set the bar higher than the Serbs could accept.")

After the commercials, I said: "We've heard, in this last few minutes, another example of how fine American journalists are very good at articulating the premises of U.S. foreign policy, but guess what? That's not supposed to be their job as journalists. They're supposed to function independently. They're not just supposed to show us a window on the world that is tinted red-white-and-blue, but unfortunately that's most of what we're getting."

"Judith, is the window on the world tinted red-white-and-blue?" the host asked.

"No," Miller answered, "I think Norman's is tinted anti–red-white-and-blue, but that's irrelevant."

———

The champion of bombing Yugoslavia was the first president from the baby-boom generation. Vast quantities of hype had told how he idolized JFK and mindfully walked in his footsteps, a motif aided by the fleeting footage of a boyhood Rose Garden encounter with President Kennedy. But Bill Clinton, "the man from Hope," could not outrun his psychological past, and neither—as he wielded power—could any of us. Dynamics of narcissism kept trumping less self-transfixed considerations. (For instance, President Clinton's inability to keep his pants on resulted in a chain of events that helped to pull George W. Bush into the White House.) This was hardly peculiar to any generation or century, but the fruits of "New Democrat" neo-liberalism were supposed to be a better harvest.

As usual for successful politicians, the recipe for Clinton's favorite image was a concoction with plenty of heavy syrup. The symbolic touch of John F. Kennedy was just one more grand confection for PR machinery. The imagery was lofty, but results could be devastating for people on the ground. Clinton loved to talk about "opportunity" for all. But industrial workers who lost jobs or wages due to NAFTA would not have an opportunity to call him to account. Neither would the families kicked off welfare rolls due to Clinton's signature domestic achievement.

A full decade after he signed "welfare reform," the media's references to the law commonly hailed a smashing success. But "ten years after the so-called welfare reform, mothers are being forced into full-time jobs that do not pay wages that allow them to make ends meet," said a scholar on poverty, Gwendolyn Mink. "The wage gap for mothers is growing, and economic insecurity for mothers and children gets worse. Indeed, the persistent insecurity enforced by sub-poverty wages—combined with harsh welfare rules and the lack of child care and health provision—makes families fragile and puts mothers' custody of children at risk."

For the vulnerable, as Clinton crowed, the era of big government was over—except for prisons, police, and the Pentagon. For the powerful, such as military contractors, the era was still going strong. And for investors, new glories awaited.

———

Time's lengthy cover story "GetRich.com" was effusive in the early autumn of 1999. The spread had its share of sardonic asides, but reverence for the magnitude of quick money in dot-com-land seemed to dwarf any misgivings. Although the magazine explained that "it's not all about the money," the punch line arrived a few dozen words later: "But mostly, it's the money." And there was plenty of it moving into new digital enterprises. At the time, Silicon Valley executives were holding stocks and options valued at $112 billion—more than the GDP of Portugal. Computer-literate job seekers were riding high: "Never before have the unemployed been so cocky. . . . E-commerce niches are getting claimed so quickly that there might not be time for business school anymore." Said one Stanford grad who was enjoying the rush of launching his own dot-com firm, "It's all about the buzz. I can't explain it. It's like magic."

"GetRich.com" was part of a long-running media binge. Fourteen months earlier, *Time* saw general prosperity on the cyber-horizon: "The real promise of all this change is that it will enrich all of us, not just a bunch of kids in Silicon Valley." While media outlets reported on the dot-com phenom, they were also glorifying and egging it on.

But the bounties of a tech-driven economy were hardly being shared equitably. From 1977 to 1999 the wealthiest 1 percent of U.S. households averaged a boost of 119.7 percent in after-tax income—compared to a loss of 12 percent for the bottom fifth of households and a loss of 3.1 percent for the middle fifth during the

same period. Meanwhile, corporations were carrying a smaller proportion of the tax burden; by the start of the twenty-first century,
the nation's corporate tax payments had dropped to 8 percent of all
federal tax revenues, down from 13 percent in 1980 and 23 percent
in 1960. Those kinds of trend lines rarely seemed to bother the
journalists avidly recounting the fortunes of big investors.

"We can have democracy in this country or we can have great
wealth concentrated in the hands of a few," Supreme Court Justice
Louis Brandeis had commented several decades earlier, "but we
can't have both."

———

July 2000:

Every day at noon, a couple of blocks from the convention complex
where delegates are holding their caucuses, destitute men line up
for lunch on the sidewalk along Race Street in front of the Ministry
to the Homeless. It's not a photo-op.

About fifteen thousand journalists are here in Philadelphia to
cover the Republican National Convention. But midway through
the week, an aide at the Ministry tells me, not a single reporter has
dropped by to inquire about the bedraggled spectacle.

"We feed homeless guys," the staff member says. "Yesterday, we
fed 223." At least three-quarters of them, he estimates, are living on
the streets in the City of Brotherly Love. Is this kind of situation
unusual for an American city? He shakes his head. "There's home-
lessness wherever you go."

That night, I overhear delegates discussing news coverage of the
convention. About the only negative theme emerging, they agree, is
that the event has been carefully staged. "If the criticism is that it's
scripted," says one, "well, God bless it."

The next morning, the Fox TV broadcast network airs a live interview with the beautician in charge of Lynne Cheney's hair.
"That's a pretty big responsibility," the Fox correspondent says. The
key issue is: "hair spray versus gel?"

Suitably sophisticated, media outlets make a habit of pausing to remark that the convention is an elaborately produced TV show—but that doesn't stop networks from effectively serving as coproducers.

At midweek, under the punched-up hot lights and color-coordinated decor inside the amphitheater, I wonder whether the big news outlets will ever get around to reexamining the assumption that killing people in some other country is the best patriotic credential imaginable. This is military theme night for the convention, and Senator John McCain steps to the podium.

McCain built his political career while news accounts routinely called him a "war hero." In the last year of the twentieth century, major U.S. newspapers published 160 articles using that phrase to describe him. The stories included frequent references to captivity and torture that he bravely withstood after a missile brought him down from a plane he was piloting over Hanoi. But media outlets rarely noted the fact that McCain was participating in an air war that killed large numbers of Vietnamese civilians.

McCain's speech is part of an evening dedicated to celebrating America's military exploits. All night, any mention of a war—past or prospective—touches off enthusiasm among the delegates so ecstatic that it often seems delirious.

———

The Clinton-Gore administration turned out to be so disappointing—on matters ranging from poverty to trade to environmental protection to Pentagon budgets—that many progressive voters were ready to respond with an electoral kick in the pants. An added impetus for staying home or voting for Ralph Nader on Election Day 2000 was that too many prominent Gore enthusiasts who knew better (or should have) were touting him as a paragon of progressive virtue. That was a farfetched case to make after nearly eight years of Al Gore's compliant behavior as vice president while Bill Clinton triangulated away, positioning himself between Republicans to his right and congressional Democrats to his left.

The best argument for Gore in the general election centered on the fact that he was the only way to keep the Republicans out of the White House. The Nader campaign was, as Nader 2000 supporter Barbara Ehrenreich wrote four years later, "tragedy . . . and I will admit now, with hindsight, that it was." As another former Nader supporter, I agreed. But at the time, with the Clinton presidency akin to Republican Lite in so many ways, the consequences of a George W. Bush administration could seem abstract. We learned too late.

10

GREASED PATH TO IRAQ

The authoritative word came that September 11 had "changed everything." So it was unremarkable when, at the end of 2001, the *St. Louis Post-Dispatch* stated in an editorial: "The unspeakable, the unthinkable, the inconceivable horror of that day changed everything." Meanwhile, the front page of the *San Francisco Chronicle* proclaimed: "Attack on the U.S. changed everyone and everything everywhere." Perception as reality. Five years later, it was time-honored matter of fact, as when the *New York Times* led off a news article this way: "Before September 11 changed everything, President Bush wrestled publicly with the issue of embryonic stem cell research . . ."

Not long after 9/11, I wrote a column urging that U.S. news media adopt a single standard for use of the "terrorist" label. If buildings and civilians are destroyed with planes or bombs in the service of a political agenda, I contended, then journalists should call it "terrorism"—or, if the word couldn't be used evenhandedly in the journalistic voice, it shouldn't be used at all.

In response I received an email from Jonathan Storm, the TV columnist at the *Philadelphia Inquirer*, saying: "The media's preoccupation with revenue has seeped into the editorial department of most newspapers. The feeling is that you fail to use this type of language at a peril to the bottom line." Four years later, I asked Storm for permission to quote his comment. "Go right ahead," he wrote back. And he added: "You put yourself in peril now if you fail to do certain types of stories, much less use certain types of language."

For many years the global news agency Reuters had been refusing to use the words "terrorist" or "terrorism" as a reportorial judgment. But no major U.S. news outlet would follow suit. The American experiences and vantage points were at the core of objectivity. What Osama bin Laden ordered to be done with hijacked airliners was certainly terrorism—and, in mainstream U.S. media, what George W. Bush ordered to be done with gigantic bombs could be nothing of the kind. The implicit media message: *Don't even think about it.*

Post-9/11 fear became the key and the lock. A dream scenario for manipulation: we were attacked, and just about anything is justified as a reaction. With enough fear, any rationale might look appropriate.

———

Partway through the summer of 2002, I realized that an invasion of Iraq was probably in the cards. The bellicosity from the White House wasn't the only big tip-off. Joseph Biden, the Democrat chairing the Senate Foreign Relations Committee, excluded invasion opponents from the list of witnesses for two days of hearings. The same committee that thirty-five years earlier had publicly scrutinized the rationales for the war in Vietnam was now playing ball with a president bent on using 9/11 fears to start a war in Iraq. I wrote a piece that appeared in the *Los Angeles Times* in early August, decrying the committee's assist for launching an invasion. But I knew that op-ed articles would count for little.

Heightening my alarm was information from the Washington office of the Institute for Public Accuracy, which put out news releases warning against war on Iraq. Many policy analysts were challenging the momentum for an invasion, but war enthusiasts held the whip and dominated the media debate.

Clearly the Bush administration had no interest in talks with Saddam Hussein's regime. But when I discussed the situation with my colleagues at the Institute for Public Accuracy, we agreed that

someone in Congress should break the ice. In late summer, the
Institute contacted many congressional offices and offered to sponsor a trip to Iraq. A former U.S. senator, James Abourezk, helped
with the outreach and committed himself to being part of a delega-
tion. Finally, a member of the House agreed to take the political risk.

We landed in Baghdad the night of September 13, 2002. Later, I
wrote about our arrival at the Al-Rashid Hotel:

> Television crews had staked out the front entrance. It was a little
> past two in the morning, and the lights from their cameras
> bathed the hotel's mosaic entryway with an eerie luminescence.
> At the curb, the congressman in the delegation hesitated, frown-
> ing as he looked at the entrance. Nick Rahall, a Democrat from
> West Virginia completing his thirteenth term in the U.S. House
> of Representatives, was a long way from home—the first mem-
> ber of Congress to set foot in Iraq during the presidency of
> George W. Bush.
>
> Rahall eyed the TV cameras, and then looked once again at the
> marble mosaic. A sinister likeness of an earlier American presi-
> dent, George H. W. Bush, spanned the floor of the hotel entrance,
> along with tiles forming block letters that proclaimed "BUSH IS
> CRIMINAL." Carefully, the congressman edged sideways into the
> hotel lobby, screened by others to avoid the problematic photo-op.

Meetings with high-level Iraqi officials went well. And the
American media coverage was mostly straightforward, in part because Congressman Rahall spoke carefully to avoid inflaming hyper-
patriots back home.

I'd brought along a little book, *Neither Victims Nor Executioners*,
by Albert Camus. "And henceforth," he wrote, "the only honorable
course will be to stake everything on a formidable gamble: that
words are more powerful than munitions." I showed that passage to
a BBC reporter as we talked in my twelfth-floor hotel room—sitting
at a large window with a panoramic view of a city that already
seemed destined for heavy bombardment. I liked the quote, but the

"formidable gamble" seemed like quite a long shot, no matter how much anyone wanted words to be more powerful than weaponry. The situation at hand in mid-September 2002 was a grim case in point. I was pessimistic, but not fatalistic. War amounted to organized violence, imposed from the top down. Stopping war meant nonviolence, percolating from the bottom up. War required widespread passivity, and peace depended on extraordinary activism.

While Rahall was en route back to Washington, the Baghdad government announced that it would allow U.N. weapons inspectors to return to Iraq. We'll never know whether his visit had anything to do with the decision.

———

Late September 2002:

It's the morning when the "Buddhist Bicycle Pilgrimage" begins in Marin County. Fresh autumn beauty is stunning under Northern California sunshine. I'm dropping off two cyclists at the starting point, a retreat center named Spirit Rock, and the kickoff ceremony is inviting. A bald man in robes with a delightful sense of humor is on the slightly raised platform, next to a sculpture of the Buddha, talking about the two days ahead—definitely not a race—the cyclists will get there when they get there! (How Zen can you get?) He describes how geese fly together, in a V formation, and if one falls to the ground then others will swoop down to see what has happened, to find out if they can help. I try to keep the lovely image in my mind. But when I think of a V formation, what I see are planes over Baghdad, where I was last week, and I think of people there, no better or worse or more or less precious than anyone here, and I think of the carnage to come and what has become of the V formation.

———

Only one more congressional trek to Iraq occurred during Saddam's rule. I watched the TV coverage from home in early fall. Congressman Jim McDermott said during a live ABC interview from Baghdad, "I think the president would mislead the American people."

The comment set off angry denunciations from pundits and politicians who ripped into McDermott for impugning the integrity of George W. Bush while standing on "enemy" soil. After that uproar, the responses to invitations for travel to Iraq grew chillier on Capitol Hill, and even colder when the House and Senate voted in mid-October to approve a war resolution.

With all signs pointing toward an invasion, the odds seemed very long that any other member of Congress would jump into a media crossfire by visiting Iraq. At the Institute for Public Accuracy we widened the search to include other prominent Americans, such as celebrities in the arts, who might be willing to stick their necks out to help avert war.

––––––––––

In late November 2002, inspections resumed in Iraq for the first time in four years. "U.N. weapons inspectors say Iraq has been cooperative," Wolf Blitzer told CNN viewers on December 3, "but the Bush administration is by no means convinced. Many experts say what happens next depends on what happens this weekend. Sounding off now, from San Francisco, the syndicated columnist Norman Solomon, and here in Washington, Jonah Goldberg with National Review Online."

BLITZER: The Bush administration would seem to be in an awkward position, if the Iraqis continue to cooperate, as they have been, at least during this first week.

SOLOMON: It is an awkward position when the Bush administration really does not want to take yes for an answer. We had the president saying that the signs are not encouraging. I think actually what is really discouraging is the stance of Bush and Cheney and the rest of the team which has been throwing cold water on what appears to be a surprisingly smooth, and so far very successful, inspection operation.

Now, I was in Baghdad in September, and at some meetings with Tariq Aziz and other Iraqi officials. It was clear that they were hesitant at that point to allow unfettered access. They have gone that extra mile, the presidential palace being inspected this morning, unprecedented access. Really, the U.N. inspectors having run of the country with very sophisticated surveillance equipment.

So I think the real question is whether the president means what he says when he said today he wants peace and security. It seems more likely from all indications that the administration wants war that will create great insecurity for the region and beyond.

BLITZER: All right. Jonah Goldberg . . . what Norman Solomon just said was why can't the Bush administration take yes for an answer from the Iraqis? They're cooperating. Why not leave it at that?

GOLDBERG: Well, it seems to me that the only reason we've had the progress that we have had so far is precisely because the Bush administration has taken a hard line, has shown that it is very serious about being committed to actually using force if necessary, including sending troops and equipment to the region, working out these deals. So Mr. Solomon [is] exactly right that the Bush administration is firmly intending to go to war no matter what, but even if it weren't firmly intending to go to war no matter what, it would have to take this line because this line is the only thing that got inspectors back in there in the first place.

BLITZER: Norman Solomon, he makes a valid point. If the Bush administration weren't making these threats, do you believe the Iraqis would be cooperating as they are?

SOLOMON: Well, I think they certainly are under pressure. I think what is clear and the key point now is that they are cooperating. They have gotten to this point, and it's enormous U.N. pressure as well, because the U.S. felt compelled to at least go through the Security Council.

I think it's very important, whether government officials or pundits or others are addressing this "use of force" question, which is a phrase that kind of rolls off the tongue. What are we talking about here? The Medact organization, a medical group, worldwide global health monitoring organization based in Lon-

don, did a report last month saying that if a regime-change war
is undertaken by the United States, the casualties—the deaths
will range between 48,000 and 260,000. That's up to a quarter of
a million people or more killed during the war or its immediate
aftermath, and let me quote from the report. "The majority of
casualties will be civilians." I think that's worth repeating: The
majority of casualties will be civilians. Now, what kind of message is that from the Bush administration against terrorism and
against violence for political ends?

BLITZER: Jonah Goldberg, do you accept that assumption in
that report on these huge casualties, including a lot of children, if there were an effort to go forward with so-called
regime change in Baghdad?

GOLDBERG: Frankly, I don't. I mean, I haven't looked at the exact
report, and I think that there are a lot of groups out there that
inflate a lot of these numbers precisely because they're against
the war no matter what. We certainly heard a lot of that
around on the table last time. Before the Gulf War, we were
told there were going to be tens of thousands of casualties.
But it would also be silly to say that there wouldn't be casualties. Of course, there would be. The question is whether or not
you're willing to go through with this anyway. And to me, it
seems like a legitimate thing to do . . .

———

A few days into December—after fruitless months of inviting
high-profile Americans to visit Baghdad—I received a call from
Sean Penn's office. Moments later he was on the line: cordial,
straightforward, and very interested in making the trip as soon as
possible. I felt like I was getting a response to a note that I'd put in a
bottle and tossed in the ocean.

———

A moment of clarity came with fatigue and apprehension inside a
plane circling Baghdad at dawn. Light had begun to filter through
windows, just above puffy gray. While the jet descended into the

clouds, a little Iraqi girl was in the row just ahead; Sean and I could hear her melodious voice. "When I start to wonder why I'm making this trip," he said quietly, "I see that child and I remember what it's about."

––––––––

December 13, 2002:

We're visiting the cancer and leukemia ward of the Al-Mansour Children's Hospital. The kids are on austere little beds, their dark eyes haunted, and haunting. "You don't even want someone to slam a *door* too loud around these children," Sean says, "let alone imagine a bomb exploding in the neighborhood."

––––––––

The same muzak as in September was looping through the Al-Rashid Hotel's sprawling lobby, still with frequent rotation of an instrumental version of a Moody Blues song from the *Knights in White Satin* album. In my subjective head (jet-lagged and free-associating) it was a surreal audio track, a washed-out melody that I'd often heard on the verge of low-grade hallucinations during the summer when I turned eighteen, in 1969, around the time President Nixon—proclaiming that "we shall look to the nation directly threatened to assume the primary responsibility for its defense"—announced what came to be known as "Vietnamization." (A year later, I. F. Stone wrote that the doctrine "will be seen in Asia as a rich white man's idea of fighting a war: we handle the elite airpower while coolies do the killing on the ground." And he predicted, "Not enough Asians are going to fight Asians for us even if the price is right.")

Now, visiting Baghdad close to the end of 2002, I had no expectation of the steps toward "Iraqization" that would come years later, but I did expect that a U.S. invasion would be coming soon, within months. The Moody Blues melody kept returning at medium volume, flooding much of the ground floor, which included a couple of restaurants with solicitous waiters and shops selling Iraqi souvenir knickknacks, including Saddam Hussein watches with Mr. Big's face on the dial, while in the entry area, near the inlaid tiles at the threshold still spelling out "BUSH IS CRIMINAL" (though a reference to Bush the elder, also foreshadowing), Iraqi men wearing checkered headdresses sat on their haunches smoking a hookah, as if—so it seemed to me, anyway—waiting for something to happen yet in no particular hurry. To my eyes, the scene was a cross between *Arabian Nights* and the caterpillar episode of *Alice in Wonderland*, with international intrigue of *Grand Hotel* thrown in; but this was gruesomely real.

I looked at Iraqi people and wondered what would happen to them when the missiles arrived, what would befall the earnest young man managing the little online computer shop in the hotel next to the alcohol-free bar, who invited me to a worship service at the Presbyterian church that he devoutly attended; or the sweet-faced middle-aged fellow with a moustache very much like Saddam Hussein's (a ubiquitous police-state fashion statement) who stood near the elevator and put hand over heart whenever I passed; or the sweethearts chatting across candles at an outdoor restaurant as twilight settled on the banks of the Tigris.

December 15, 2002:

We sit at breakfast, pita bread and hummus on the table. Sean is writing a statement for the news conference, scrawling on a pad.

"I believe in the Constitution of the United States, and the American people," he tells a room full of journalists and cameras a few hours later. "Ours is a government designed to function 'of,' 'by,' and 'for' the people. I am one of those people, and a privileged one." Sean continues: "I am privileged in particular to raise my children in a country of high standards in health, welfare, and safety. I am also privileged to have lived a life under our Constitution that has allowed me to dream and prosper." And then he says:

> In response to these privileges I feel, both as an American and as a human being, the obligation to accept some level of personal accountability for the policies of my government, both those I support and any that I may not. Simply put, if there is a war or con-

tinued sanctions against Iraq, the blood of Americans and Iraqis alike will be on our hands.

My trip here is to personally record the human face of the Iraqi people so that their blood—along with that of American soldiers—would not be invisible on my own hands. I sit with you here today in the hopes that any of us present may contribute in any way to a peaceful resolution to the conflict at hand.

―――――――――

December 16, 2002:

Before dawn we land in Amman, and Sean dashes to catch a plane so he can get to Tennessee to start work on *21 Grams*. By now the denunciations are well underway back home—led by Rupert Murdoch's *New York Post* and Fox News Channel, with other media outlets joining in.

I'm staying overnight in Amman. At the hotel a call comes in, inviting me to tape an MSNBC show via satellite. I end up in a makeshift studio, doing the interview with a program host who doubles as the news channel's editor-in-chief. Later I see the transcript of what MSNBC viewers heard:

JERRY NACHMAN, HOST: First question. From everything I have heard and read, Sean Penn has tried to be very measured in his public statements and his behavior in Iraq. Can you confirm that?

NORMAN SOLOMON: Well, that's what I saw throughout our visit in Baghdad. He was very conscious of the need to be sensitive to the feelings of Americans and, for that matter, people everywhere. He wasn't trying to go in and be a hotshot. As he said, point blank, "I'm here to learn, not to teach." And I think he fulfilled that mission.

NACHMAN: The *New York Times* today said that the situation with Jane Fonda a generation ago in North Vietnam was very much on his mind. Can you talk about that?

SOLOMON: Mr. Penn showed a lot more maturity and I think complexity of thought than what Ms. Fonda displayed back during the Vietnam War, when she went to North Vietnam.

SEAN PENN (videotape): There is no question in my mind that this conflict can be resolved peacefully. I think it's going to take an enormous amount of work from both—the entire global community, but from both the United States and from Iraq.

NACHMAN: He went so far as to say, again, according to the *New York Times*, that "I don't imagine I will be apologizing as she did at some far point in the future."

SOLOMON: Yeah, I think that's a key point, because he wasn't zigzagging, he wasn't trying to showboat. He was showing a lot of attention to nuance, frankly, that often goes by politicians and, with due respect, personnel at major networks.

NACHMAN: Was he given any sort of star treatment? People at his level live in very rarefied [unintelligible]. They travel with entourages, they get suites, they get whatever they want in the M&M bowl. Was he there more or less as just a guy?

SOLOMON: Well, you know he was on a ten-hour flight with me from San Francisco to Amsterdam on the way over to Baghdad, and we flew coach. He was in a hotel in Baghdad that was the same room journalists and myself were in, hardly very plush. And in contrast to people in the United States, people in Iraq, for the most part, did not recognize him, but some people did. So no, he wasn't pampered at all.

NACHMAN: He described our position—or the government's position as—and I'm quoting now, "a simplistic and inflammatory view of good and evil." What is simplistic about portraying Saddam Hussein and his regime as evil? Is there anything subtle or nuanced there?

SOLOMON: Well, actually you have conflated two things. I mean, he was talking about the entirety of U.S. foreign policy. In his ad that he took out in the *Washington Post*, an open letter to President Bush in October of this year, Sean Penn explicitly referred to Saddam Hussein as a tyrant, and he is clearly on the record. And anybody with half a brain knows that Saddam Hussein is a vicious tyrant.

The fact is that U.S. policy has continued to support many tyrants around the world who torture their citizens. The human rights situation in Egypt, for instance, has deteriorated in the last year, many people being tortured. A country that gets billions of dollars in aid from the United States, for instance. So if we are going to get on our high horse, we may as well look at the downside of U.S. foreign policy in terms of human rights.

NACHMAN: Norman, I want to go back to my original question. And maybe you can flesh it out. Spending that much time on an airplane and a couple of days in hotel rooms, how sensitive was Sean Penn to being mischaracterized or having his patriotism questioned? Again, the Jane Fonda issue. What did he say?

SOLOMON: Oh, he knew it. He knew what he was walking into. He knew that the Fox news channels of the world were going to be bashing him from day one as soon as he set foot in Baghdad. And it was a risk that he understood was inherent in the situation. But he was far more concerned about the prospect of living in a country that was responsible for a lot of deaths in Iraq that could be avoided.

And we went, I have to tell you, to a number of schools, escorted by UNICEF officials. We met with the director of UNICEF in Baghdad, and we saw hundreds and hundreds of children and interacted with them. And you know it's one thing to say, well that's the price you've got to pay for war. I wish more Americans would go and look into the faces of young children and then talk about whether they want to launch a war on those kids.

NACHMAN: I think both you and Sean would probably have more credibility if we heard a word or two about the atrocities attributed to Saddam against his own people, including children, including gassing and chemical weapons.

SOLOMON: Jerry, are you having a little earwax in your ears? I mean, I just quoted from Sean Penn's open letter to President Bush published in October of this year in the *Washington Post*, where he explicitly referred to Saddam Hussein as a vicious tyrant. So, you know, maybe that was on your list of questions and you forgot to scratch it off.

NACHMAN: Well, no, but it was a kiss-off, I think, without getting contentious. It's one thing to talk about it, but it's another thing not to give something like equal weight to both sides. It's exactly what you accuse the media . . .

SOLOMON: Well, that's your projection and your formulation of equal whatever to both sides. I don't know where that came from.

NACHMAN: Norman, if we put this conversation on a scale and measured the words you've used critical of U.S. policy versus Saddam policy, there would be a real disequilibrium. I'm trying to hear something representing balance.

SOLOMON: Jerry, you know, I think your question is a bit of a cop-out. I'm a citizen of the United States of America. It's my tax dollars that I pay that are going to result in the actions that are taken by the Pentagon.

I am supposed to be living in a democracy. When I speak up or you speak up or Sean Penn speaks up, we're exercising our First Amendment rights . . .

NACHMAN: Norm, I'm the wrong guy to give a lecture on the First Amendment. I know it very well. I'm not saying you don't have a right to say what you want to say. I'm saying that the credibility gets affected by the skew in terms of the length and types of comments critical of U.S. policy versus kind of the bromides about what Saddam has done to his own people, which is virtually unprecedented in the modern world.

SOLOMON: Well, let me ask you a question in response to that. Do you think that I as an American citizen could have more effect on the policies of my own government, the U.S. government, or the policies of Saddam Hussein? I think that question answers itself.

NACHMAN: Well, I don't have a problem answering your question. And my answer would be, I think you would have stronger credentials as a critic if your comments seemed somewhat more balanced and disinterested, as the lawyers say.

SOLOMON: Well, you know, here's a situation where it's supposed to be our government of the United States of America.
   And if every time an American makes a criticism of the president or the Congress, you're going to say, well, gee, you have
   to spend an equal amount of time denouncing North Korea
   or Libya or Saddam Hussein or whatever, I mean, it might
   clog up discourse a bit. We're supposed to have some effect
   over the policies of our own government and we need to engage in democratic discourse to that end.

NACHMAN: All right. Norm, I got to go because the satellite bill
   is getting prohibitive. Thank you very much for being with
   us. And thank you for answering all my questions in a forth-
   coming manner.

SOLOMON: Thank you, Jerry.

NACHMAN: Well, interviewing is becoming an intellectual taffy
   pull today, but that's the nature of the business.

———————

Two days later, I was back in San Francisco, and the U.S. media
firestorm was looking fierce. When I went on MSNBC's *The
Abrams Report*, the host (destined to become the network's general
manager) started off the show by announcing, "After his contro-
versial visit to Baghdad, actor Sean Penn has become a weapon in
Iraq's propaganda war"—while the White House was "set to de-
clare Saddam Hussein guilty, saying his latest declaration is filled
with lies and omissions about weapons of mass destruction."

   Dan Abrams introduced me after telling viewers that Sean Penn
had aligned himself with the Iraqi government: "Just showing up in
Iraq implies, I think, that he is on their side," Abrams said. "And by
focusing on the U.S. role in this conflict, Penn seems to be forgetting that it is the U.N. that is confronting Saddam." The first question was: "Can anyone be surprised, Sean Penn, you, that Iraq is
now twisting Sean Penn's words to make it seem like he is basically
supporting Iraq's position?"

   "Well, Dan," I responded, "from the jump-start, you just said
that Sean Penn going to Iraq implies his support for the Iraqi posi-

tion. I'm actually quite surprised at someone with your level of expertise saying something so ludicrous. Our institute and I myself accompanied Congressman Nick Rahall, a twenty-six-year veteran in the United States Congress, to Iraq in September, much of the same itinerary as Sean Penn's. Are you also saying that his visit to Baghdad implied his support for Saddam Hussein?"

"It is a different time," Abrams replied. I tried to cut in, but he continued: "You asked me a question. Let me answer it. You said, do I think it's the same? And the answer is no. It is a different time now. There is no question, I think, that, at this point, even months later, as the rhetoric is heating up, as the U.N. demands, as the U.N. timeline is now moving forward, it is very different for someone to go to Iraq now than even four months ago."

"Well, September or November or December, it is still the same basic situation of an American going there. I would point out to you and the viewers that, in October of this year, Sean Penn took out a full-page ad in the *Washington Post*, an open letter to President Bush. Let me read you one sentence from that letter: 'There can be no acceptance of the criminal viciousness of the tyrant Saddam Hussein'—unquote. I think that makes his position rather clear about the Iraqi government."

"But, see, the problem is, you can read me a line from a letter, but the bottom line is, Sean Penn being there means something," the MSNBC host retorted. "It has an impact. And the bottom line is, now he is being used as a tool in the propaganda war."

———

That winter, movers and shakers in Washington shuffled along to the beat of a media drum that kept reporting on Iraqi weapons of mass destruction as a virtual certainty. At the same time, millions of Americans tried to prevent an invasion; their activism ranged from letters and petitions to picket lines, civil disobedience, marches, and mass rallies. On January 18, 2003, as the *Washington Post* recalled years later, "an antiwar protest described as the largest since the Vietnam War drew several hundred thousand . . . on the eve of the

Iraq war, in subfreezing Washington weather. The high temperature reported that day was in the mid-20s."

The outcry was global, and the numbers grew larger. On February 15 an estimated 10 million people demonstrated against the impending war. A dispatch from Knight-Ridder news service summed up the events of that day: "By the millions, peace marchers in cities around the world united Saturday behind a single demand: No war with Iraq." But the war planners running the U.S. government were determined.

———

March 9, 2003:

This time I'm debating someone from the Foundation for the Defense of Democracies, a group headed by a former official of the Republican National Committee. The CNN anchor on duty, Anderson Cooper, introduces the segment: "A war of words has erupted over documents the U.S. used to help make its case against Iraq. It concerned some papers Secretary of State Colin Powell showed to the U.N. Security Council when he laid out evidence against Baghdad last month. Well, Friday, chief nuclear inspector Mohamed ElBaradei said he thinks some of those documents were fake, and today he explained why."

The brouhaha is "much ado about nothing," says the Foundation's spokesman, David Silverstein. He adds: "The fact remains that no matter what kind of bad intelligence might have been fed to the United Nations from U.S. or British or other sources, there is no erasing the fact that Saddam has violated U.N. resolutions for twelve years, that he's used poison gas on his own people, that he continues to murder them at will. There is no getting around that. There is no getting around the fact that he's a threat both to U.S. interests in the region and to our allies there. And so whether or not this turns out to be a forgery is almost immaterial. The time has come for Saddam to be removed."

When my turn comes, I say: "It's clear that it is a forgery and it's very important. The reason that the *New York Times* today editorialized that the statements on Friday at the U.N. Security Council were devastating from Blix and ElBaradei is that this is part of a pattern. Forged documents claiming that the Iraqis were seeking uranium to enrich for their weapons program turn out to be absolute falsehoods. The much-ballyhooed claim for aluminum tubes for a nuclear program, again, falsehood. A poison factory we heard so much about from Secretary Powell again doesn't hold up when reporters go there."

The discussion plunges downhill soon after Cooper says: "Norman seems to be indicating that he at least believes the U.S. administration knew that these documents perhaps were not accurate. Do you think that is at all a possibility?"

"Well," Silverstein replies, "I'm sure Norman subscribes to the notion that there is this vast right-wing conspiracy out there that controls the minds of people and that we should all be walking around with tin foil on our heads to prevent it. . . ."

Silverstein is one of those TV debaters who has mastered the strategy of constant interruption. For the rest of the segment, it's a battle to complete even a single thought.

SOLOMON: We have a slow motion Gulf of Tonkin incident here where document after document has been proven to be forgery.

SILVERSTEIN: Is that the best you can do, Norman? Come on.

SOLOMON: Gulf of Tonkin incident here—

(crosstalk)

SOLOMON: If you'll stop interrupting me, sir.

SILVERSTEIN: —you can do better.

SOLOMON: This war is telegraphed ahead of time to be based on lies, and we know it now. We have to stop this war—

SILVERSTEIN: He murdered Iraqis, he murdered millions of Iraqis.

11

WAR TO THE HORIZON

After the 2003 invasion of Iraq, I met author Anthony Swofford, whose book *Jarhead* is a vivid account of his participation in the 1991 Gulf War as a young Marine sniper. We talked for several hours. Along the way, he mentioned the common use of pornography in the psych-up process that revs young men just before military action. More generally, he had come to believe that scenes of battle and bloodshed in popular movies—even ones like *Platoon* with a reputedly antiwar tone—actually jack up the lure of war. Media products with sex and violence are not only compatible with warfare; they promote it.

What about the term "warnography," I asked. Without hesitating, Swofford said that it was a reality. Venturing farther, and with a little trepidation—after all, he'd fought in war and I hadn't—I asked what he thought of a word I'd just seen recently for the first time: "wargasm." Was it valid and useful for our understanding? His answer: Absolutely.

When a small Woodstock reunion convened for a few days in August 2004 near the original site, on the bill for the thirty-fifth anniversary were four original members of Country Joe and the Fish. Their current repertoire included "Cakewalk to Baghdad," a caustic song based on prewar boasts (from such experts as Richard

155

Perle and Ken Adelman) that the U.S. military's quest for victory in Iraq would be a "cakewalk."

> Now moms and dads don't worry 'bout
> Your soldier boys and girls
> We're just sending them cakewalkin'
> Around the world
> When the coffins come home and the flag unfurls
> Cheer for Bush, Cheney, Rumsfeld, Wolfowitz and Perle.

And still, somehow in the air was the song that Joni Mitchell wrote long ago about Woodstock, the one that tells of a dream about bombers in the sky turning into butterflies above our nation.

On August 30, 2005—the day that levees broke in New Orleans—the president spoke to troops alongside a nuclear-powered aircraft carrier at a naval air station in Southern California. He warned that unless the U.S. military prevented terrorist leaders from grabbing control of Iraq, they would "seize oil fields to fund their ambitions." As floodwaters rose over 80 percent of New Orleans, the outrageous failures of the federal response to Hurricane Katrina became painfully apparent. Most of the victims were black and poor. Less obvious was the fact that the priorities of the warfare state contributed to the horrors engulfing people in New Orleans and elsewhere along the coast.

The Iraq war had made people in the hurricane path more vulnerable. "At least nine articles in the [New Orleans] *Times-Picayune* from 2004 and 2005 specifically cite the cost of Iraq as a reason for the lack of hurricane- and flood-control dollars," *Editor & Publisher* magazine noted. When Katrina struck, more than a third of Mississippi's and Louisiana's National Guard troops were deployed for the war effort in Iraq. Some vital equipment was also tied up. Humvees and high-water vehicles, previously in Louisiana, had gone to Baghdad along with National Guard units.

"With thousands of their citizen-soldiers away fighting in Iraq, states hit hard by Hurricane Katrina scrambled to muster forces for rescue and security missions yesterday—calling up army bands and water-purification teams, among other units, and requesting help from distant states and the active-duty military," the *Washington Post* reported on August 31. The newspaper added that the Mississippi National Guard "has a brigade of more than 4,000 troops in central Iraq" while "Louisiana also has about 3,000 Guard troops in Baghdad." A spokesman for the Mississippi National Guard said: "Missing the personnel is the big thing in this particular event. We need our people."

"They can go into Iraq and do this and do that," Martha Madden, former secretary of the Louisiana Department of Environmental Quality, said two days after Bush's war-boosting speech, "but they can't drop some food on Canal Street in New Orleans, Louisiana, right now? It's just mind-boggling."

When the long-running PBS panel show *Washington Week* announced Boeing as a new underwriter in 2006, it caused no stir. Boeing's decision to plunk down money for the influential program was understandable; sales of the firm's military aircraft and weaponry have always depended on favorable action in political Washington—exactly the landscape covered each week by the half-hour telecast. That none of the journalists around the table would go negative against the "military-industrial complex" was a safe bet, made perhaps a little safer by the influx of cash from Boeing. For good measure, *Washington Week* soon added Chevron as another underwriter. It would have been hard to find two companies with more at stake in the nation's capital.

Journalists, including producers, are no more brave than people in other professions. Few bite the hand that signs the paycheck. And the usual assumption in the news media is that objectivity includes acceptance of American militarism, while rejection of it would indicate bias.

With yearly revenues above $50 billion, Boeing could afford to throw plenty of money around with the aim of enhancing its image. War had been very, very good to Boeing. When the firm became a *Washington Week* sponsor, its latest annual report was emphasizing the company identity as the world's largest manufacturer of military aircraft, with products such as "electronic and defense systems, missiles, satellites, launch vehicles, and advanced information and communication systems." The corporation trumpeted its capacities for "integrating military platforms, defense systems, and the war-fighter through network-centric operations."

From Boeing headquarters, press liaison Dan Beck told me that support for the show "is a way to reach out to informed and interested audiences and extend the brand of this global aerospace company." Others becoming associated with the prestigious broadcast were more effusive. A few weeks into 2006, when *Washington Week* entered into a partnership with *National Journal*, the print outlet's publisher John Fox Sullivan quickly hailed the match-up as a "natural editorial fit." Both the magazine and the television program, he said, were "for people who have brains and actually exercise their brains and people who have power and influence and exercise their power and influence." Combined, Boeing and Chevron were reportedly supplying more than a million dollars to *Washington Week* for the year—a bargain to link up with a demographically upper-crust TV program reaching close to 1.8 million viewers each week, including those "who have power and influence and exercise their power and influence."

Meanwhile, public television's nightly flagship program, the *NewsHour with Jim Lehrer*—seen on more than three hundred PBS stations—was a supposed exemplar of journalistic independence. In 2007 the show's list of major funders included agribusiness giant Archer Daniels Midland, the insurance firm Pacific Life, AT&T, and Chevron.

The Baghdad bureau chief of the *New York Times* could not have been any clearer. "The story really takes us back into the eighth

century, a truly barbaric world," John Burns said, speaking on the
NewsHour with Jim Lehrer. The date was June 20, 2006, and the
bodies of two U.S. soldiers had just been found in Iraq. They were
victims of atrocities, and the words of horror used by Burns to describe the "barbaric murders" were totally appropriate. Yet there
was a big, ongoing problem: Burns and his media colleagues would
not talk that way when the cruelties were inflicted by the U.S.
military.

Such prominent journalists maintain a double standard in their
language—allowing themselves moral outrage when Americans
suffer but not when victims of the U.S. military suffer. The result is
more flackery than journalism. Reporters for the *New York Times*
and other large U.S. media outlets would not dream of publicly describing what American firepower did to Iraqis as "barbaric."

An eyewitness account from American author Rahul Mahajan,
during the U.S. attack on Fallujah in April 2004, said: "During the
course of roughly four hours at a small clinic in Fallujah, I saw
perhaps a dozen wounded brought in. Among them was a young
woman, eighteen years old, shot in the head. She was having a
seizure and foaming at the mouth when they brought her in; doc-
tors did not expect her to survive the night. Another likely terminal
case was a young boy with massive internal bleeding." Hundreds of
civilians died in that assault on Fallujah, and many more lost their
lives when U.S. troops attacked the city again seven months later.

The American air war escalated in Iraq, often putting urban
neighborhoods in the crosshairs. Just days before Burns denounced
the jihadists as "barbaric," the independent U.S. journalist Dahr
Jamail had written: "A hospital source in Fallujah reported that
eight Iraqis, some of whom were women and children from the
same family, were killed and six wounded when U.S. warplanes
bombed a home in the northeastern Ibrahim Bin Ali district of the
city." These sorts of deaths were routine.

We heard, of course, that the U.S. government tried to avoid
killing civilians—as if that made killing them less consequential.
But the slaughter from the air and from other U.S. military actions

was a certain result of the occupiers' war (which had been based on deception from the outset). What would we say if, in our own community, the police force killed shoppers every day by spraying blocks of stores with machine-gun fire—while explaining that the action was justifiable because no innocents were targeted and their accidental deaths were an unfortunate necessity in the war on crime?

———————

While an air war kept escalating in Iraq, the U.S. media assumed that almost any use of American air power was to the good. (Exceptions came with fleeting news of mishaps like dropping bombs on wedding parties.) What actually happened to human beings every day as explosives hit the ground would not be conveyed to the reputedly well-informed. What we didn't know presumably wouldn't hurt us or our self-image. Thomas Merton's observation still held: We did think ourselves better—incomparably better—because we burned people with modern technology from high in the air. Car bombs and detonation belts were for the uncivilized.

I wanted to see the air war up close, though not close enough to be on the ground under bombs; so I contacted the U.S. Air Force press office in New York City, which often arranged journalists' trips to Iraq. A few months later, in the spring of 2006, Captain Matthew Bates emailed me an invitation to cover "how patients are transferred from the battlefield quickly" to medical centers at bases in the vicinity of Baghdad and Mosul. On the phone Captain Bates indicated he knew that I was against the war, but he commented pointedly that the Pentagon's media offices were taxpayer-funded and weren't just in business to serve the likes of Fox News.

I was wearing my hat as a columnist for Creators Syndicate, a mainstream outfit that had been distributing my weekly column on media and politics for many years. Credentials for the trip seemed to be no problem. Soon I was in frequent communication with the press office at Lackland Air Force Base in San Antonio, where the trip would originate. A sergeant there sent me guidelines and a checklist of required items, including body armor and a Kevlar helmet. I submitted a formal application. "From our end it is a go," she emailed back on June 14. "The rest I can't guarantee as it is up to the diplomatic processes for the clearance request."

Describing the pilots I would meet at air bases in Iraq, the sergeant explained: "They can tell you general information about how they are prepared for flights into possible hostile territory but no specifics. They can tell you about the emotions [that] go through their minds as they prepare. They can tell you general information about how they avoid collateral damage and casualty to area populations but not specifics."

The original departure date out of San Antonio got rescheduled. Then the new date was also scrubbed. More weeks went by, and finally in late summer I got a call from Captain Bates' supervisor, Major John Thomas. He had contacted air force officers at bases in Iraq about my trip, he told me, and they read some of my columns on the web that were negative about the use of air power—so they didn't want to put any time into helping me visit. The major sounded a bit embarrassed at the turn of events. Like his colleagues, in previous conversations he had exuded a tone of evenhanded professionalism; shutting me out of the trip due to the content of my columns didn't square with the concept.

As our discussion went on, Major Thomas suggested various angles that I could pursue without going to Iraq. He told me that cutting-edge technology was now making it possible for much of the air war to be operated in real time from the United States, and he gave an example: An air force officer could go to work in Nevada, spend the day directly guiding planes as they dropped bombs in Iraq, and get home in time to tuck his kids into bed.

Major Thomas let me know how to sign up for an air force listserv that included an "airpower summary" from U.S. Central Command. And so, a daily compendium of official news releases and reports began to arrive in my email box. As months went by, I did not want to open them, and when I did they were enough to make me wish I hadn't.

One of the methodical quirks of the air force news releases about

Iraq was that they consistently referred to insurgents as "anti-Iraqi forces"—even though almost all of those fighters were Iraqis. So, in a release about activities on Christmas Day 2006, the air force reported that "Marine Corps F/A-18Ds conducted a strike against anti-Iraqi forces near Haqlaniyah." Meanwhile:

> Air Force F-16 Fighting Falcons and F-15E Strike Eagles provided close-air support to troops in contact with anti-Iraqi forces near Baghdad.
>
> In total, coalition aircraft flew 28 close-air support missions for Operation Iraqi Freedom. These missions included support to coalition troops, infrastructure protection, reconstruction activities and operations to deter and disrupt terrorist activities.

The next day, it was the same story, as it would be for a long time to come—with U.S. Air Force jets bombing "anti-Iraqi forces" on behalf of missions for "Operation Iraqi Freedom" in order to "deter and disrupt terrorist activities."

———

I live in a semirural area of Northern California where George W. Bush got very few votes. Antiwar sentiment is strong, though usually implicit rather than outspoken; from the start the Iraq war was widely abhorred.

This cluster of towns is interspersed with ranches, dairies, and farms, quite a few of them organic. Sales outlets feature high-quality organics—fruit, vegetables, milk products including exotic cheeses, olive oil, and much more—catering to tourists and locals alike. A countywide organics trade association has gained clout as it markets and promotes an array of wonderful food.

There seems to be no conflict, only complementary affirmation of life's goodness, between the shared enthusiasm for organic foods and the predominant antiwar outlook. But sometimes I wonder.

In the autumn of 2005 the news broke that Prince Charles and the duchess Camilla would be coming to town, ceremonially shopping at the weekly farmers market.

Before arriving in California, the prince went to a formal White House dinner, where he offered a toast to "the commitment, courage, and comradeship of our two great nations." He didn't mention the Iraq invasion or the ongoing war effort led by those two nations.

I wrote a brief leaflet and distributed it around town:

> Prince Charles seems like a nice person. Unfortunately, he's here representing a British government that joined with the U.S. government to launch a war based on deception. While the war continues in Iraq, top officials in London and Washington keep trying to justify their indefensible actions. They are squandering billions of pounds and billions of dollars for killing instead of meeting human needs. This is what Martin Luther King called "the madness of militarism."

Like many other people, I was in the habit of shopping for fruit and vegetables at the farmers market on Saturday morning. This time it was more crowded than ever. I bought some beautiful chard, glistening green-and-red in the early November sunshine. The hubbub of the scene felt familiar yet strangely not. This was a big opportunity to promote the local organic food industry, and a lot of people wanted to make the most of it. Compared to that, the war in Iraq—then in its thirty-second month—seemed to be widely viewed as irrelevant, an abstraction, on the very day that our community might have been able to make a more clear and far-reaching statement against the war than it ever could before or since.

I'd printed up ten-by-ten-inch green signs that said "War Is Not Organic," and I offered them to farmers and merchants setting out their wares early, but I just seemed to be provoking indifference or annoyance. Few of the shoppers were any more interested. The imminence of a genuine royal visit had just about the entire town in a protracted swoon.

After I stood for a few minutes holding my sign, next to the stall where I bought the chard, a woman I'd never seen before approached and told me it was time to go across the street, where metal barricades had been erected for the occasion. I said that I preferred to stay where I was. She called over a man who also told me it was time to go. Both became more insistent. The man informed me that they were from the U.S. State Department and that the concern was security. I offered to be searched to eliminate any security concern, but the State Department representatives insisted that I'd have to leave.

Minutes later, the prince and the duchess arrived. But I missed them. I'd been dragged out of the farmers market.

The *Times* of London ended its article on the royal visit this way:

> The couple left town as organic heroes to visit a farm and nibble organic canapés over discussions about sustainable agriculture. But there are imperfections in Paradise, even when it's in California.
>
> Norman Solomon had been staging a perfectly peaceful protest against the Iraq war when he was bundled away by overzealous security men and held in the back of a police car until the royal couple had left.
>
> His offense had been to stand in the crowd holding up a banner reading: "War is not organic."

Little did I know. The next year, a county-based firm named Green Beans Coffee Co. nearly doubled its revenue, to $15 million, on the strength of serving organic coffee—mochas, cappuccinos, espresso chai lattes, and other gourmet drinks—to soldiers at U.S. military bases in Iraq, Afghanistan, and elsewhere. And the war market for organic coffee kept exploding. In early 2007, the biggest growth area was Iraq, where new Green Beans Coffee outlets were set to open soon on American bases at nine locations including Ramadi, Mosul, and Fallujah.

An edition of the *New York Times Style Magazine*—more than a hundred pages of ads and articles dedicated to tastefully conspicuous and pricey consumption—included an essay with an incisive passage about haute organic cuisine of the sort heavily concentrated in the San Francisco area and diffused to broad American enclaves. "I worry that we have begun to reflexively equate an aesthetically beautiful lifestyle with a morally good life," wrote chef Daniel Patterson, "and that the way we cook and eat has become bound up in that mix." Recalling a two-hundred-dollar dinner for two at the legendary Chez Panisse restaurant in Berkeley, he asked: "How can we build an egalitarian society based on a lifestyle that so few can afford?" In short, "something has gone awry."

Awry or not, a synergy had kicked in for the personal politics of environmental protection and self-absorption. Elevating organic food to the stature of a "movement" was always dubious, all the more so after the 2006 announcement from Wal-Mart that its Always megastores (as in "Always low prices") would jump into the battle for organics market share. To be sure, healthy-food boosters sometimes complained, on solid grounds, that the corporate version of organic food inside supermarket chain stores was expanding in tandem with degraded standards for regulatory certification. And some critics pointed out that the relatively high prices of organics— and of nonorganic fruits and vegetables, for that matter, in comparison to most packaged goods along the aisles—were largely due to the federal government's enormous subsidies for corn that amounted to underwriting of high fructose corn syrup, the base ingredient of countless junky-food products. But the fact remained that organic food—healthier and tastier while also better for an Earth already choking on chemical fertilizers and pesticides—was, for many people, becoming a kind of substitute for political action, a way of justifying what might otherwise seem like inordinately self-centered fixations. I can elevate my preoccupation with what I put in my mouth, and in the mouths of my family and friends, to the status of global principle.

A special issue of *Time* magazine in the summer of 2006 was explicitly devoted to the process of turning "sustainability" into a fashion statement—and a declaration of values. By then, "Nirvana" was the word standing out in big type on the bottles of spring water being sold at Ben & Jerry's stands across the United States. For years, the global Ben & Jerry's brand had no longer been under the control of the two countercultural icons from Vermont; in 2000 they sold the whole Ben & Jerry's Homemade company, known for such flavorful product imaging as Cherry Garcia and Peace Pops, to the Unilever conglomerate. In the admixture of MBA and Grateful Dead ambiences, the big corporate wheeler-dealers had proved more adept at truckin' for the long haul.

In spring 2006 the owners of two other well-known companies went with huge firms after decades of publicly emphasizing commitments to "social responsibility." Anita Roddick sold her worldwide Body Shop chain to the French cosmetics firm L'Oreal, a move that drew sharp criticism from consumer activists who pointed out that 28 percent of L'Oreal was owned by Nestle—long notorious for aggressively marketing baby formula in Third World countries to the serious detriment of public health. And Tom's of Maine, with toothpaste and other products signed "your friends Kate and Tom," was suddenly no longer an independent company after its sale to Colgate-Palmolive.

In these and other instances, the years of initial marketing had relied on counterculture images while steadily integrating into corporate culture. Pursuit of the bottom line often advanced by implying that the bottom line was of scant concern. The alchemy of the marketplace could turn the hip alternative into a parody of itself.

Meanings could easily be inverted. So, during the World Series in October 2001, halfway through the seventh inning, the national TV audience saw a Wranglers jeans commercial that started with the American flag on the screen and the familiar opening chords of Credence Clearwater Revival's old song "Fortunate Son." Moments later, the lyrics began: "Some folks are born, made to wave the flag/ Ooh, they're red white and blue." Then—suddenly—the soundtrack of the song dropped out of the commercial, as if the next lines didn't exist: "And when the band plays Hail to the Chief/They point the cannon right at you." The splice turned the song's meaning upside down, so that "Fortunate Son" could fit in with the "USA Number One" military fervor that was sweeping America.

Slicing up a song is one way to destroy its meaning. Another is to trivialize. In 2006, I heard the opening notes of "All You Need Is Love" on a cable news channel; moments later I realized that I was watching a commercial for Chase credit cards. The Beatles song continued. "Love is all you need."

This wasn't new. Way back in 1974, the hit song "Anticipation" by Carly Simon began its lengthy run as a jingle for Heinz ketchup. In 1987 a sportswear company relying on sweatshop labor used the Beatles song "Revolution" in commercials for Nike running shoes. Another megafirm known for exploiting workers in poor countries, The Gap, has featured Donovan's dreamy "Mellow Yellow." (While introducing one of his best songs, "Catch the Wind," at a 2005 concert in San Francisco, Donovan referred to the fact that it had been heard of late on Volvo commercials. "Safe song, safe car," he quipped, a bit sheepishly I thought.) The Who's combative anthem to perpetual skepticism, "Won't Get Fooled Again," served ads for the Nissan Maxima. The Band's most haunting song, "The Weight," became part of a Cingular Wireless ad campaign. The Beatles kept singing "Come Together"—on Nortel commercials.

On a coast-to-coast flight, the two people sitting next to me seemed delighted to discover that they were both in the same specialized field of the computer industry. One, a middle-aged woman, owned her own company. The other, about the same age, was a guy with very long hair who worked for a software firm. After a few hours of their rapid-fire conversation, I asked whether there were any government contracts their companies would decline. The man suddenly went silent. The woman's answers were roundabout, on one hand and the other hand, but as near as I could tell it was unlikely that her outfit would turn down a war-related contract. Before we landed, they both made clear that they were antiwar; the woman reminded me that, after all, she was Canadian.

For both, the big hero was Bill Gates. They admired his recent outsize philanthropy for humanitarian causes. The fact that just a few weeks of Pentagon spending added up to the equivalent of Gates' total accumulated wealth, including all the money he kept or gave away, seemed to hold very little interest. When Warren Buffett announced in June 2006 that he would donate $31 billion—the bulk of his entire fortune—to the Bill & Melinda Gates Foundation, it was an enormous boost to the foundation's work for education and against fatal diseases in poor countries. Buffett's gift doubled the assets of the foundation. But even then, the new total of $60 billion in assets for the Bill & Melinda Gates Foundation—far and away the largest in the United States—amounted to about five weeks of the Pentagon's real budget. And of course the Defense Department coffers are fully replenished each year, in sharp contrast to the standard foundation process that disburses just a fraction of total assets. Compared to the taxpayer funds lavished on the U.S. military, the Gates Foundation and the American philanthropies that it dwarfed would not be providing much money for humanitarian causes.

The guy with long hair said that he had friends in the computer industry who'd realized that they could follow suit and do the most good by becoming as wealthy as possible. This, on the entire flight from San Francisco to Dulles Airport, was what depressed me most—the reverence for capital accumulation, combined with a lack of interest in public space or governmental remedies; the privatization and diminished scope of social imagination.

June 2006:

Near the border of Berkeley and Oakland, on Ashby Avenue sloping down toward the bay, there's a multicolored mural on a wall. I'm on the sidewalk, giving the mural just a mental nod—but in moments it calls me back from the next block. At first glance the painted picture is just agitprop; but as I stand under the sun looking, there are qualities that rivet me to the spot where it depicts a small group of people walking and holding signs. The biggest is a banner that says "We Can Bomb the World to Pieces, But We Can't Bomb it into Peace.—Michael Franti." And several signs, including: "Guernica 1937–Iraq 2003." "One World One Love." "Stop the War Against Iraq." "I'm Shocked But Not Awed."

Cars are roaring by, it's a hot afternoon, and I'm staring at the mural. On the right, at the corner, a face has big dark eyes and under them are tears. On the left, a baby has been tossed and is tumbling through the air, head ominously below feet.

I glance at the sign marking a cross street—Otis St., and I think of "Dock of the Bay." Forty years after Otis Redding recorded it, the song is in the present, not the slightest sound of relic. Only a few minutes ago, near the BART subway station, an African-American man with a cane, who looked a few years younger than me, approached, asking for help; could I give him five dollars. I offered him the drink in my bag, a smoothie from a Whole Foods Store, but he needed a place to stay, he said, he'd been recently released from somewhere or other (I couldn't catch the details). He was clearly in desperate straits, at the dock of the bay and worse. "I have sciatica," he said, in a vaguely menacing tone, "you know what sciatica is?" As it happened, I'd been dealing with sciatica recently, from a back injury. And I thought to myself: *Yeah, I know what sciatica is. It means I get to go to an excellent physical therapist and get better, and you're out on the streets in pain, begging for five dollars.*

Michael Berg picked me up at the Wilmington airport. His son Nicholas had been beheaded in Iraq a year earlier. We went to Michael's house, where I met his wife. A photo of their boy was on the living-room wall. The pain in the household air was thick. I sat at their little dinner table; we made small talk over meatloaf and salad until it was time to go to a public meeting at the church down the street. The parents had responded to the catastrophe in very different ways: the mother moving inward, wanting the world to go away and leave her diminished family alone, the father reviving a former incarnation as a peace activist. When the media camped out on their lawn during those first traumatic days, Michael told me, after a while he couldn't stay quiet. That's when he went in front of the microphones and blamed the president and secretary of defense for his son's death.

At the church, I stood next to a twenty-five-year-old veteran, Mike Hoffman. He was with a Marine unit that fought its way into Tikrit and Baghdad two years earlier. Back home, he cofounded Iraq Veterans Against the War. One of the young men who joined the organization, Robert Acosta, had reentered civilian life in early 2004, six months after losing his right hand when a grenade landed next to him in a vehicle on a Baghdad street. Acosta was twenty-one when I interviewed him near the end of 2004. He told me: "I was there and I'm proud of my service. But I really questioned the war once I was in the hospital. . . . I feel like we—the guys who went in to do the job—were lied to. . . . A lot of people don't really see how the war can mess people up until they know someone with first-hand experience. I think people coming back wounded—or even just mentally injured after seeing what no human being should have to see—is going to open a lot of eyes."

January 20, 2006, marked the thirty-eighth anniversary of the day Ron Kovic was shot during his second tour of duty as a Marine in Vietnam—"a date I can never forget, a day that was to change my life forever. . . . As I now contemplate another January 20th I cannot help but think of the young men and women who have been wounded in the war in Iraq. They have been coming home now for almost three years, flooding Walter Reed, Bethesda, Brooke Army Medical Center, and veterans hospitals all across the country. Paraplegics, amputees, burn victims, the blinded and maimed, shocked and stunned, brain-damaged and psychologically stressed, over 16,000 of them, a whole new generation of severely maimed is returning from Iraq, young men and women who were not even born when I came home wounded to the Bronx veterans hospital in 1968."

Ron wrote about a present past:

Do the American people, the president, the politicians, senators and congressmen who sent us to this war have any idea what it really means to lose an arm or a leg, to be paralyzed, to begin to cope with the psychological wounds of that war? Do they have any concept of the long-term effects of these injuries, how the struggles of the wounded are only now just beginning? How many will die young and never live out their lives because of all the stress and myriad of problems that come with sending young men and women into combat?

It is so difficult at first. You return home and both physically and emotionally don't know how you are going to live with this wound, but you just keep trying, just keep waking up to this frightening reality every morning. *"My God, what has happened to me?"* But you somehow get up, you somehow go on and find a way to move through each day. Even though it is impossible, you go on. Maybe there will be a day years from now, if you are lucky to live that long, when it will get better and you will not feel so overwhelmed. You must have something to hope for, some way to believe it will not always be this way. This is exactly what many of them are going through right now.

They are alone in their rooms all over this country, right now. Just as I was alone in my room. . . . I know they're there—just as I was. This is the part you never see. The part that is never reported in the news. The part that the president and vice president never mention. This is the agonizing part, the lonely part, when you have to awake to the wound each morning and suddenly realize what you've lost, what is gone forever. They're out there and they have mothers and fathers, sisters and brothers, husbands and wives and children. And they're not saying much right now. Just like me they're just trying to get through each day. Trying to be brave and not cry. They still are extremely grateful to be alive, but slowly, agonizingly they are beginning to think about what has really happened to them.

"It has been two years that I have waited for his return, for a miracle that would bring him to our door smiling and at peace,"

Fernando Suarez del Solar said in late March 2005. "The same door through which three uniformed men entered two years ago to give us the horrible news that he had died. The same door through which he left to fulfill his destiny, through which our grandson passes only to see still photos of his father and not understand why those photos do not move and speak and play with him. Our grandson does not understand and so I ask myself if he will understand someday that his father was victimized by an immoral war and that he was used by people like Bush for their own interests. I hope to God that someday my grandson will understand and still not hate but forgive and love his fellow man as his father loved humanity."

Months earlier, in his second inaugural address, President Bush had said: "Some have shown their devotion to our country in deaths that honored their whole lives, and we will always honor their names and their sacrifice."

How to reconcile the statements from Fernando Suarez del Solar and George W. Bush?

On the front page of the *New York Times*, a dispatch from Fallujah reported: "Nothing here makes sense, but the Americans' superior training and firepower eventually seem to prevail."

––––––––––

Early April 2005:

Through the darkness, on an outer wall of the Cesar Chavez Library, a projection shows the mounting revenues from Salinas taxpayers helping to pay for the war in Iraq—already more than $80 million. The odometer image keeps spinning while authors and others read aloud into the night as part of a protest against the planned closure of the public libraries in a city that John Steinbeck once called home.

Fernando Suarez del Solar is here, with his sweetness and dedication and grief. His son Jesus has been dead for more than two years. Since then, Fernando has been traveling widely, speaking at antiwar demonstrations, being present at vigils, talking to families with loved ones in Iraq. Whenever he can, he gets into high-school classes, addressing teenagers who might enlist, telling the story of his son. Every time I see Fernando, his eyes are tired and still racked with mourning, he speaks passionately about children he has never seen.

The dozens of tents pitched across the library's lawn bring to mind the encampment that I saw thirty-seven years ago on the mall not far from the White House: the Poor People's Campaign, demanding economic justice at a time of war. "A nation that continues year after year to spend more money on military defense than on programs of social uplift is approaching spiritual death," Martin Luther King said. Today, blocks from the library named after a visionary leader of farm workers, the need for social uplift is painful. Children play on concrete between rows of shabby trailers. On the streets, drab signs of extreme poverty are everywhere. In the mostly Latino neighborhoods, bereft of resources, the plan for closing the public libraries is an ultimate rebuff to aspirations.

———

I met Marla Ruzicka once, in 2000, when she was helping Medea Benjamin campaign as the Green Party's candidate for senator from California. We stood in the back of a room and chatted while Medea was mixing with the crowd. Like many other young people involved in social justice efforts, Marla seemed to look at the world with fresh idealism. I never could have imagined that five years later I'd be at her funeral.

American news outlets provided extensive—and mostly laudatory—coverage after she died at age twenty-eight in Baghdad on April 16, 2005. With an inspiring spirit, Marla was determined to gain acknowledgment and aid for civilians harmed by the war. "Their tragedies," she said, "are our responsibilities." Her funeral, at a church in her hometown of Lakeport, California, was mostly friends and coworkers paying tribute to a woman whose tremendous moral energies led her to take big risks along the way to great accomplishments.

During the last two years of her life, Marla set aside previous antiwar activism. "I decided not to take a position on the war but to try to do the right humanitarian thing," she told the *San Francisco Chronicle* in December 2003. And she found common ground with the Pentagon in her laudable pursuit of "compensation" for Iraqi civilians—for the wounded and families of the dead. Yet I think of Irma Thomas, tearful in her living room downwind of the Nevada nuclear test range, saying: "They couldn't pay anyone for the loss of a child. I hope they realize that."

Mainstream media coverage of Marla Ruzicka's death and life would not have been nearly so favorable if she had been a vocal critic of the U.S. military occupation during the previous two years. It was not only Marla's warmth and charm that endeared her to American generals in Baghdad and policymakers in Washington. It was also the fact that her work could be helpful to the war effort. Five days after Marla died, *Philadelphia Inquirer* columnist Trudy Rubin wrote: "Civilian casualties are an inconvenient stain on the storyline of Iraq liberation." The column went on: "Ruzicka understood that helping civilian victims is not just the right thing to do, but also is militarily essential."

After Marla's funeral, the *Los Angeles Times* noted that "her efforts, carried in Congress by Senator Patrick Leahy, resulted in an unprecedented $30 million in aid to victims." Within weeks, President Bush officially renamed that line item The Marla Ruzicka Fund. But about $80 *billion* had just gone through Congress as an extra appropriation into the war pipeline, and a lot more of such funding was on the horizon.

———

Days before the first round of Iran's presidential election in mid-June 2005, excitement was in the air at the campaign headquarters of the frontrunner, Ali Akbar Hashemi Rafsanjani. A pistachio tycoon and all-around rich guy—notorious for using corrupt means to become Iran's wealthiest man—former president Rafsanjani was the centrist in the race. He'd been making noises lately about wanting incremental democratic reforms and better relations with the

West. His son Mehdi, a campaign manager, seemed relaxed and good-humored as he sat with three American visitors around a conference table, parrying questions with twinkles in his eyes. When I asked about Iranian enthusiasm for atomic energy, my question became long-winded about dangers of the nuclear fuel cycle, from uranium mining to radioactive waste. I told him that nuclear power has been a terrible mistake in the United States. He replied: "We like your mistakes."

June 18, 2005:

The gloom feels unnervingly familiar. The TV screen keeps showing vote totals, getting worse; already a night of nightmare, fully awake. Our Iranian host turns on a CD player, a tenor saxophone begins, the sound of Coltrane, and we sit in the living room as Tehran's dusk falls on heat. The first round of the presidential election is over, with a rigid fundamentalist surging; there will be a runoff, but the momentum is now his.

In the kitchen, the sound of pots and plates.

"A love supreme. A love supreme."

Ahead, a negative synergy not daring to speak its name, an axis of fanatics in Tehran and Washington, presidents egging on rationales for belligerence, speaking different and similar languages.

Our host stands and changes the music, "so we don't all start crying," he says.

August 2006:

After six years behind bars due to his writings, Akbar Ganji seems remarkably gentle and free of bitterness. He was released from an Iranian prison a few months ago. He's currently traveling around the United States.

In Washington, at the National Press Club, he said: "I am a journalist and reporting is my profession. For some time, my task has been to report on political assassinations, imprisonments, and torture. I report in order to instigate protest." Two weeks later he wrote in the *New York Times*: "Freedom-loving Iranians inside and outside the country are against American military intervention in Iran. Such a war would be of no help in our fight for freedom; in fact, it would only contribute to our further enslavement, as the regime would use war as an excuse to suppress any and all voices of opposition."

Now he's in garden shade, talking to a few Americans. We're sitting around a picnic table. One of the first things he says is: "In the Middle East the extremism from all sides—Christian fundamentalism, Jewish fundamentalism, Islamic fundamentalism—are fanning the flames. Helping each other."

When Israel launched a huge assault on Lebanon in the summer of 2006, I thought again of my friend sitting at the breakfast table twenty-four years earlier, weeping as she read about the massacres at refugee camps near Beirut.

Now, after getting out of Lebanon, a writer named June Rugh told Reuters: "As an American, I'm embarrassed and ashamed. My administration is letting it happen [by giving] tacit permission for Israel to destroy a country." The news service quoted another American evacuee, Andrew Muha, who had been in southern Lebanon. He said: "It's a travesty. There's a million homeless in Lebanon and the intense amount of bombing has brought an entire country to its knees." Embarrassed. Ashamed. A travesty. Those words began to describe how I felt. But others seemed more apropos. Government criminality. High-tech terror. Murder from the skies.

Of course Israeli officials talked about murderous crimes against civilians by Hezbollah and Hamas. And Hezbollah and Hamas officials talked about murderous crimes against civilians by Israel. Plenty of real crimes to go around. The continual dynamic was based on a chain of tacit lies, none more important than the insistence that a religion could make one life worth more than another; render a human death unimportant; elevate certain war-inflicted agonies to spiritual significance.

"There are terrorists who will blow up innocent people in order to achieve tactical objectives," President Bush said on July 13, 2006, referring to actions by Hezbollah and Hamas. We were supposed to believe that Israel did not also "blow up innocent people in order to achieve tactical objectives." But the Israeli leaders ordering the air assaults on Gaza and Lebanon, and the American leaders who backed them, had to know that many civilians would be killed, many others wounded, many more terrorized. (Overall, by any measure, Israelis were doing a lot more killing than dying.) The smug moral stance that the bombing didn't target specific civilians amounted to moldy political grist—in human terms, irrelevant to the totally predictable results where the bombs fell.

––––––––––

Superior violence, according to countless scripts, was righteous and viscerally satisfying. Television and movies, ever since childhood, presented greater violence as the ultimate weapon and final fix, uniquely able to put an end to conflict. Leaving menace for dead— you couldn't beat that. But at home in the USA and far away, the practical and moral failures of violence became irrefutable: most of all for the generation officially tasked to kill and be killed in Vietnam. Later, much later, when the U.S. occupation of Iraq was starting to unravel, the eminent pundit George Will wrote that "the first task of the occupation remains the first task of government: to establish a monopoly on violence."

If Washington's war-makers were seeking a "monopoly" on violence, they could only be hostile to trustbusters. In Iraq, sources of unauthorized violence met with escalating American violence. In the United States, war opponents met with presidential contempt. And in the immediate aftermath of the 2006 midterm election, the Bush administration moved to countermand the antiwar message of the results. The votes had scarcely been counted before the launch of a huge spin assault on the option of withdrawing U.S. troops.

The media barrage was dense within a week of the election. Right-wing outlets like Fox News and the *Wall Street Journal* editorial page were secondary. Many of the most effective salvos came from page one of the *New York Times*. Under the headline "Get Out of Iraq Now? Not So Fast, Experts Say," the newspaper's front page reported that "a number of military officers, experts and former generals" were against proposals from congressional Democrats to begin withdrawal of U.S. troops within four to six months. ("Experts" with contrary views did not make the cut.) The reporter who wrote the piece, Michael Gordon, appeared on CNN hours later to morph into a commentator who sounded much like a White House spokesman. He insisted that withdrawal was "simply not realistic" and warned against a pullout. That was conventional media wisdom.

As William Dean Howells wrote long ago: "What a thing it is to have a country that *can't* be wrong, but if it is, is right, anyway!"

Today:

In my kitchen is a dark-red little carpet with black designs, imported from Baghdad. I bought it there one afternoon in late January 2003 at the bazaar (not so different, to my eyes anyway, from the market I later visited in Tehran). My traveling companion was a former high-ranking U.N. official, Denis Halliday, who had lived in Baghdad for a while during the 1990s before resigning as head of the "oil for food" program in protest against the draconian sanctions that caused so much devastation among civilians. Denis was revisiting some of the shopkeepers he had come to know. After warm greetings and pleasantries, an Iraqi man in his middle years said that he'd heard on the BBC about a French proposal for averting an invasion. The earnest hope in his voice made my heart sink, as if falling into the dirty stretch of the Tigris River that Denis and I had just hopped a boat across, where people were beating rugs on stones alongside the banks.

Often when I look at the carpet in the kitchen I think that it is filled with blood, remembering how one country's treasures become another's aesthetic enhancements. I had carted home the rolled-up carpet and less than two months later came "shock and awe," and now four years afterward the daily papers piled up on the breakfast table a few feet away tell of the latest carnage. I don't think the rug has ever given me pleasure since the day it unfurled across the hardwood floor. It hasn't been cleaned since presumably it soaked up the Tigris water during its last washing. There's blood on the carpet and no amount of trips to the dry cleaners could change that.

Macbeth, Act V, Scene 1:
Out, damned spot! out, I say! . . . What need we fear who knows it, when none can call our power to account?—Yet who would have thought the old man to have had so much blood in him? . . . What, will these hands ne'er be clean? . . . Here's the smell of the blood still: all the perfumes of Arabia will not sweeten this little hand.

12

MEANWHILE, BACK AT THE NUCLEAR RANCH

June 2006:

It's the last day of the month, the midpoint of the year, and I've just arrived in the mountains of northern New Mexico to stay at a house for a few weeks of solitude to work on this book. The morning is bright with sky blue over browns and greens, a big country panorama of high desert. I walk past fields with dry brush, and occasional horses look at me over barbed wire. When I introduce myself to a neighbor, he exudes warmth. Lived in this area his whole life, he tells me, and there's nowhere he'd rather be. Looking around the 360 degrees of this "land of enchantment," I can glimpse why. Now that he's retired, he spends a lot of time fixing up his house, the biggest one around, and tending to the land near it.

His first name is one I remember from *The Iliad*; it has spread with the rise and fall of many empires. His ancestors were Spanish and Indian. He proudly tells me about his children, off at college. We gaze across a large picturesque valley, and he points to the small towns of Cordova and Chimayo a few miles away, and farther the more sizeable Espanola. Off in the distance, under a mountain range, is Los Alamos. I ask how long a drive it is from here, and he says about forty-five minutes. I ask how near the laboratory site is to the town, and he says maybe a mile. He adds that he worked there, at Los Alamos National Laboratory, for twenty-three years. Later, I recall something that Nestor said while we were standing in front of his house, looking out at the wonderful surroundings: "It's so peaceful here."

————

July 7, 2006:

Today is my fifty-fifth birthday, and the feeling that despite all the changes so little has changed really torments me. Turn on a television and there's the president, giving hypocrisy a bad name, and this is normal. Always has been, in my lifetime. Turn on the TV when I was fifteen and there's the president, some kind of perverse fount of lies. That was when I started to get it and not get over it. If I'd been born ten years earlier, it would have started with Ike instead of LBJ.

A year ago I was in Philadelphia, talking about my book on media manipulation for war, and a radio host asked a question that I appreciated because it got close to a very difficult truth that so many of us in the United States have been living with for a long time now: Isn't it upsetting and frightening to perceive that the people at the top of the government can't be trusted—that they're just fundamentally deceitful and dangerous? For an interviewer on a big station she was being unusually clear and perceptive. She'd read between the pages of my book that, below the careful documentation, I'd written through gritted teeth. Take away all the categories—left right moderate, pro and anti, this or that—and come back to the basic matter of the continuum, from one president to another, one commander in chief to another: that they've all been ready to demolish us in an instant. That fact, alone, from Harry S Truman to George W. Bush and whoever comes next, is so ghastly that we can't really look at it, like "brighter than a thousand suns" just before the mushroom cloud.

I think of the atomic veterans I've met, who talked about what it was like to kneel in the desert or on a ship and then suddenly see the bones in their hands covering their eyes—and when I think of those skeletoned hands, I remember the scientist at the Nevada test site back in 1980 who had something to say but wouldn't say it until I turned off the tape recorder: "I don't think anyone who has ever seen a nuclear explosion has ever not asked the question: *My God, what have we done?"*

Those of us who haven't ever seen a nuclear bomb go off should be asking, too. Despite all horrors, the world has been lucky enough to not have a nuclear war since 1945, but that's by definition: until it comes and then that's the end of the luck forever. Just a few days ago, the North Korean government launched a test missile, and yesterday President Bush boasted that if the missile hadn't misfired the American military probably could have shot it down. Dubious bravado from a technical standpoint, but that aside: wrong answer. We don't want that kind of dice rolling, do we? But the system is deranged. Not just suicidal but globally homicidal in the sense that the pledge has already been made, the mechanisms are in place: willing to use these weapons. What has made the presidents so transparent has been their simultaneous enthusiasm for and condemnation of violence.

That made me first realize how deeply the essence was amiss, when President Johnson would get on TV and deplore the riots and preach against violence; here was a guy who told us how bad people with Molotov cocktails were while he was cheering on the B-52 bombers as they systematically turned the bodies of adults and children into corpses and ashen remains. Ever since, one president after another has counseled nonviolence while ordering the opposite, like Clinton deploring the Columbine High School shootings on a day when the U.S. bombing of Yugoslavia happened to be heavier than ever. "We do know," the president said with the straightest of straight faces, "that we must do more to reach out to our children and teach them to express their anger and to resolve their conflicts with words, not weapons."

Now, looking across the mesa at these dry scrub mountains, I remember fireworks a few nights ago, for the Fourth, along a swath of horizon near Los Alamos; as I watched, there was a lightning storm behind the fireworks, making them look puny while gigantic jagged bolts stabbed down from the sky, flickering the darkness, before thunder. It's really beautiful out here in the high desert

as I start to see what seemed just arid and harsh a week ago; on foot
it's easy to notice rabbits with very big ears and squirrels and chip-
munks, scurrying through the brush, and wildflowers and an occasional blooming cactus close to the ground, and butterflies (as
graceful and colorful as the ones I used to chase in a field near our
house where my older brother launched water-propelled rockets),
and grasshoppers . . .

———————

The local phone book listed the Los Alamos National Laboratory
under "University of California."

On the way, a road climbed above canyons with awesome vistas
of rock layers; uncountable shades of browns, oranges, yellows.
Then, at about seven thousand feet, came the city of Los Alamos.
Along Central Avenue, at frequent intervals, blue banners said "LOS
ALAMOS: WHERE DISCOVERIES ARE MADE."

Not even a tiny town was here, on finger-shaped mesas near a
giant dormant volcano, until the Manhattan Project arrived in April
1943. While the crash program to build an atom bomb was far-
flung, Los Alamos served as headquarters for the brains behind it.
Scientists at the lab oversaw the first atomic bomb explosion, code-
named Trinity, in a forlorn stretch of New Mexico desert on July 16,
1945. American nuclear testing continued, in the atmosphere and
then underground, until 1992. After the detonations finally ended,
the Los Alamos and Lawrence Livermore laboratories still had
plenty of nuclear weapons work to do.

Inside a modest business complex, at the communications office
of the Los Alamos National Laboratory, "media relations team
leader" Kevin Roark greeted me with cordial professionalism. His
silvery hair, moustache, and goatee were short; his eyes looked
through steel-rimmed glasses. He wore an open-collar olive shirt
and blue jeans.

The conference room was in use, and Roark motioned across the
hall to what looked like a break room. When I asked if it was okay to
turn on my tape recorder, he nodded. Of course.

The University of California was fully in charge of managing the Los Alamos laboratory for more than sixty years, until recent security problems led to a shift. In June 2006 the lab went under new management—widened to also include Bechtel National, BWX Technologies, and Washington Group International—a team of "three private companies and a university system," as Roark put it. His badge said "U.S. Department of Energy," and I assumed that he was working for the U.S. government. But Roark corrected me. "We're not a federal agency," he said. "I work for a contractor. I'm not a federal employee. I'm an employee of this team."

So, I asked, what's the "legal entity" managing the Los Alamos lab?

"It's a limited liability corporation," he replied.

"Really. Is that what they call it?"

"Yeah. It's called Los Alamos National Security LLC."

I repeated the name, to make sure I'd heard correctly.

"Right," he said, though the contractor's legal name was rarely used in public. "We don't really go by that. We just go by the name Los Alamos National Laboratory."

Moments later, he was showing me head shots of the lab's new top managers and describing their backgrounds, but I was still trying to wrap my mind around the concept of "limited liability" for managers of a nuclear weapons laboratory.

When I tuned back in, Kevin Roark was describing the laboratory site: "We're uniquely suited to our activities because we are in a remote area, which means we can do high explosives work, et cetera. We're a very large area, roughly the size of D.C., thirty-eight square miles." And: "Despite what you might read in the newspapers sometimes, we do have *ex*cellent relationships with our neighbors, because we are the—aside from state government—we are the largest employer in the state." The total number of workers at the Los Alamos laboratory, including students and contractors, was around twelve thousand.

"Los Alamos National Laboratory quite literally changed the way applied science is done in the world," Roark said. "Previous to

1943, almost all science was done in an academic setting. Some corporations had an R & D function, but it was very focused on one thing—the bottom line. The idea that Oppenheimer had, and brought to fruition, was this idea of you bring in an extremely diverse technical workforce and you have everybody working with everybody." Usually, in academia, "you hardly ever saw a physicist working with an engineer, especially a *theoretical* physicist. . . . Oppenheimer changed all of that."

Roark pointed out the digital debt to Los Alamos. From the Manhattan Project days of slide rules and punch cards to the lab's present-day computers, with one able to do upwards of 100 trillion calculations per second, "this laboratory has been at the forefront of computing research and development." A need emerged to turn data into "something you could watch," and that need propelled the lab into finding "a way to translate reams and reams and reams and reams of numbers into a movie." As a result, he said, "To a very great degree, all computer visualization is an idea born here." He added: "The Pixar movies are the same basic idea."

My host talked about a theme central to Los Alamos public relations: "Our primary mission has never changed—and that is, assuring the reliability and safety of this nation's nuclear deterrent." Since nuclear test explosions are no longer part of the process, "reliability and safety" are more dependent than ever on computer modeling and simulation. The tolerances are breathtakingly small. "Part of the problem—and this isn't fully appreciated by people much either—is that nuclear weapons are highly *highly* complex systems, on the order of six thousand parts, each one very highly tuned . . . very high-quality manufacturing techniques, a huge number of parts all of which have to work exactly as designed, every time, and most of which weren't designed to last longer than twenty years." With its annual budget of more than 2 billion dollars mostly devoted to nuclear weapons, the Los Alamos laboratory has remained heavily focused on weapons manufacturing, experimental programs, and "high performance computing."

Today, for scientists at the labs, mere atomic bombs are so 1940s.

Long ago the standard became what was first, at mid-century, called a "super bomb": the fission-fusion hydrogen weapon, more powerful than the A-bomb by a factor of a hundred or even a thousand. "Basically, the way a nuclear weapon works is that you have a *ther-monuclear* weapon—which all of ours are," Roark said. "There aren't any just basic atom bombs anymore, they're all two-stage. There's a primary and a secondary. The primary is the pit. It's a plutonium shape, which we can't get into, a hollow shape that's surrounded by high explosives, there's enough plutonium in that shape to have a critical mass, enough mass in the right configuration to cause a runaway nuclear reaction." The atomic implosion is just the beginning. "It gives off a huge amount of radiation, heat, and pressure, and that is directed towards the secondary, which is squeezed by that radiation, heat, and pressure, and causes hydrogen nuclei to fuse."

Roark described himself as "a journalist" when I asked about his background. "I went to the University of New Mexico, got a degree in journalism, worked at a local TV station here, worked at a local TV station in Miami, went to a local TV station in Pittsburgh, and then kind of came to the lab. Not in that exact order, but I'm a television news photographer by trade, if not profession, and didn't even know I had an affinity for science until I came here." After working at Los Alamos on and off for sixteen years, his current job "is to lead the team that handles the media."

I asked whether he perceived two "different worlds" in terms of basic outlook—with some people "who see nuclear weapons production and deployment as an unfortunate but absolutely rational best-case scenario in the world we live in, and then you have other people who feel that it's nuts. Do you think there's any chance for dialogue or intersection between those two points of view, or are they just totally different?"

"This would be my own personal opinion," he said. "Because I don't think the lab would have a position on something like that. But my own personal feeling on that is that, from what I've seen, the 'two worlds' as you describe them *do* exist, much as the way you describe them; I would agree with your characterization, and they don't intersect. It's like, I hate to use an oversimplified analogy—you know the old joke is, there are two kinds of people in the world, people who group people into two kinds and people who don't—but there are two kinds of people in the world, there's the kind of person who wears a buck knife on his belt, and when you ask him 'Why do you carry that knife?' it's like 'I carry the knife because I might need it some day. And if you see me carrying the knife, you're not going to mess with me.' And there's this other guy who thinks"—Roark's voice suddenly became high-pitched and a bit hysterical—"*Carrying the knife is insane, because the first time somebody pushes you, you're going to pull it out and stab him, and it's cra-zee. You don't need to stab a guy. It's insane. Take it all off. If you take your knife off and drop it, everyone'll take their knives off and drop them. Don't you get it?*"

"But I don't see you wearing a knife here. Kevin."

"Well, that was an analogy. I am a knife carrier under that scenario."

"In a way, you see it as a difference between realists and non-realists?"

"My other joke about me is that I am *not* a cynic, I'm a realist. And I'm good-natured about it. But yeah, I see the world as a place where a nuclear deterrent is abso*lute*ly necessary. I believe strongly in the mission of this laboratory. Because I've lived in the world, I've been to the Third World, I've been to Russia a couple of times, I've traveled extensively, and the world is a dangerous place without some level of deterrent. Do I want to see the world back away from that? Absolutely. I don't think there's a person at this lab who doesn't believe that what we're doing is in the spirit of one of our former director's statements, that's Norris Bradbury, who said: 'What we do here is not make war. What we do here is buy time for the politicians to find a better way.' That's what we do. And it's clear that this is going to take a lot of time."

"Is there a chance, do you think, that the very R & D and deployment for 'deterrence' might end up being a catalyst for exactly what everybody wants to avoid?"

"If anybody, not just the United States, if anybody uses a nuclear weapon in anger, we have failed in our mission. Pure and simple. Our mission, in the very broadest sense, is to prevent nuclear war. Bottom line."

I asked about his childhood recollections of the Bomb.

"I gained my consciousness in the early days of the Cold War, in the early '60s, mid-'60s," he said. "I mean, I remember, as a little guy, 'duck and cover,' in my school. And I remember the Cuban Missile Crisis, to a degree—I was a first grader, but I remember. . . ."

"Do you think it freaked out people to be in 'duck and cover' and the Cuban Missile Crisis? . . . Our parents' generation assumed there was going to be a future. Our generation couldn't assume that. Was that an important difference?"

"See, I never got that feeling as a kid," Roark said. "I never doubted—I never believed there would be a nuclear war."

"Did you believe there would never be a nuclear war?"

"I believed there would never—I still believe there will never be a nuclear war."

"You believe there will never be nuclear weapons used in anger?"

"That's a different story, especially in today's environment."

"Okay, let's say a nuclear exchange. Do you think there will—"

"No."

"You think there'll never be a nuclear ex—"

"No."

"And where did that come from? It sounds like you've always had that belief. Where does it come from?"

"Because I know a lot about nuclear weapons," Roark answered. He paused for a few seconds. Then he said, with sudden intensity: "People have no idea."

The comment seemed cryptic. I waited for him to say more. When he didn't, I spoke. "'We're buying time,' you said."

"Um-hmm."

"But it's not only about nuclear weapons," I went on. Then I referred to the computer-world axiom of Garbage In, Garbage Out. "It's about the—you know, it's the GIGO principle, ultimately. You said buying time for the politicians."

"Right."

"Do you have as much confidence in the 'stockpile reliability' of the judgment of the politicians?"

The question hung in the air for a moment, before he replied quietly: "You have to." More silence. "You have to," he repeated.

"But this is a place of science," I replied. "That sounds almost like faith."

"I'm not a person of faith. But you know, everybody—again, this is just me personally—I believe that almost all people perceive from a position of essentially detached self—what's the word I'm looking for—self-interest. . . . I think a politician's detached self-interest is essentially he wants a lot of people to love him. And a lot of people aren't going to love you if you push the nuclear button."

I asked whether it would be fair to compare the scientists at the laboratory with officers in the military, ultimately following orders from the Joint Chiefs and the president.

"It's not at all like that. It's more like an academic setting. . . . It's not at all like a military environment."

"And yet there is a hierarchy that this academic environment is answerable to, in a way that a college campus somewhere wouldn't be the case."

"I wouldn't go that far," he said. "No. No. College campuses have boards of governors, boards of regents, they have major fundraisers, they have major contributors, they have the same kinds of driving forces that a laboratory like this has. Maybe a different environment, more free, and a laboratory like this doesn't have an endowment to tap into when you want to do something sort of outlandish, but—no, I think it's a very academic-like environment."

As we got to our feet, he showed me an internal Los Alamos laboratory publication, *Nuclear Weapons Journal*. "One of the things

that's almost always lost on people is that the science here is real,"
he said, more than a little passionately. "They don't get it. They
think it's just a buncha eggheads in rooms, talking about stuff. But
this is a way to give you an idea that the science we do is real—
especially in the weapons programs."

He flipped through the magazine and pointed to a piece headlined "Modeling Coupled Fluid-Solid Response in Low-Density
Cellular Material Systems" as an example of the rigorous content.
"Just a quick read of this will give you an idea of what kind of level
of complexity we're talking about. . . ." He handed me the magazine.

"You ever heard anybody at the lab say, 'That's a sweet
problem'?"

"Oh yeah. All the time. In fact, I've heard people say, 'You know,
all the interesting math is now nonlinear.' Things like that. You
know, nobody wants to do linear math anymore because all the interesting linear math has really been done."

I asked whether *Sputnik*, which went into orbit the year he was
born, had much effect on him.

"My personal frame of reference isn't *Sputnik*," he responded.
"It's the moonwalk."

"The moonwalk. What did that mean?"

"That meant you could come up with just about the most challenging technical problem you could think of, and the United States
of America could come up with a solution—could solve that problem and make it happen."

"What did it mean to you when it was the summer of '69 and
the moonwalk happened?"

"I was twelve, and it was a really *really* big deal, to me," Roark
said. "It really meant that there are technical solutions to just about
any problem. I didn't even realize at the time the technical problems, and I've only come to learn how out there on the ragged edge
we were for that endeavor."

He added: "I don't think you can turn to technology for everything. But you can turn to technology for almost everything."

13

OBSTINATE MEMORY

*There is too little recognition of the vast difference
between the world as described and the world
as sensed . . .*

Alan Watts

Only in omniscient fictions can the pieces fit together with anything that approaches tidy. Our lives lack the smooth arc of drama's
acts, while actual memory is on the chaotic side: tangled, in innumerable shades of gray and color, with double and triple and
quadruple exposures, and moments that are uncountable.

You have them too, of course: memories that don't stay for long
in plain sight but never quite really leave, any more than a well-
kept lawn or tended tree makes the soil beneath disappear. Every
loose leaf turned like page into humus, each season fading into chill,
disappearing into realms we know and don't know, somehow disin-
tegrating, somehow not gone. For memories that have no apparent
function, obsolescence is the supposedly natural fate. As if topsoil is
only for burial.

You have them too: muddy creeks upstream, hazy with sedi-
ment that can stir into thick sentiment, forgotten and not forgotten,
the moments that are just too old to dwell on and too intense to ex-
punge. Still part of you.

Think of where you were a decade or two or three ago, and
maybe there's an ineffable scent that can be overpowering: your
life, being and going by. We live in a time when nearly everything is

supposed to have a point, a proximity to advancement or self-improvement; yet memory, deceptively simple and infinite and fourth dimensional, clear and murky, is an opposite of neat, cannot configure in the furrowed rows of field or brow. Looking back, we see mostly that we can't; memory is largely spaces, of all descriptions and thin description.

The new digital technologies with prodigious "memory" are, ironically enough, maybe corrosive for human memory, which is much of what makes us human: the capacity to reflect, to remember with uniquely textured nuance the unnumbered dimensions of feelings past and not past, mixed like infinite shades of paint. While overt fascination goes to gigabyte machines—"remembering" vast quantities for us—we struggle for the most elemental and sometimes simple memories, almost all we really have.

Every memory is a partial truth. Every forgetting might be a kind of lie; retroactive innocence, maybe not so innocent. Forgetting is a necessity and at times a betrayal—opting for convenience and omission, survival and abnegation. The future may be possible but the past is impossible, in part a leaden weight of missed opportunities and disintegration, compounded by immutability.

Sand keeps piling up a mountain in hourglass, the past and not quite, our own little big stories, almost any and all of them later to be lost in vast ocean. ("Life is like stepping onto a boat that is about to sail out to sea and sink."—Shunryu Suzuki) In the meantime, there is nothing that can't be forgotten at least temporarily, and plenty can be forgotten seemingly forever, but somewhere under the carpet are grains of truth swept neatly or chaotically, every buried memory a trove of uncertain value.

What can be remembered can be buried. But is the reverse true? Memory excavation looks like a messy business. Yet the alternative to digging is withering. The writer Eduardo Galeano has commented that the greatest truth is the search for truth. But the reigning inclination is to toss aside the shovel (as if a sign says, "No digging here without permission from the power company"). Ahead is the possibility of abject failure to truly learn much more—overturning all that granite to find deeper truth and finding only more of the same flinty rock.

———————

In themselves, words and visual images and objects are clues that are virtually clueless, just memorabilia—what Patsy Cline called "these little things"—not to be confused with actual memories. Yet the possibilities of retrospective wisdom are compelling. Love and death: Can we understand and participate in the possible before the inevitable?

———————

"All memory is individual, unreproducible—it dies with each person," Susan Sontag wrote. But the reality that any and all memory is individual, and can't be the same for even two people, cuts against the grain of media pretense. The same events, or more precisely the same gist of news coverage, may be remembered by millions of people, and with mostly similar emotions. Yet it's a myth that the public holds a memory like a big umbrella. "People talk a great deal these days about collective memories and shared history," psychologist Susan Engel notes. And it's true that in some ways "memories are shaped by the people you share them with, and the situations in which you share them." But ultimately, "the memory is a mental representation that resides within a person's mind."

The mass-marketing of synthetic "memory" provides off-the-shelf products that discourage people from asserting the relevance of their more authentic perceptions. Not acknowledging the complexity of memories is part of a process of steamrollering them. Flat results are available from the morning paper, the evening newscast, the 24/7 cable news channels. What makes the public renderings of life so routinely thin—and so helpful for toning down outraged human responses to vile official actions in our names—is bound up in narrow media limits that virtually infantilize the listeners, viewers, and readers. The widely replicated screens end up screening us, from ourselves and from each other.

What quickly passes for common memory, and then shared history, is a very big prize for political interests. Media consumers are told what is memorable; that, in turn, becomes what "everybody knows." We live in a world of media prompts—with millions of them encountered by each person over a lifetime—mass loops heavily programmed by a degraded and degrading media environment.

The flip side of synthetic memory is media-produced forgetting. So, after he died, the antiwar and socialist-oriented Martin Luther King Jr. had to be dumped—by a "shared history" of omission—before he could be memorialized as a national-holiday icon.

———

"Garbage In, Garbage Out" came as an early caveat for the computer age. But GIGO is rarely mentioned these days amid all the fascination with the next new digital thing. That fascination keeps overshadowing the purposes (or lack of purpose) to which the dazzling arrays of technology are being put. With bearings unclear, we get lost. "Our problem today is that we have allowed the internal to become lost in the external," Martin Luther King wrote in 1967.

> We have allowed the means by which we live to outdistance the ends for which we live. So much of modern life can be summarized in that suggestive phrase of Thoreau: "Improved means to an unimproved end.". . . When scientific power outruns moral power, we end up with guided missiles and misguided men. When we foolishly minimize the internal of our lives and maximize the external, we sign the warrant for our own day of doom. Our hope for creative living in this world house that we have inherited lies in our ability to re-establish the moral ends of our lives in personal character and social justice. Without this spiritual and moral reawakening we shall destroy ourselves in the misuse of our own instruments.

In what became known as his "Beyond Vietnam" speech, on April 4, 1967, King said: "We must rapidly begin the shift from a thing-oriented society to a person-oriented society. When machines and computers, profit motives and property rights, are considered more important than people, the giant triplets of racism, extreme materialism, and militarism are incapable of being conquered."

———

"Machines are already becoming better at communicating with each other than human beings with human beings," R. D. Laing commented in 1967. "The situation is ironical. More and more concern about communication, less and less to communicate." The theatrical teacher Lee Strasberg observed: "Our society has spent so much time and has achieved such startling results with the discovery of new mechanical processes of communication, but we have somehow forgotten that the process of living demands the ability to respond, to make contact, and to communicate one's experience to another human being."

———

Timeworn media storylines are descriptive *and* prescriptive. They keep orienting, suggesting, and role-modeling. Standard journalism runs parallel to the "industrially produced fiction" that Ariel Dorfman has described: "Although these stories are supposed merely to entertain us, they constantly give us a secret education." We receive tacit instruction on "how to succeed, how to love, how to buy, how to conquer, how to forget the past and suppress the future. We are taught, more than anything else, how not to rebel."

Late in the summer of 2001 a *New York Times* obituary about a former state prison official made a passing reference to "the bloody Attica uprising in 1971, which left 43 people dead." It was a small instance of the kind of newspeak that presents itself as journalism. Thirty years earlier, on September 13, 1971, in upstate New York, a four-day standoff at the Attica Correctional Facility ended when Governor Nelson Rockefeller ordered an assault—and five hundred state troopers attacked the prison compound, firing 2,200 bullets in nine minutes. The raid killed twenty-nine inmates and ten guards held as hostages, while wounding at least eighty-six other people. At the time, media outlets across the country reported that the rebellious prisoners slit the throats of the hostages when the troopers began their assault.

Horribly inhumane prison conditions had prompted the Attica uprising, which began as an undisciplined riot and grew into a well-focused articulation of rage from men who chose to take a fateful step. While the rebellion was multiracial, most of the 1,281 prisoners involved were black. Reflexively assuming that the powerful white guys in positions of authority would be truthful, reporters got the story backward. Autopsies later revealed that no throats had been cut; only then did authorities admit that officers of the state had done the killing.

Actual events at Attica never really took hold for the American public. The initial, sensational lies received way more publicity than the later corrections. Journalism—sometimes called "the first draft of history"—instantly remembered for America what didn't happen and then forgot for us what did.

A twenty-six-year-long civil action, brought by Attica inmates, made possible the release of more than a million Attica-related files that state authorities kept claiming did not exist. The prisoners collectively won a $12 million settlement. But thirty-five years after the Attica uprising, our nation's jails and prisons held more people than any other country, over 2 million—mostly very poor and 63 percent black or Latino—while media sunlight rarely exposed brutality common for prisoners. It's a huge social reality: past, present, and forgotten.

"We work hard to create and maintain a sense of inner cohesion and consistency in our self-concept," the psychologist Susan Engel observes. And after horrendous actions, most research indicates, "people repress unbearable truths about their past, or distort in ways that make those actions seem justifiable."

14

CONSEQUENCES AND TRUTHS

Interviewed in 2006, the author of *David and the Phoenix* said that he regretted making the Scientist the villain. When I asked why, Edward Ormondroyd mentioned the current attacks on science from the Bush administration. Fifty years after he finished writing the book, disdain for the empirical that couldn't be readily jiggered or spun was evident at the top of the executive branch in Washington. The country was mired in a discourse that echoed the Scopes trial dramatized in *Inherit the Wind*. Mere rationality would mean lining up on the side of "science" against the modern yahoos and political panderers waving the flag of social conservatism. (At the same time that scientific Darwinism was under renewed assault, a de facto alliance between religious fundamentalists and profit-devout corporatists moved the country further into social Darwinism that aimed to disassemble the welfare state.) Entrenched opposition to stem-cell research was part of a grim pattern that included complacency about severe pollution and global warming—disastrous trends already dragging one species after another to the brink of extinction and beyond.

No longer was the scientist presumably rushing up the mountainside and shooting at the phoenix. More likely, the scientist was documenting the effects of pollutants and habitat destruction that were closing in on the rare bird. True, many scientists still worked for companies or agencies with a much higher premium on boosting profit margins than preserving species. But most scientists didn't pretend that essential facts could be made to disappear by virtue of patriotic faith.

Actually, few Americans and no major political forces are "anti-science" across the board. The ongoing prerogative is to pick and choose. Those concerned about the ravages left by scientific civilization—the combustion engine, chemicals, fossil-fuel plants, and so much more—frequently look to science for evidence and solutions. Those least concerned about the Earth's ecology are apt to be the greatest enthusiasts for science in the service of unfettered commerce or the Pentagon, which always seeks the most effectively "advanced" scientific know-how. Even the most avowedly faithful are not inclined to leave the implementation of His plan to unscientific chance.

So, depending on the circumstances, right-wing fundamentalists could support the use of the latest science for top-of-the-line surveillance, for command and control, and for overall warfare—or could dismiss unwelcome scientific evidence of environmental harm as ideologically driven conclusions that should not be allowed to interfere with divinely inspired policies. Those kinds of maneuvers, George Orwell wrote in 1984, help the believers "to forget any fact that has become inconvenient, and then, when it becomes necessary again, to draw it back from oblivion for just so long as it is needed, to deny the existence of objective reality and all the while to take account of the reality which one denies."

In the first years of the twenty-first century, the liberal script hailed science as an urgent antidote to Bush-like irrationality. That was logical. But it was also ironic and ultimately unpersuasive. Pure allegiance to science exists least of all in the political domain; scientific findings are usually filtered by power, self-interest, and ideology. For instance, the technical and ecological advantages of mass transit have long been clear; yet foremost engineering minds are deployed to the task of building better SUVs. And there has never been any question that nuclear weapons are bad for the Earth and the future of humanity, but no one ever condemns the continuing development of nuclear weapons as a bipartisan assault on science.

On the contrary, the nonstop R & D efforts for thermonuclear weapons are all about science.

When scientists found rapid climate change to be both extremely ominous and attributable to the proliferation of certain technologies, the media and political power centers responded to the data by doing as they wished. The GOP's assault on science was cause for huge alarm when applied to the matter of global warming, but the unchallenged across-the-aisle embrace of science in the weaponry field had never been benign. When it came to designing and manufacturing the latest doomsday devices, only the most rigorous scientists need apply. And no room would be left for "intelligent design" as per the will of God.

The neutrality of science was self-evident and illusionary. Science was impartial because its discoveries were verifiable and accurate—but science was also, through funding and government direction, largely held captive. Its massively destructive capabilities were often seen as stupendous assets. In the case of ultramodern American armaments, the worse they got the better they got. Whatever could be said about "the market," it was skewed by the buyers; the Pentagon's routine spending made the nation's budget for alternative fuels or eco-friendly technologies look like a pittance.

———

I was walking on Timber Ridge Road one scintillating fall afternoon in 2006 when I remembered what Raymond Mungo, freshly liberated from Liberation News Service, had written back in 1969 about trees. Later in the day, I looked at his exact words: "I wish everybody would pay as much attention to trees as I do, but since everybody won't listen, I'll just go my solitary way and strive to enjoy what may well be the last days of this beautiful but deteriorating planet."

Mungo's plea for tree mindfulness might seem like unwitting self-satire. My eyes roll a bit. Yet no amount of scoffing can quite obscure the wisdom in the sentiment. Essential to life on the planet, trees can be seen as incarnations of a golden rule for survival, just as war is the opposite. And what could be more antithetical than a tree and a nuclear bomb? The radioactive ashes in humanity's mouth would negate all life, including trees.

We're social beings, as evolution seems to substantiate. Blessings and curses revolve largely around the loving and the warlike, the nurturing and the predatory. We're self-protective for survival, yet we also have "conscience"—what Darwin described as the characteristic that most distinguishes human beings from other animals. Given the strength of our instincts for individual and small-group survival, we seem to be stingy with more far-reaching conscience.

Our capacities to take humane action are as distinctive of our species as conscience, and no more truly reliable. As people, we are consequences and we also cause them: by what we choose to do and not do. The beneficiaries of economic and military savagery are far from the combat zones. In annual reports, the Pentagon's prime contractors give an overview of the vast financial rewards for shrewdly making a killing. To surrender the political battlefield to such forces is to self-marginalize and leave more space for those who thrive on plunder.

The inseparable bond of life and death should be healthy antipathy.

When columnists Russell Mokhiber and Robert Weissman let readers know about the recent deaths of their mothers due to cancer, they wrote:

> We have been taking care of our moms.
> And then mourning our loss.
> And in our sorrow, we have pondered this question—why decency often doesn't translate into policy.
> We know that many of you are working hard to figure this one out.
> But let us first admit it—we have not figured it out.
> Our society has figured out how to get to the moon and back.
> And we've figured out how to build weapons of mass destruction and use them.

And we have figured out how to pack 5,000 songs in a single I-Pod.

And plug it into a tape deck so we can listen to any or all of them on our car stereo.

And we have figured out how to build in the television into the back seat of the mini-van so the kids don't bother us on our trips to the beach for vacation.

And we have figured out how to order any of thousands of DVDs off of Netflix—and have them delivered to our homes—with no late fees.

And we have figured out how to take pictures on our cell phones—and email those pictures instantaneously halfway around the world so our friends and family can see them.

And get instant ESPN sports reports on those cell phones.

But we haven't figured out how to translate our fundamental decency into policy.

So that we are all covered with one system of national health insurance.

So that war becomes a relic.

So that poverty is eradicated.

In honor of our moms, we dedicate our lives to figure this out.

2006:

I drive my father to an orthopedic clinic in Bethesda. His feet have been giving him trouble for a long time. He's eighty-seven years old, and his short-term memory has slipped. But he can recall vivid details from when he was one of four kids in the family. "We were invisible," he tells me. "It was like we didn't exist. That was my childhood."

Around the corner from the clinic is the block where Freedom House briefly existed thirty-seven years ago. I steer the car in that direction and slow down. The county parking garage that I emblazoned with an antiwar slogan in 1969 is still there, painted bright white. The bungalow that was across the street has been gone for decades; in its place now is a Zagat-rated restaurant.

When we get back to the apartment, my mother is in the recliner, feet up as the doctor has urged to reduce the swelling in her
legs. She struggles to get around with a walker. Her own memory is
fading. Yet what she says can stop me in my tracks. Like, "Life is
magical, sometimes." And, "Dead people can be very real." And, remembering something her uncle used to say: "We're only human,
and sometimes not even that."

I think of her father, a dedicated socialist with a sparkling sense
of humor, whom she adored. He died when she was in her thirties,
when I was just a few years old. Now she likes to hear a recording
of Yiddish songs; she knows some of them from meetings of the
Workmen's Circle branch where her father often brought her during the 1920s and '30s in Brooklyn. Next to the recliner is a book of
such songs; when she picks it up, she sings a few, still remembering
the melodies. One, written in 1889, has a verse that goes: "We are
driven and despised, we are tortured and persecuted, for we cherish
the poor and the weak."

No buzzards were gliding overhead, but several helicopters circled,
under black sky tinged blue. On the shore of a stunning bay at a
placid moment, the state prepared to kill.

Outside the gates of San Quentin, people gathered to protest the
impending execution of Stanley Tookie Williams, a former gang
leader. Hundreds became thousands during the last minutes of
December 13, 2005, as the midnight hour approached. Rage and
calming prayers were in the air.

The operative God of the night was a governor. "Without an
apology and atonement for these senseless and brutal killings, there
can be no redemption," Arnold Schwarzenegger had just declared.

But at the prison gates, there were signs.

"The weak can never forgive."

"No Death in My Name."

"Executions teach vengeance and violence."

The execution was scheduled for 12:01 A.M. Twenty-five minutes before then, people outside the gates began to sing "We Shall Overcome."

"We shall live in peace . . ."

Overhead, the helicopters kept circling; high-tech buzzards.

"An eye for an eye makes the whole world blind," said one sign.

Elsewhere in the crowd, another asked: "Are we blind yet?"

At seven minutes to midnight, it occurred to me how much the ritual countdown to execution resembles the Doomsday Clock invented by atomic scientists several decades ago to estimate the world's proximity to nuclear annihilation.

From the stage, speakers praised Williams' renunciation of violence, his advocacy for nonviolence.

At two minutes before midnight, a TV news correspondent stood on the roof of a white van, readying a report for the top of the hour. At midnight the standup report began. It ended at 12:02 A.M.

"No to Death Machine Careerism," a sign said.

"As you do unto the least of these, you do unto me," another sign said.

Full silence took hold at 12:24 A.M.

Then, an old song again. ". . . We shall . . . overcome . . . some . . . day."

An announcement came at 12:38 A.M.; Stanley Tookie Williams was dead.

The country was no safer. Just more violent. The sanctity of life not upheld, just violated.

"It's over," said a speaker. "But it's not over."

From San Quentin to Iraq, in the name of the murdered, the state murdered; in the name of the fallen, more killed and fell. The warfare state taught vengeance and violence most profoundly with the daily lessons of acceptance, example, and budget.

"They have destroyed and are destroying hundreds of thousands of lives and do not know it and do not want to know it," James Baldwin wrote. He added: "But it is not permissible that the authors of devastation should also be innocent. It is the innocence which constitutes the crime."

––––––––

While the U.S. military occupation fueled Iraq's descent into civil war, American news media often returned to the well of sorrows being plumbed by the long trial of Saddam Hussein and top subordinates. In 2006 one of the front-page *New York Times* stories concentrated on former deputy prime minister Tariq Aziz; a color photograph showed him wearing what the article described as "an open-necked hospital gown, with a patient's plastic identification tag on his wrist." He looked gaunt, very different from the last time I saw him—at a January 2003 meeting in his Baghdad office, eight weeks before the invasion began—when he was still portly in one of his well-tailored business suits.

Under Saddam's command, Aziz had been Iraq's most visible diplomat. A very smooth talker. Up close, he seemed equally comfortable in a military uniform or a suit, using his language skills the way a cosmetician might apply makeup to a corpse. The urbanity of evil.

We may assume that such abysmal moral fiber is a world away from the truly civilized and decent—that U.S. leaders are cut from entirely different cloth. But so many have comfortably supported a succession of indefensible wars. In some respects, the terrible compromises and crimes of Tariq Aziz are more explainable than ones that are routine in U.S. politics. Aziz had good reason to fear for his life—and the lives of loved ones—if he ran afoul of Saddam. In contrast, many American politicians have gone along with lethal policies because of fear that dissent might cost them reelection, prestige, money, power.

––––––––

More than three decades after Fred Branfman worked to stop the bombing of Laos, he wrote about "the effect on the biosphere of the interaction between global warming, biodiversity loss, water aquifer depletion, chemical contamination, and a wide variety of other new threats to the biospheric systems upon which human life depends."

Branfman was far from optimistic: "It is a new problem for humans, and we have not only been slow to respond but are in fact accelerating our long-term suicide. When I look at this issue alone, let alone the likelihood of increasingly technologically sophisticated terrorism and its impact on Western societies, and the threats facing the Third World, I find it hard to have much 'hope' that the species will better itself in coming decades." He went on:

> But I have also reached a point in my self-inquiries where I came to dislike the whole notion of "hope." If I need to have "hope" to motivate me, what will I do when I see no rational reason for hope? If I can be "hopeful," then I can also be "hopeless," and I do not like feeling hopeless. I came to see "hope" as just one more of the many games that we humans devise to keep us occupied.
>
> When I looked more deeply at my own life, I noticed that my life was not now and never had been built around "hope." Laos was an example. I went there, I learned to love the peasants, the bombing shocked my psyche and soul to the core, and I responded—not because I was hopeful or hopeless, but because I was alive.

In the United States it's easy to get the impression that we're supposed to be—or at least *seem*—optimistic. Commonly, the optimism is forced, the despair private. The media and political landscapes of the country are inhospitable to broad pessimism. "American politics is about optimism," a leading pundit, Mark Shields, declared on national television a few months into the twenty-first century. "Americans are the most optimistic people on the planet." That sounds like a description, but functions more like a prescription. Such cheery statements end up instructing the public as to proper attitudes. Touring the Gulf Coast a year after Hurricane Katrina hit, President Bush proclaimed: "Optimism is the only option."

Often an implicit message is that Americans who lack the appropriate optimism are of insufficient mettle, resilience, or patriotism. Like a smile forced to override private despair, an exterior of optimism can be a way of coping with personal alienation—and a

zone for passivity in the face of impending catastrophe. Sunny evasions are apt to make life more disorienting. Pressure to appear
hopeful pushes us farther from the genuine.

———

Forced optimism may be all the more welcome because it's so es-
tranged from current realities. The planet is now at its worst in
terms of prospects for human survival. Of course the very nature of
life involves death, but now death has within its reach the simultaneous end of everyone. Maybe whistling past graveyards has come
to seem natural.

However much and whatever ways the specter of the Bomb af-
fixed itself to our psyches, we mostly absorbed it out of plain sight.
It was there and not there, too horrendous to be insignificant and
too horrendous to be taken out and looked at on a regular basis. Our
foreboding was, in the long run, numbing and liable to be boring,
yet embedded in deep folds of ourselves, with full articulation of its
terrifying constant almost impossible. An end-of-the-world movie
like *On the Beach* could have chilling effects on viewers but probably little staying power except for a wispy sense of doom. (I can
never hear or think of the song "Waltzing Matilda" without recalling its haunting role on the movie's soundtrack. But for that matter,
these days I can't hear Gershwin's "Rhapsody in Blue" without
thinking of being on hold with United Airlines.) With the national
leadership serving as a sort of atomic priesthood, faith in ultimate
weaponry has withstood the strongest challenges in our midst.

With prominent individuals and groups like Physicians for
Social Responsibility evoking the horrors of thermonuclear holocaust, the nuclear freeze movement of the early 1980s jarred many
Americans. But, overall, the effects were not long-lasting. Fear—
particularly about a matter so visceral yet somehow abstracted as
nuclear dangers—has proved to be a shoddy basis for sustaining
political momentum. The efforts of many "arms control" advocates,
opting for a moderate path, turned into backpedaling arguments
over the best ways to manage nuclear arsenals. On the other hand,

fifteen years after people heard Dr. Helen Caldicott eloquently warn
that humanity had just ten years to turn the arms race around or all
would be finished, she was in danger of sounding more like Chicken
Little than Cassandra. There would be no way to overstate the ultimate peril, but there were plenty of ways to render oneself less per-
suasive over time.

The latest technology for doomsday has remained as tuned-up
as ever. In 2006, when the National Nuclear Security Administration announced that the U.S. government had just eliminated its
final W56 nuclear warhead—a 1.2 megaton model from the
1960s—self-congratulation was in the air. Several hundred W56s
had been at the tip of Minuteman intercontinental ballistic missiles, aimed at silos in the Soviet Union, until removal from the U.S.
arsenal at the end of the Cold War; now not a single W56 would
exist. "Dismantling the last W56 warhead," an official statement
said, "shows our firm commitment to reducing the size of the nation's nuclear weapons stockpile to the lowest levels necessary for
national security needs." Meanwhile, the *Washington Post* reported, Congress and the White House were resolutely moving
ahead with plans for "a new generation of U.S. nuclear weapons"
under the rubric of the Reliable Replacement Warhead program:
"The nation's two nuclear weapons design centers, the Los Alamos
and Lawrence Livermore national laboratories, are competing to design the first RRW. . . . A second RRW design competition may provide an opportunity to the losing lab." In 2007 the United States
had retained at least ten thousand nuclear bombs and warheads.

We've had no way of really knowing how near annihilation might
be. But our lives have flashed with scarcely believable human-made
lightning—the evidence of things truly obscene, of officialdom
gone mad—photos and footage of mushroom clouds, and routinely
set-aside descriptions starting with *Hiroshima*. Waiting on the nuclear thunder.

Five decades after *Sputnik*, such apocalyptic dangers are still present, but from Americans in my generation the most articulated fears have to do with running out of money before breath. The USA is certainly no place to be old, sick, and low on funds. Huge medical bills and hazards of second-class care loom ahead. For people whose childhoods fell between victory over Japan and evacuation from Saigon, the twenty-first century has brought the time-honored and perfectly understandable quest to avoid dying before necessary—and to avoid living final years or seeing loved ones living final years in misery. Under such circumstances, self obsession may seem unavoidable.

There must be better options. But they're apt to be obscured, most of all, by our own over-scheduled passivity; by who we figure we are, who we've allowed ourselves to become. The very word "options" is likely to have a consumer ring to it (extras on a new car, clauses in a contract). We buy in and consume, mostly selecting from prefab choices—even though, looking back, the best of life's changes have usually come from creating options instead of choosing from the ones in stock.

When biologist George Wald said that "we are under repeated pressure to accept things that are presented to us as settled—decisions that have been made," the comment had everything to do with his observation that "our government has become preoccupied with death, with the business of killing and being killed." The curtailing of our own sense of real options is a concentric process, encircling our personal lives and our sense of community, national purpose, and global possibilities; circumscribing the ways that we, and the world around us, might change. Four decades after Wald's anguished speech "A Generation in Search of a Future," many of the accepted "facts of life" are still "facts of death"—blotting out horizons, stunting imaginations, holding tongues, limiting capacities to nurture or defend life. We are still in search of a future.

And we're brought up short by the precious presence and unspeakable absence of love. "All of us know, whether or not we are able to admit it, that mirrors can only lie," James Baldwin wrote, "that death by drowning is all that awaits one there. It is for this reason that love is so desperately sought and so cunningly avoided. Love takes off the masks that we fear we cannot live without and know we cannot live within." This love exists "not in the infantile American sense of being made happy but in the tough and universal sense of quest and daring and growth."

The freezing of love into small spaces, part of the numbing of America, proceeds in tandem with the warfare state. It's easier to not feel others' pain when we can't feel too much ourselves.

If we want a future that sustains life, we'd better create it ourselves.

Notes

EPIGRAPHS

xv   Cormac McCarthy, *No Country for Old Men* (New York: Alfred A. Knopf, 2005), p. 227.

"Eve of Destruction" was written by P. F. Sloan.

Thich Nhat Hanh, *Our Appointment with Life* (Berkeley, CA: Parallax Press, 1990); excerpted in Jean Smith, ed., *365 Zen: Daily Readings* (New York: HarperSanFrancisco, 1999).

CHAPTER 1: COLD WAR CHILDHOOD

1   "America is the greatest force": Eisenhower, April 5, 1954; quoted in Norman Solomon, *The Power of Babble* (New York: Dell, 1992), p. 108.

1   "Without God there could be no": Eisenhower, February 27, 1955; quoted in Solomon, *The Power of Babble*, p. 108.

1   "a new era in history had begun": *Time*, October 14, 1957.

2   "The U.S. had lost its lead": ibid.

2   "And in six months we may all": quoted in *Washington Post and Times Herald*, October 16, 1957.

2   "does not raise my apprehension": quoted in *New York Times*, October 20, 1957.

2   "outer-space raspberry to a decade": quoted in *Time*, October 28, 1957.

2   Symington statement: *Washington Post and Times Herald*, October 15, 1957.

2   Thrust of first-stage rockets: *U.S. News & World Report*, October 18, 1957.

2   "The few who are allowed": Lippmann, *Los Angeles Times*, October 11, 1957. The newspaper headlined the syndicated column "Analysis by Light of the Sputnik."

3   "the mild panic that has seized": *New York Times*, October 20, 1957.

3   "In a free society such as ours": *New York Times*, October 13, 1957.

3   The first U.S. space bureau was named the Advanced Research Projects Agency.

4   "a big Communist 'fear' campaign": *Los Angeles Examiner*, March 24, 1955.

4   "Evidence of a world-wide propaganda": *Washington Post*, March 1955.

4   "The Nevada tests are being conducted": *Chicago Daily News*, March 25, 1955.

4   "it is not impossible to suppose": quoted in *Life*, June 1980, p. 38.

4   The Borden milk-products company was a big sponsor of the Disney television show.

5   "Linus Pauling published an article": Pauling, "How Dangerous Is Radioactive Fallout?" *Foreign Policy Bulletin*, June 15, 1957, p. 149.

5   "we have reduced fallout from bombs": quoted in *New York Times*, June 27, 1957; cited in Wim A. Smit and Peter Boskma, "Laser Fusion," *Bulletin of the Atomic Scientists*, December 1980, p. 34.

5   For an account of the petition drive by scientists to halt atmospheric nuclear explosions, see Linus Pauling, *No More War* (New York: Dodd, Mead, 1958), pp. 160, 171–178.

8   "Some schools derive 90 percent": quoted in Robert Jungk,
       Brighter Than a Thousand Suns (New York: Harcourt Brace,
       1958), p. 248. Morrison spoke at an annual forum sponsored
       by the *New York Herald Tribune*.

8   "In 1939 when we tried": quoted in George Fielding Eliot, *The
       H Bomb* (New York: Didier, 1950), pp. 118–119.

9   "It is clear that the use": quoted in Herbert York, *The Advisors:
       Oppenheimer, Teller, and the Superbomb* (San Francisco: W. H.
       Freeman and Co., 1976), p. 155.

12   "I'm ashamed I had any part": quoted in Christopher Paul
       Denis and Michael Denis, *Favorite Families of TV* (New York:
       Carol Publishing, 1991), pp. 50–52.

13   "Excuse me, Mrs., but": John Hersey, *The Child Buyer* (New
       York: Alfred A. Knopf, 1960), p. 12.

13   "in charge of materials procurement": ibid., p. 23.

13   "When a commodity that you need": ibid., p. 33.

14   "squarely on the table": ibid., pp. 129–130.

14   "As you know, we live in": ibid., p. 238.

14   memorandum, released into the hearing record: ibid.,
       pp. 204–208.

15   "I guess Mr. Jones is really": ibid., pp. 256–257.

15   "I was wondering about that": ibid., p. 258.

16   "the Soviet military build-up": October 22, 1962, "Radio-TV
       Address of the President to the Nation from the White House";
       Associated Press, "Twenty Years After the Cuban Missile Cri-
       sis," October 22, 1982. Some circulated versions of the quote are
       not fully accurate, most importantly substituting "risk the
       course" for "risk the costs" of worldwide nuclear war. See also
       Lawrence Chang and Peter Kornbluh, eds., *The Cuban Missile
       Crisis, 1962: A National Security Archive Documents Reader*
       (New York: New Press, 1992), pp. 150–154.

17   "as if a feast had been": Charles Dickens, *Great Expectations*
       (New York: Oxford University Press, 1993), chapter XI, p. 84.

CHAPTER 2: INNOCENCE ON THE EVE OF DESTRUCTION

19   "the courageous decision that Communism's advance": quoted in Edward Jay Epstein, *Between Fact and Fiction* (New York: Vintage Books, 1975), p. 215.

19   Bob Dylan's performance at the Washington Coliseum was on November 28, 1965.

20   Norman Mailer, *Why Are We in Vietnam?* (New York: G. P. Putnam's Sons, 1967).

21   "There was the shared enthusiasm": Jeff Nuttall, *Bomb Culture* (London: Paladin, 1970), p. 129. The book was first published in 1968 by MacGibbon & Kee Ltd.

22   "the military-industrial complex": Eisenhower, January 17, 1961.

22   "well known as the leader": "Sputnik Biographies—Wernher von Braun (1912–1977)," NASA website, http://history.nasa .gov/sputnik/braun.html.

23   "The scientist is not responsible": quoted in York, *The Advisors*, p. 71.

23   "technically sweet problem": quoted by Sehdev Kumar in an article headlined "Scientists reveled in the mathematics of the bomb and ignored its evil power," *Kitchener-Waterloo (ON, Canada) Record,* August 5, 1995. Oppenheimer also said: "If you are a scientist you believe that it is good to find out how the world works; what the realities are; that it is good to turn over to mankind at large the greatest possible power to control the world and to deal with it according to its lights and values." (Brian Easlea, *Fathering the Unthinkable: Masculinity, Scientists, and the Nuclear Arms Race* [London: Pluto Press, 1983], p. 129; cited in Gray Brechin, *Imperial San Francisco: Urban Power, Earthly Ruin* [Berkeley: University of California Press, 1999], p. 355)

23   For a detailed account of the intersection between the civil rights movement and the Vietnam War, see Taylor Branch, *At Canaan's Edge: America in the King Years 1965–68* (New York: Simon & Schuster, 2006).

26   While serving as Maryland's governor, Spiro Agnew became
      Richard Nixon's running mate in 1968 and then vice president
      of the United States—a position he held for nearly five years
      until resigning in October 1973 as part of a plea-bargain agree-
      ment with the U.S. Justice Department. The deal spared him jail
      time for failing to pay income tax on graft he received while he
      was governor.

26   "Christ and Moses standing": Lenny Bruce, *How to Talk Dirty
      and Influence People* (Chicago: Playboy Press, 1965), p. 184.

27   "My defense? I was a soldier": Bruce's bit was based on the
      poem "A Devout Meditation in Memory of Adolf Eichmann,"
      which appeared in Thomas Merton's book *Raids on the Un-
      speakable* (New York: New Directions, 1964), p. 46.

27   "By bombing North Vietnam": *Silver Spring Gazette* (Sum-
      mer 1966).

CHAPTER 3: REVULSION AND REVOLT

29   "the largest building in Southeast Asia": Paul N. Edwards, *The
      Closed World: Computers and the Politics of Discourse in Cold
      War America* (Cambridge, MA: MIT Press, 1996), pp. 3–4.

30   In his book *Famous Long Ago: My Life and Hard Times with
      Liberation News Service* (Boston: Beacon Press, 1970), LNS co-
      founder Raymond Mungo did not shy away from making nega-
      tive comments about fellow '60s activists. But the book de-
      scribed Bill Higgs in only glowing terms—"our faithful lawyer
      friend" (p. 63) "who aided us, scraped up money for us, advised
      us, housed our reporters, wrote for us, and, from time to time,
      criticized us" (p. 145), "the saintly Bill Higgs" (p. 168).

31   I lost track of Bill Higgs for about ten years, until one wintry
      day in 1980 when we literally crossed paths on Capitol Hill. Bill
      looked and sounded more weary than I could remember. He
      told me that he'd be relocating to Mexico soon. I got the im-
      pression that the move had to do with the cost of living.

32   "Both Israelis and Arabs": I. F. Stone, "Holy War," *New York Re-

view of Books, August 3, 1967; reprinted in Neil Middleton, ed., *The I. F. Stone's Weekly Reader* (New York: Random House, 1973), pp. 287–291; quoted in Taylor Branch, *At Canaan's Edge: America in the King Years 1965–68* (New York: Simon & Schuster, 2006), p. 618.

33 "It was as if dismalness": D. H. Lawrence, *Lady Chatterley's Lover* (New York: Modern Library, 1993), pp. 227–228.

34 "Around us are pseudo-events": R.D. Laing, *The Politics of Experience* (New York: Ballantine Books, 1968), p. 11.

34 "Our social realities are so ugly": ibid.

34 "In order to rationalize our": ibid., pp. 57–58.

35 "At this moment in history": ibid., p. 78.

35 "The flower children were all": James Baldwin, *No Name in the Street* (New York: Dial Press, 1972), pp. 183–184.

36 "Their flowers had the validity": ibid., p. 184.

36 "Since Martin's death . . . something has altered in me, something has gone away," James Baldwin wrote. "Perhaps even more than the death itself, the manner of his death has forced me into a judgment concerning human life and human beings which I have always been reluctant to make—indeed, I can see that a great deal of what the knowledgeable would call my lifestyle is dictated by this reluctance. Incontestably, alas, most people are not, in action, worth very much; and yet, every human being is an unprecedented miracle. One tries to treat them as the miracles they are, while trying to protect oneself against the disasters they've become. This is not very different from the act of faith demanded by all those marches and petitions while Martin was still alive. One could scarcely be deluded by Americans anymore, one scarcely dared expect anything from the great, vast, blank generality; and yet one was compelled to demand of Americans—and for their sakes, after all—a generosity, a clarity, and a nobility which they did not dream of demanding of themselves. . . . Perhaps, however, the moral of the story (and the hope of the world) lies in what one demands, not of others, but of oneself." (*No Name in the Street*, pp. 9–10)

37   "They were in the streets": ibid., p. 187.

38   "What has happened is that the pressure": Nuttall, *Bomb Culture*, p. 9. The author added: "It is the violence of Che Guevara, his life, his rapacious good looks, his fabulous death, which constitute his appeal. Nobody decorates their bed-sitter with posters of Bolivian miners."

38   "We had espoused an evil": ibid., pp. 18–19.

38   "No longer could teacher, magistrate": ibid., p. 19.

39   "At the point of the dropping": ibid., p. 20.

40   "LNS Backs Stones in Ideological Rift": quoted in Mungo, *Famous Long Ago*, p. 187. As with many an "ideological rift" of the era, time would tell a different tale. In the late 1960s, Mick Jagger enjoyed tweaking John Lennon in public, suggesting among other things that Lennon would benefit from reading Marx. But Jagger turned out to be much more accommodating to war and corporate priorities than John Lennon, whose peace activism sparked intensive FBI surveillance and harassment during 1971 and 1972. For several decades afterward, the Rolling Stones combined stellar rock 'n' roll with a steady embrace of corporatism; Stones tour concerts, led by Jagger and sponsored by multinational beer brands and the like, cashed in with top-dollar ticket prices and commercial tie-ins. Politically conscious Stones songs proved to be rare. The band's 2005 antiwar tune denouncing top neo-conservatives, "Sweet Neo Con," was refreshing but hardly a profile in courage.

42   "School Officials Will Meet": *Washington Star*, January 14, 1969.

43   "REVOLT For Peace" photo: *Washington Post*, June 4, 1969.

45   George Wald spoke at MIT on March 4, 1969.

CHAPTER 4: TO THE MOON AND TO WOODSTOCK

50   "We took space back quickly": Michael Herr, *Dispatches* (New York: Vintage International, 1977), p. 71.

51   "Between 100,000 and 250,000 persons": Mungo, *Famous Long Ago*, p. 20.

52   "I guess we all agreed": ibid., p. 24.

53   "we came over to the New Age": ibid., p. 187.

53   "I no longer have *any* kind": ibid., p. 189.

55   "The drugs, whilst accelerating": Nuttall, *Bomb Culture* , p. 241.

57   "What satisfaction is now possible": Ginsberg, *International Times* (London), No. 6, January 1967; quoted in Nuttall, *Bomb Culture*, p. 192.

57   "No one pointed out to Ginsberg": Nuttall, *Bomb Culture*, p. 192. Nuttall observed: "Possibly the gravest of the psychological gashes inflicted by the bomb is the way in which the hunger for regenerative spirituality becomes discolored into a vapid pseudo-oriental anti-materialism which says 'Why worry about the world and the human species? They're not real anyway.'" (p. 134)

57   "I want to say that drugs": ibid., p. 238.

57   "My retrospective attitude to LSD is that when one has received the message, one hangs up the phone," Alan Watts insightfully wrote in the early 1970s. "I think I have learned from it as much as I can, and, for my own sake, would not be sorry if I could never use it again. But it is not, I believe, generally known that very many of those who had constructive experiences with LSD, or other psychedelics, have turned from drugs to spiritual disciplines—abandoning their water-wings and learning to swim. Without the catalytic experience of the drug they might never have come to this point, and thus my feeling about psychedelic chemicals, as about most other drugs (despite the vague sense of the word), is that they should serve as medicine rather than diet." (Alan Watts, *In My Own Way: An Autobiography* [New York: Pantheon Books, 1972], p. 347)

58   "were giving way to tract homes": John Markoff, *What the Dormouse Said: How the 60s Counterculture Shaped the Personal Computer Industry* (New York: Viking, 2005), p. 1.

58 For information on Pentagon and NASA funding for key computer research at Stanford Research Institute, see ibid., especially pp. 78, 213.

58 "Computer speed and capacity": ibid., p. x.

59 "It's the next thing after acid": quoted in ibid., p. 165.

59 "Sandy Miranda, a self-styled": ibid., pp. 204–205.

59 employees whose jobs included such activities as: ibid., p. 205.

60 *Washington Post*, September 29, 1969. The headline was "He 'Had to Be Free': Maryland Dropout Defends Integrity." In retrospect, maybe the most interesting quote in the article was this one: "The most outstanding thing about me is that I don't know what I am."

63 The title of the Jefferson Airplane song was "We Can Be Together."

63 "plays the key role": Charles A. Reich, *The Greening of America* (New York: Random House, 1970), p. 304.

64 "The revolution must be cultural": ibid., p. 306.

64 "The political activists have had": ibid., p. 302.

64 "The great error of our times": ibid., pp. 356–357.

64 "The whole edifice of the Corporate": ibid., p. 216.

64 "It comes into being the moment": ibid., p. 225.

65 "The new generation cannot be": ibid., p. 311.

65 "the whole Corporate State rests": ibid., p. 348.

65 "By the standards of history": ibid., p. 393.

CHAPTER 5: WAR ON THE HOME FRONT

68 "All Aboard" was written by McKinley Morganfield, a.k.a. Muddy Waters. Most of the twenty tracks on *Fathers and Sons* were recorded during a three-day session at the Chess Records studios in Chicago, and the rest were performed live the following night—April 24, 1969—at an event in the same city with the Zeitgeist name "Super Cosmic Joy-Scout Jamboree."

71   "intend to put the blood": Transcript, Senate Foreign Relations
       Committee, February 27, 1968.

72   "The American majority is against": *Saturday Review*, Novem-
       ber 13, 1971. The title of Schrag's article was "The Ellsberg
       Affair."

72   Fred Branfman sent me those recollections in May 2006. He
       added: "I cannot, even now, describe the shock, outrage and hor-
       ror that I experienced hearing these reports from the refugees.
       I could not, and even today cannot, fathom how humanity had
       reached the point when the richest and most sophisticated of
       the species could carry out a policy of what was in fact system-
       atic murder of the poorest and weakest of the species—inno-
       cent, subsistence-level farmers who had not only not commit-
       ted any offense against their murderers, but DIDN'T EVEN
       KNOW WHO THEY WERE.
           "The first level of shock was simply realizing that my coun-
       try, the United States, was conducting these massive bombing
       raids without the world even knowing. At that time, September
       1969, the official U.S. position was that U.S. planes had never
       dropped a single bomb in Laos. (It wasn't until March 1970 that
       Richard Nixon finally admitted this was a lie and that the U.S.
       had been bombing in Laos for the previous six years, although
       he and the U.S. government continued to maintain the most
       monstrous lie of all until today: that the U.S. only bombed "mili-
       tary" targets and avoided hitting civilians.) I knew from South
       Vietnam that my leaders were lying and murdering their way
       into history. But realizing it in this personal way, in a Laotian
       refugee camp, with the victims two feet away, transformed this
       intellectual knowledge into a deeply felt emotional experience."
           Branfman worked in Southeast Asia and back in the United
       States for many years to end the bombing and halt the U.S. war.
       Looking back, he wrote: "I firmly believe that the peace move-
       ment as a whole was a restraining influence on the Johnson and
       Nixon administrations, which we know from the tape-recorded
       conversations of Johnson and Nixon themselves. There is also
       no question that the peace movement as a whole played a key

role in the two key U.S. decisions of the 1971–75 period, when I was active. The movement played a major role in the close [congressional] vote to end U.S. bombing of Cambodia in the summer of 1973 and the decision to reduce aid to [South Vietnam's war-waging Premier] Thieu from $1.2 billion to $700 million in the winter of 1975."

74   "How many did we kill in Laos?": quoted in Daniel Ellsberg, *Secrets: A Memoir of Vietnam and the Pentagon Papers* (New York: Viking, 2002), p. 418.

74   "I'll see that the United States": quoted in ibid., p. 419.

75   "I have asked our Vietnam staff": quoted in Edward Jay Epstein, *Between Fact and Fiction* (New York: Vintage Books, 1975), pp. 227–228.

75   Vietnam bombing tonnage: Sidney Lens, *The Forging of the American Empire* (Sterling, VA: Pluto Press, 2003), p. 429.

76   "the explosive equivalent of": Ellsberg, *Secrets*, p. 420.

CHAPTER 6: REGROUPING IN THE '70S

85   "The United States knows that peaceful": Eisenhower speech to U.N. General Assembly, December 8, 1953.

86   "Protesters Vow to Close Trojan N-Plant": *Oregonian*, August 7, 1977.

86   "Oregon state police Monday arrested": *Oregonian*, August 9, 1977.

87   "A District Court jury last night": *New York Times*, December 18, 1977.

88   After the mass acquittal at the first trial of Trojan protesters, the liberal *Oregon Times* magazine noted, "The *Oregonian* was so upset that they editorialized not once, but twice, against the verdict, headlining it 'Travesy at Trojan.' . . . What really hurt was the defense's well-advertised boast that they would 'put nuclear power on trial.'"

88   In May 2006—after being a symbol of nuclear power on the banks of the Columbia River along Interstate 5 for more than

thirty years—the Trojan plant's 499-foot cooling tower under-
went detonation. It instantly became a fifteen-foot-tall pile of
rubble. By then, decommissioning of the plant had cost upwards of $400 million.

CHAPTER 7: AGENCIES OF ANNIHILATION

93   Columbia High School near Hanford changed its name to Rich-
     land High School in 1982.

93   "It is the sane ones, the well-adapted ones": Merton's brief
     essay titled "A Devout Memory of Adolf Eichmann."

93   For details on U.S. soldiers sent into Nagasaki and Hiroshima
     after the atomic bombings, see Harvey Wasserman and
     Norman Solomon, *Killing Our Own: The Disaster of America's
     Experience with Atomic Radiation* (New York: Delacorte Press,
     1982), pp. 6–30.

93   Information on the frequency of Factor VIII deficiencies came
     from my interview with Clapp's hematologist, Dr. Scott Good-
     night of the Oregon Health Sciences Center.

95   Another veteran I got to know in 1979 was James J. McDaniel,
     a longtime Weyerhauser Company mechanic from southwest-
     ern Washington state who had been among the few hundred
     Marines quartered in a bombed-out waterfront hotel near the
     Nagasaki blast center, where they were ordered to do cleanup.
     In 1975 he was diagnosed with Waldenstrom's macroglobuline-
     mia, a rare cancer of bone marrow involving overproduction of
     blood protein.

96   *Science,* August 19, 1983. Under the article's title "Study
     of Atomic Veterans Fuels Controversy," the subhead stated:
     "Criticism of a study of U.S. soldiers in Hiroshima and
     Nagasaki illustrates the pitfalls of dressing up a political
     study as purely a scientific investigation."

99   Ten months after interviewing Irma Thomas in her living
     room, I heard a speech by Rose Mackelprang at the University
     of Utah. Mackelprang was from a small town in northern Ari-

zona, an area hit hard by fallout from a dozen years of aboveground nuclear testing in Nevada. "My husband and I moved to
Fredonia in 1948," she said. "It's just a little town, and we have
a very happy atmosphere down there. We did rather, anyway.
They raise their own gardens and most of 'em have their own
cows, a lot of them do, and they have gardens and bottle their
own food, put it up, store it, that's just the life of a small community." Rose Mackelprang's husband, Gayneld, became a
teacher in the public schools of Fredonia, where the lumber industry was taking on economic importance alongside farming
and livestock. "At that time, when they started the testing in
Nevada, it'd be at dawn when the tests would go off and we
could see this big light and then the ground would shake, it'd
billow up, you could see the big mushroom cloud go way up
and it was really quite exciting, it was different, we didn't really
know that much about it. As far as we knew, why, it was really
going to help us out, it was really something that our government was doing and it would be for our own good. We trusted
the government, we figured that it was necessary because, after
all, the government does look after us, and they're over the people and they will take care of anything that needs to be taken
care of to see that it's healthy, or otherwise. . . . So we didn't
worry about it." (National Conference for a Comprehensive
Test Ban, Salt Lake City, December 12, 1980)

99   In 1960 the population of Fredonia was 643. By 1965 four had
passed away from leukemia—a truck driver, who died at age
forty-eight; a fourteen-year-old girl; a lumber crane operator,
thirty-six; and Gayneld Mackelprang, by that time forty-three
years old and superintendent of the Fredonia Public Schools. A
secret memorandum by the U.S. Public Health Service's leukemia unit director, Dr. Clark W. Heath Jr., noted: "This number
of cases is approximately 20 times greater than expected." In
the entire previous decade 1950 to 1960 no cases of leukemia
had been reported among Fredonia residents. The memo, dated
August 4, 1966, and sent to the head of the federal agency's
Communicable Disease Center, was marked "FOR ADMINISTRA-

TIVE USE ONLY, NOT FOR PUBLICATION." (Wasserman and Solomon, *Killing Our Own*, p. 63)

100   "Seven years ago, government scientists": Norman Solomon, Pacific News Service, *San Francisco Sunday Examiner & Chronicle*, October 18, 1981. In Canada, the *Toronto Star* published the article on the same day.

101   "The atomic bomb is a marvelous gift": quoted in Carol Felsenthal, *The Sweetheart of the Silent Majority: The Biography of Phyllis Schlafly* (New York: Doubleday, 1981), p. 51.

102   "Very late one autumn night": Robert Scheer, *With Enough Shovels: Reagan, Bush, and Nuclear War* (New York: Vintage Books, 1983), p. 18.

102   "My fellow Americans, I am pleased": Ronald Reagan, August 11, 1984.

103   "As the war was dragging on": From the *Chicago Sun-Times* wire service, the piece appeared in the *Oregonian* on August 23, 1982.

104   "a break in the momentum": quoted in *New York Times*, September 4, 1983.

105   "In Franz Kafka's classic novel": *Oakland Tribune*, November 2, 1984.

107   "voted to end this insane": quoted in United Press International, April 3, 1984.

108   "I support the air-launch cruise missile": quoted in *New York Times*, October 22, 1984.

CHAPTER 8: COLD WAR SEQUEL

110   "reacted with an indifferent": quoted in *Times Herald-Record* (Middletown, NY), November 24, 1985. Other accounts of the demonstration at West Point appeared in the *Newburgh Evening News* and the Rockland *Sunday Journal-News*.

111   "to express concern about rights violations": *New York Times*, February 26, 1985.

112   "The U.S. government killed my brother": quoted by author in *Houston Chronicle*, April 30, 1987.

112   "The Central Intelligence Agency is very": quoted by author in *Witness Magazine*, June 1987.

113   For details on media spin about the Gorbachev moratorium on nuclear testing, see Martin A. Lee and Norman Solomon, *Unreliable Sources: A Guide to Detecting Bias in News Media* (New York: Carol Publishing, 1990), pp. 274–275.

114   "Two American peace activists": Associated Press, February 19, 1986.

114   "urging President Reagan to accept": *Chicago Tribune*, February 20, 1986. The brief article, by the *Tribune*'s Moscow bureau chief, included basic inaccuracies. In the newspaper's account, I became Anthony Guarisco and vice versa: So, reportedly, Guarisco "was hauled out the door, fireman-style, over the shoulder of a U.S. marine guard." And I was paraphrased as saying that I "was exposed to harmful amounts of radiation during a postwar U.S. atomic test" and was suffering "kidney, bladder and prostate problems caused by the fallout." The person who "walks with a cane" and "exited the building under his own power" was reported to be me, not Anthony. I called the foreign desk of the *Chicago Tribune* and urged a correction—but an editor told me that none was needed because the mistakes were inadvertent. More than twenty years later, that *Tribune* article was intact on electronic databases without any correction. The reporter who wrote the story, Thom Shanker, had long since moved on. In 2007, Shanker was in his tenth year at the *New York Times*, covering U.S. military policies from Washington.

116   A few weeks earlier in the fall of 1987, the current Soviet leader Mikhail Gorbachev had declared: "The guilt of Stalin and his immediate entourage before the party and the people for the wholesale repressive measures and acts of lawlessness is enormous and unforgivable. It required no small courage of the party and its leadership, headed by Nikita Khrushchev, to criticize the [Stalin] personality cult and its consequences."

118   "a marvel" and "two days of almost": quoted in Lee and
      Solomon, *Unreliable Sources,* paperback edition, p. xvii.

118   "a term meaning dead or wounded": quoted in ibid., p. xviii.

119   "was virtually flawless": quoted in ibid., p. xix.

119   Associated Press cited sources: AP, March 22, 1991.

119   "It's really not a number": Colin Powell quoted in *New York
      Times,* March 23, 1991.

119   "Coverage of the Gulf crisis": Lee and Solomon, *Unreliable
      Sources,* p. xxiii.

CHAPTER 9: SLICK TORCH

121   "a merger of governmental": Charles A. Reich, *Opposing the
      System* (New York: Crown Publishers, 1995), p. 17.

122   "we deny and repress the fact": ibid., p. 41.

122   "There will be no relief": ibid., p. 74.

122   "It is economic deprivation that comes": ibid., p. 101.

122   "Most of the important things": ibid., p. 184.

124   "is without question the most": *Arkansas Democrat-Gazette,*
      November 5, 1995.

125   "The hidden hand of the market": Thomas Friedman, *The
      Lexus and the Olive Tree* (New York: Farrar, Straus & Giroux,
      1999), p. 373.

126   "While there are many obvious downsides": *New York Times,*
      April 23, 1999. Friedman's column was headlined: "Stop the
      Music."

130   For information on the Rambouillet negotiations and Appendix
      B, see Norman Solomon, *War Made Easy: How Presidents and
      Pundits Keep Spinning Us to Death* (Hoboken, NJ: John Wiley
      & Sons, 2005), pp. 41–44.

130   "deliberately set the bar higher": quoted in *The Nation,* June
      14, 1999, in an article by George Kenney, a former Yugoslavia
      desk officer at the U.S. State Department. Kenney wrote that

the quotation was transcribed by "an unimpeachable press source who regularly travels with Secretary of State Madeleine Albright." A similar account came from Jim Jatras, a foreign policy aide to Republicans in the Senate, who also said he had obtained a quote transcribed by a journalist who had been present at the interview: "We intentionally set the bar too high for the Serbs to comply. They need some bombing, and that's what they are going to get." Jatras cited the quote in a speech at the Cato Institute in Washington on May 18, 1999. For details, see also: "What Reporters Knew About Kosovo Talks—But Didn't Tell," news release, Fairness & Accuracy In Reporting (FAIR), June 2, 1999, www.fair.org/index.php?page=1900.

131   "ten years after the so-called welfare reform": quoted in news release, Institute for Public Accuracy, June 20, 2006, "An Impoverished Minimum Wage?"

132   "it's not all about the money": *Time*, September 27, 1999.

132   1977 to 1999 economic figures: Chuck Collins and Felice Yeskel, *Economic Apartheid in America* (New York: New Press, 2000), p. 41.

133   corporations were carrying a smaller proportion: economist Richard Du Boff, news release, Institute for Public Accuracy, March 26, 2004, "Bush's Housing Policies; Budget; Kerry's Corporate Tax Cut."

133   "We can have democracy": quoted in George Seldes, ed., *The Great Quotations* (New York: Lyle Stuart, 1960), p. 112.

135   "tragedy . . . and I will admit now": op-ed column, *New York Times*, July 18, 2004.

CHAPTER 10: GREASED PATH TO IRAQ

137   "The unspeakable, the unthinkable": *St. Louis Post-Dispatch*, December 30, 2001.

137   "Attack on the U.S. changed everyone": summary headline at top of last Sunday edition of 2001 in *San Francisco Chronicle*.

137 "Before September 11 changed everything": *New York Times*, July 16, 2006.

139 "Television crews had staked out": Norman Solomon and Reese Erlich, *Target Iraq: What the News Media Didn't Tell You* (New York: Context Books, 2003), pp. 3–4.

139 "And henceforth, the only honorable course": Albert Camus, *Neither Victims Nor Executioners* (Philadelphia: New Society Publishers, 1986), p. 55.

140 "I think the president would mislead": *This Week*, ABC, September 29, 2002. Pundit George Will blasted McDermott minutes later on the same TV program and via his syndicated column appearing in the *Washington Post* on October 1, 2002.

144 "will be seen in Asia": I. F. Stone, *Polemics and Prophecies, 1967–1970* (New York: Vintage Books, 1972), p. 139.

144 "Not enough Asians are going": ibid., p. 141.

146 Days after Sean Penn left Iraq in mid-December 2002, an official Iraqi news agency reported that he had said during his visit that Iraq had no weapons of mass destruction. The Iraqi claim was false. Penn had not said any such thing.

151 "An antiwar protest described": *Washington Post*, January 25, 2007.

CHAPTER 11: WAR TO THE HORIZON

155 "Cakewalk to Baghdad" was written by Bruce Barthol.

156 "seize oil fields to fund": quoted in *Los Angeles Times*, August 31, 2005.

156 "At least nine articles in": *Editor & Publisher* website, August 31, 2005. The article was by Will Bunch.

157 "Missing the personnel is": quoted in *Washington Post*, August 31, 2005. The spokesman was Lt. Andy Thaggard.

157 "They can go into Iraq and": quoted in *Washington Post*, September 2, 2005.

158 "for people who have brains": quoted in *New York Times*, January 30, 2006.

159 "During the course of roughly": Empire Notes blog, www.empirenotes.org/fallujah.html, April 12, 2004.

159 "A hospital source in Fallujah": Truthout, www.truthout.org, June 19, 2006.

160 "how patients are transferred from": email to author from USAF Captain Matthew C. Bates, Air Force National Media Outreach, June 1, 2006.

161 "From our end it is a go": email to author from USAFR Sergeant Collen A. McGee, NCOIC 433rd Airlift Wing Public Affairs, June 14, 2006.

162 "Marine Corps F/A-18Ds conducted a strike": "CENTAF releases airpower summary for December 26, 2006," Air Force Link, official website of the United States Air Force.

162 The next day, it was the same story: "CENTAF releases airpower summary for December 27, 2006," Air Force Link, official website of the United States Air Force.

164 "The couple left town as organic heroes": *Times* (London), November 7, 2005.

165 "I worry that we have begun": *New York Times*, November 6, 2005. The article was by Daniel Patterson.

165 "sustainability": The cover of the special edition "Summer 2006 Supplement to *Time*" posed the question, "Green Living: Is Sustainability the New Luxury?"

166 Anita Roddick sold her worldwide Body Shop chain: *Independent* (London), May 11, 2006.

167 It's unlikely that Simon was short on cash. She came from a wealthy family, part of Simon & Schuster publishers.

167 A few high-profile rock 'n' rollers, including Bruce Springsteen, Tom Petty, R.E.M., and Neil Young, steadfastly refused to lease any of their songs to commercials. In 1988, Young put out a caustic tune, "This Note's for You," with lyrics vowing not to sell songs to advertisers; MTV found the video unsuitable for

airing. By the first years of the twenty-first century, a chronic problem for those in charge of putting together commercials was finding beloved songs that hadn't already been used in major advertising campaigns. At the McCann Erickson ad agency, executive Mike Boris commented: "A lot of the big, known songs and baby-boomer hits that we have grown up with have been used." (*Wall Street Journal*, June 9, 2006) The power of big money had already converted much of the most memorable rock music into grist for the corporate mill.

168 The magnitude of Buffett's philanthropy was hardly representative of an overall trend among the USA's wealthy, as David Cay Johnston reported in the *New York Times* (July 2, 2006): "His megagifts, like many of his investments, buck the popular trend. Giving by the richest Americans has fallen in recent years, with the biggest declines at the very top, based on deductions Americans take on their tax returns. Among Americans who at death left a taxable fortune of $20 million or more, the average charitable bequest fell by $2 million, or 9 percent, from 1995 to 2004."

169 Two years after the beheading of Nicholas Berg, a U.S. air strike killed Abu Musab al-Zarqawi. The American news media responded with extensive coverage. CNN quickly invited Michael Berg for a live interview with anchor Soledad O'Brien on June 8, 2006. This edited portion of the interview appeared the next day in the Minneapolis *Star Tribune*:

Q. Mr. Berg, thank you for talking with us again. It's nice to have an opportunity to talk to you. Of course, I'm curious to know your reaction, as it is now confirmed that Abu Musab al-Zarqawi, the man who is widely credited and blamed for killing your son, Nicholas, is dead.

A. Well, my reaction is I'm sorry whenever any human being dies. Zarqawi is a human being. He has a family who are reacting just as my family reacted when Nick was killed, and I feel bad for that. I feel doubly bad, though, because Zarqawi is also a political figure, and his death will reignite yet another wave of revenge, and revenge is something that I do not follow, that I do not ask for, that I do not wish for against anybody. And it can't end the cycle. As long as people use violence to combat violence, we will always have violence.

Q. I have to say, sir, I'm surprised. I know how devastated you and your family were, frankly, when Nick was killed in such a horrible and brutal and public way.

A. Well, you shouldn't be surprised, because I have never indicated anything but forgiveness and peace in any interview on the air.

Q. No, no. And we have spoken before, and I'm well aware of that. But at some point, one would think, is there a moment when you say, "I'm glad he's dead, the man who killed my son"?

A. No. How can a human being be glad that another human being is dead?

Q. You know, you talked about the fact that he's become a political figure. Are you concerned that he becomes a martyr and a hero and, in fact, invigorates the insurgency in Iraq?

A. Of course. When Nick was killed, I felt that I had nothing left to lose. I'm a pacifist, so I wasn't going out murdering people. But I am—was not a risk-taking person, and yet now I've done things that have endangered me tremendously. . . .

Now, take someone who in 1991, who maybe had their family killed by an American bomb, their support system whisked away from them, someone who, instead of being fifty-nine, as I was when Nick died, was five years old or ten years old. And then if I were that person, might I not learn how to fly a plane into a building or strap a bag of bombs to my back?

That's what is happening every time we kill an Iraqi, every time we kill anyone, we are creating a large number of people who are going to want vengeance. And, you know, when are we ever going to learn that that doesn't work?

170 "a date I can never forget": Ron Kovic, "The Forgotten Wounded of Iraq," Truthdig.com, January 18, 2006.

171 "It has been two years that": quoted in *La Prensa San Diego*, April 1, 2005.

172 "Nothing here makes sense": *New York Times*, November 10, 2004.

173 "Their tragedies are our responsibilities": email dated April 8, 2004, posted on www.civicworldwide.org, the website of Campaign for Innocent Victims in Conflict (CIVIC).

174 "I decided not to take a position": *San Francisco Chronicle,* December 30, 2003.

174 "Civilian casualties are an inconvenient": *Philadelphia Inquirer,* April 21, 2005.

174 "her efforts, carried in Congress": *Los Angeles Times,* April 24, 2005.

175 "I am a journalist and reporting": speech at National Press Club, July 17, 2006.

176 "Freedom-loving Iranians inside and outside": Akbar Ganji, op-ed, *New York Times,* August 1, 2006.

176 "As an American, I'm embarrassed and ashamed": quoted in Reuters, July 18, 2006.

176 "It's a travesty. There's a million": quoted in ibid.

177 "There are terrorists who will blow up": quoted in *New York Times,* July 14, 2006.

177 "the first task of the occupation": George Will, *Washington Post,* April 7, 2004.

178 "a number of military officers": *New York Times,* November 15, 2006.

178 "What a thing it is to have": William Dean Howells, *Editha.* The short story was published in 1905.

CHAPTER 12: MEANWHILE, BACK AT THE NUCLEAR RANCH

186 No American responded to the nuclear age with Eastern mysticism sooner than Robert Oppenheimer. He famously recounted that when he saw the flash of the first atomic explosion, at the Trinity test, he remembered from the *Bhagavad-Gita* the words "Now I have become death, the destroyer of worlds." Oppenheimer's knowledge of Hindu scriptures did nothing to under-

mine his firm support for dropping atomic bombs on Hiroshima and Nagasaki a few weeks later.

In contrast, Admiral William D. Leahy, chairman of the Joint Chiefs of Staff at the time, as well as a personal friend of President Truman, rendered his own judgment. Leahy said: "The use of this barbarous weapon at Hiroshima and Nagasaki was of no material assistance in our war against Japan. . . . [I]n being the first to use it, we . . . adopted an ethical standard common to the barbarisms of the Dark Ages." (Gar Alperovitz, "Hiroshima: Historians Reassess," *Foreign Policy*, No. 99 [Summer 1995], p. 24; quoting from William D. Leahy, *I Was There* [New York: McGraw-Hill, 1950].)

CHAPTER 13: OBSTINATE MEMORY

193   "There is too little recognition": Alan Watts, *In My Own Way: An Autobiography* (New York: Pantheon Books, 1972), p. 5.

194   "Life is like stepping onto": quoted in David Chadwick, *Crooked Cucumber: The Life and Zen Teaching of Shunryu Suzuki* (New York: Broadway, 1999), p. 202.

195   "All memory is individual, unreproducible": Susan Sontag, *Regarding the Pain of Others* (New York: Farrar, Straus & Giroux, 2003), p. 86.

195   "People talk a great deal": Susan Engel, *Context Is Everything: The Nature of Memory* (New York: W. H. Freeman and Company, 1999), p. 148.

196   "Our problem today is that we": Appearing in a chapter titled "The World House" in Martin Luther King's book *Where Do We Go From Here: Chaos or Community?* (New York: Harper & Row, 1967), this passage expanded on a portion of the Nobel Peace Prize lecture that King delivered in Oslo on December 11, 1964.

197   "Machines are already becoming better": R. D. Laing, *The Politics of Experience* (New York: Ballantine Books, 1968), p. 40.

197   "Our society has spent so much time": Lee Strasberg, from *A Dream of Passion: The Development of the Method* (New York:

Plume, 1988), quoted in Richard T. Kelly, *Sean Penn: His Life and Times* (London: Faber and Faber, 2004), p. vii.

197   "industrially produced fiction": Ariel Dorfman, *The Empire's Old Clothes: What the Lone Ranger, Babar, and Other Innocent Heroes Do to Our Minds* (New York: Pantheon Books, 1983), p. ix.

197   "the bloody Attica uprising in 1971": *New York Times*, August 25, 2001.

198   "We work hard to create": Engel, *Context Is Everything*, p. 90.

198   "people repress unbearable truths": ibid., p. 152.

CHAPTER 14: CONSEQUENCES AND TRUTHS

200   "to forget any fact that has become": George Orwell, *1984* (New York: Signet, 1981), p. 177.

204   "We are driven and despised": Labor poet David Edelstadt (1866-1892) wrote the song, "In Struggle," published in *Mir Trogn a Gezang!* (New York: Workmen's Circle, 1972), p. 80.

205   "They have destroyed and are destroying": James Baldwin, *The Fire Next Time* (New York: Vintage Books, 1993), pp. 5-6.

206   "an open-necked hospital gown": *New York Times*, May 24, 2006.

207   "American politics is about optimism": Mark Shields, *NewsHour with Jim Lehrer*, June 16, 2000.

207   "Optimism is the only option": quoted in *Chicago Tribune*, August 29, 2006.

209   "Dismantling the last W56 warhead": quoted in *Albuquerque Journal*, June 29, 2006.

209   "a new generation of U.S. nuclear weapons": *Washington Post*, June 29, 2006.

210   "All of us know, whether or not": Baldwin, *The Fire Next Time*, p. 95.

Acknowledgments

This book would not exist without the steady support of editorial director Peter Richardson and publisher Scott Jordan at PoliPoint-Press. I want to thank them along with Jonathan Harris, Carol Pott, and everyone else at PoliPoint, a publishing house where ideas and values really matter.

Jeff Cohen, Cheryl Higgins, Peter Richardson, and James Sylvester went through multiple drafts of the manuscript, offering valuable critiques and detailed suggestions. I'm also appreciative of comments from Daniel Ellsberg, Laura Gross, Roger Lippman, and Sam Spiewak. Along the way, Sam Spiewak did extensive research on *Sputnik* and tracked down a lot of elusive facts.

As always, my literary agent Laura Gross was an upbeat source of tangible help and moral support. She provided deft guidance over many hurdles.

While writing this book, I drew inspiration from my friend Martin Lee. I was also inspired by my parents, Miriam Solomon and Morris Solomon. Others who gave me a boost in various ways included James Abourezk, Loretta Alper, Medea Benjamin, Gray Brechin, Tim Carpenter, Jacqueline Cabasso, Steve Cobble, Patricia Ellsberg, Beau Friedlander, Reese Erlich, Meghan Gilliss, Barbara Keady, Kathy Kei, Kathy Kelly, Peggy Law, Jacques Leslie, Leslie Leslie, Rae Levine, Paul Loeb, Country Joe McDonald, Maisa Mendonca, Omo Odesola, Sean Penn, Peggy Prince, Elisabeth Ptak, Mervis Reissig, Steve Rhodes, Cindy Sheehan, Lesley Shiner,

Eugene Solomon, Helen Solomon, Fernando Suarez del Solar, Tony Sutton, Jennifer Warburg, Harvey Wasserman, and David Zupan. The staff of the media watchdog group FAIR was uplifting as always. For three scenic writing-retreat spots, I'd like to thank Joannie Kwit, Vicki Leeds, and Peter Barnes of the Mesa Refuge.

Working with Hollie Ainbinder, Sam Husseini, and Cynthia Skow at the Institute for Public Accuracy has been more of a joy than ever. I feel very fortunate to have colleagues of such dedication, skill, and compassion.

My wife Cheryl Higgins showed great forbearance while I disappeared for long stretches to write. Her belief in the book project was always unequivocal. Her love has elevated my life.

In a sense, work on a major facet of this book began more than a quarter of a century ago, when I approached *The Progressive* about research I was doing on U.S. Marines who had been sent to ground zero in Nagasaki after the atomic bombing. The magazine's editors Erwin Knoll and Samuel H. Day Jr. backed my efforts, then published the story and put scarce resources behind a launch that sent it around the world. Erwin and Sam are not alive anymore, but—like so many others who have challenged what Martin Luther King Jr. called "the madness of militarism"—their spirits remain with us.

Index

Weissman, Robert, 202–3
Wershba, Joseph, 96
West Point Military Academy, 110
"white train" protests, 104–7
Wilkerson, Cathy, 54–55
Will, George, 177, 230n140

Williams, Stanley Tookie, 204, 205
Woodstock, 50, 155–56
World War II, 38

Young, Neil, 231n167
Yugoslavia, 125–31

About the Author

Norman Solomon has written twelve books, including *War Made Easy: How Presidents and Pundits Keep Spinning Us to Death*. A nationally syndicated columnist on media and politics, he is the founder and executive director of the Institute for Public Accuracy. Solomon's op-ed pieces have appeared in the *New York Times*, the *Washington Post*, the *Los Angeles Times*, *Newsday*, the *Boston Globe*, *USA Today*, the *International Herald Tribune*, and many other newspapers. He has been a guest on the PBS *NewsHour with Jim Lehrer*, CNN, Fox News Channel, MSNBC, *Democracy Now*, C-SPAN's *Washington Journal*, *CounterSpin*, and various National Public Radio programs. Internationally he has appeared on outlets ranging from Voice of America and the BBC to Al Jazeera and South African radio. His book *Target Iraq: What the News Media Didn't Tell You*, coauthored with foreign correspondent Reese Erlich, has been translated into five languages. Solomon is a longtime associate of the media watch group FAIR. He received the Annual Ruben Salazar Journalism Award in 2007 and is a recipient of the George Orwell Award for Distinguished Contribution to Honesty and Clarity in Public Language.

Other Books from PoliPointPress

The Blue Pages:
A Directory of Companies Rated by Their Politics and Practices
Helps consumers match their buying decisions with their political values by listing the political contributions and business practices of over one thousand companies. $9.95, PAPERBACK.

Jeff Cohen
Cable News Confidential: My Misadventures in Corporate Media
Offers a fast-paced romp through the three major cable news channels—Fox, CNN, and MSNBC—and delivers a serious message about their failure to cover the most urgent issues of the day. $14.95, PAPERBACK.

Marjorie Cohn
Cowboy Republic: Six Ways the Bush Gang Has Defied the Law
Details the six most important ways in which the Bush administration has breached domestic and international law and offers political and legal remedies. $14.95, PAPERBACK.

Joe Conason
The Raw Deal: How the Bush Republicans Plan to Destroy Social Security and the Legacy of the New Deal
Reveals the well-financed and determined effort to undo the Social Security Act and other New Deal programs. $11.00, PAPERBACK.

Steven Hill
10 Steps to Repair American Democracy
Identifies the key problems with American democracy, especially election practices, and proposes ten specific reforms to reinvigorate it. $11.00, PAPERBACK.

Yvonne Latty
In Conflict: Iraq War Veterans Speak Out on Duty, Loss, and the Fight to Stay Alive
Features the unheard voices, extraordinary experiences, and personal photographs of a broad mix of Iraq War veterans, including Congress-

man Patrick Murphy, Tammy Duckworth, Kelly Dougherty, and Camilo Mejia. $24.00, HARDCOVER.

Phillip Longman
Best Care Anywhere: Why VA Health Care Is Better Than Yours
Shows how the turnaround at the long-maligned VA hospitals provides a blueprint for salvaging America's expensive but troubled health care system. $14.95, PAPERBACK.

William Rivers Pitt
House of Ill Repute: Reflections on War, Lies, and America's Ravaged Reputation
Skewers the Bush administration for its reckless invasions, warrantless wiretaps, lethally incompetent response to Hurricane Katrina, and other scandals and blunders. $16.00, PAPERBACK.

Nomi Prins
Jacked: How "Conservatives" Are Picking Your Pocket —Whether You Voted For Them or Not
Describes how the "conservative" agenda has affected your wallet, skewed national priorities, and diminished America—but not the American spirit. $12.00, PAPERBACK.

John Sperling et al.
The Great Divide: Retro vs. Metro America
Explains how and why our nation is so bitterly divided into what the authors call Retro and Metro America. $19.95, PAPERBACK.

Curtis White
The Spirit of Disobedience: Resisting the Charms of Fake Politics, Mindless Consumption, and the Culture of Total Work
Debunks the notion that liberalism has no need for spirituality, and describes a "middle way" through our red state / blue state political impasse. Includes three powerful interviews with John DeGraaf, James Howard Kunstler, and Michael Ableman. $24.00, HARDCOVER.

For more information, please visit www.p3books.com.